Managing the Psychological Contract

To Ruth and Zack

Managing the Psychological Contract

Using the Personal Deal to Increase Business Performance

MICHAEL WELLIN

Routledge
Taylor & Francis Group

LONDON AND NEW YORK

First published in paperback 2024

First published 2007 by Gower Publishing

Published 2016 by Routledge
4 Park Square, Milton Park, Abingdon, Oxon OX14 4RN

and by Routledge
605 Third Avenue, New York, NY 10158

Routledge is an imprint of the Taylor & Francis Group, an informa business

British Library Cataloguing in Publication Data
Wellin, Michael
   Managing the psychological contract : using the personal
   deal to increase performance
   1. Performance management 2. Organizational commitment
   3. Communication in personnel management
   I. Title
   658.3'14

Library of Congress Cataloging-in-Publication Data
Wellin, Michael.
   Managing the psychological contract : using the personal deal to increase
performance / by Michael Wellin.
      p. cm.
   Includes index.
   ISBN-13: 978-0-566-08726-4 1. Personnel management. 2. Performance
technology. 3. Organizational behaviour. 4. psychology, Industrial. I. Title.
   HF5549.W43194 2006
   658.3'14--dc22

                                                                   2006025036

ISBN 13: 978-0-566-08726-4 (hbk)
ISBN 13: 978-1-03-283786-4 (pbk)
ISBN 13: 978-1-315-59366-1 (ebk)

DOI: 10.4324/9781315593661

Contents

List of Figures

List of Tables

Acknowledgements

As an intrepid mountain walker and world traveller, I know something about journeys. The journey involved in writing this book has been amazing and rewarding. It has been a journey of discovery, learning and self-awareness. It has been a journey to which many different people, some knowingly, others unknowingly, have contributed.

I want to say something about the journey, and to thank all those who have supported and encouraged me on my voyage of discovery into the psychological contract. As with all real journeys, it is difficult to know where it will end up, but this book feels like an important staging post in my professional life. What I have written is entirely my responsibility; but without the people mentioned below, the book would never have been possible.

My first exploration of the psychological contract occurred as part of an employee opinion survey I implemented for Reuters in 1998. When I discussed the implications of the results with Martin Davids and Anne Bowerman of Reuters, the subject of the psychological contract came up. They asked me to interpret the survey data in terms of the psychological contract, and my brief discussion paper for them was my first step in this journey.

Later in 2001, a long-standing client, Lynne Gomer, Senior Manager Human Resources (HR) at Ernst &Young, mentioned that she and her colleagues wanted a different type of presentation about people at the firm's summer conference for central region professional staff. When I asked if the psychological contract would be of interest, Lynne booked me to make the presentation. This required some serious understanding of the subject, and after reading and reflecting I created the basic model of the 'personal deal' which you will see in Chapter 3. My presentation involved the audience discussing their perceived psychological contract with Ernst & Young. I received positive feedback from this presentation and decided then that the psychological contract was a subject worth pursuing.

In 2002, an old friend and professional colleague Jane Cranwell Ward, Director at Henley Management College, invited me to co-lead a workshop on the psychological contract for the Henley Learning Partnership. I made my presentation alongside two colleagues, Mike Mister of Ernst & Young and Noelle Irvine from City University. We spent the day with a diverse audience who represented many different companies. Feedback from participants suggested that while we presented some interesting ideas we left many unanswered questions. My take from this workshop was that there was much more mileage in the psychological contract, and I wanted to explore this further.

My first breakthrough in using, as opposed to just talking about, the psychological contract came when my business partner Liz Baltesz and I were invited to undertake a culture change assignment for Parkside Housing Group. Colin Sheriff, the Chief Executive, asked us to come up with ideas for implementing leadership and culture change which would help the Group sustain its 33 per cent per annum growth, and enhance customer service. Subsequent encouragement from the Parkside M-Power steering group – Adrian, Emma, Donna, Lizzie, Louise, Sean and Sue – persuaded us to include the psychological contract, or as we subsequently called it the 'personal deal', as one of the key methods for changing the culture of Parkside. See Chapter 8 for the details of what we did.

Following our success with Parkside, the Managing Director Mark Thompson and the Head of HR David Prince brought us into Royal Mail Sales to support a culture change. After researching the issues among people in the business unit, we came up with the idea of 'team deals' to help shift the culture towards becoming more commercial and customer focused. See Chapter 9 for details of what we did and the results we achieved.

In our work with Parkside and Royal Mail, and other organisations since, my business partner Liz Baltesz, has been a great colleague and mentor, enthusing me to carry on, challenging my thinking and jointly delivering assignments with me to use the psychological contract to add real value to our clients. Kim Talbot worked with Liz and me to support the work we undertook with clients.

By the middle of 2004, I knew we were on to something, and I wanted to explore my long forgotten dream of studying for a PhD. I sought out an academic psychologist I greatly admire – Professor Adrian Furnham of University College London. Adrian cunningly suggested that, rather than enrol me onto a PhD straight away, it might be better if I completed a literature search to decide if this was really something I wanted to pursue. Adrian supervised my search through a significant weight of publications (intellectual and physical) about the psychological contract. Adrian commented that with a few alterations my efforts might make an acceptable first chapter for my PhD. He then reminded me that if my goal was a PhD, then I would need to study for at least a further four and a half years, as he had never known a full-time employee complete a PhD in less time.

The idea of studying for a PhD appealed, but four and a half years' work involving one day every weekend seemed too high a price to pay, alongside my other interests including running a consulting business, being a partner to Ruth, a father to Zack, and wanting to enjoy other life journeys. The pragmatic solution for pursuing my interest in the psychological contract was therefore to write this book.

It took me two months to draft a sample chapter and produce a proposition for a publisher. Some ten months later, however, I experienced my 'dark night of the soul' (as Shakespeare would say) part of this venture. By early 2005, despite submissions to a number of publishers, no publisher was interested in my ideas for a book. Two friends counselled me: Barbara Cook reminded me in a few discussions that it was really important to believe in this venture, to revise my book proposition and resubmit it; Pam White gave me lots of practical counsel on how to present my thinking to publishers. Between the two of them, they re-energised me to completely re-write the book proposition and sample chapter.

Just as I went off on holiday in August 2005, Jackie Bailey, who later corrected my English on the first draft chapters, phoned me at the airport on my departure day to tell me that Jonathan Norman of Gower was interested in my ideas for the book. Throughout the months of writing, Jonathan has encouraged and supported my efforts.

Three other people helped me on my journey: Mike Mister of Ernst & Young made many helpful suggestions about the first draft manuscript; Rabbi Charles Emanuel, as well as his support and humour, helped me with the most appropriate biblical references; and Nita Myers helped me with editing and with other details in putting together the total manuscript.

Two important people I have yet to mention are my wife Ruth and son Zack. Both of them encouraged me to pursue my interest in the psychological contract. When the idea of the book seemed a reality, they both accepted me burying myself for one day every weekend over a six-month period while I wrote. Ruth fulfilled many different roles of coach, mentor, critic, as well as friend. Ruth and Zack have both encouraged and supported me all the way on my journey.

It has been an exciting journey and one for which I owe a debt of thanks to all those mentioned here, as well as to the many other friends who have encouraged me on this venture. I hope you think it worthwhile.

Michael Wellin

CHAPTER 1

Introduction and Why the Psychological Contract Matters

In this first chapter I will describe my purpose and aims in writing this book and make the high-level case why managing the psychological contract can create real business value.

Writing this book seemed an interesting venture after completing a number of consulting assignments where my colleagues and I used the psychological contract to add value to different business organisations. After using the psychological contract as the main vehicle for developing leadership performance in one organisation, and for changing organisation culture in another business, it occurred to me that we might have developed some innovative and practical tools for implementing organisation change.

When I explored the literature it quickly emerged that there is increasing interest in the psychological contract. It appeared however that almost nothing had yet been written on how to actually use the psychological contract as a practical method to implement change. As last year's book on the psychological contract by Conway and Briner[1] stated, there is 'an absence of "hands on" advice about how to use the concept to manage'. I hope this book begins to fill this void. In the first part of this chapter I will elaborate on this purpose.

In the second part of this chapter I will propose three reasons why the psychological contract really matters in business today. These will be explored against some of the ideas put forward by gurus such as Peter Drucker, Stephen Covey and Richard Koch. We shall also view these in the context of what two world-class organisations have achieved. While the three companies delivered very different things, the challenges faced by their people had distinct similarities.

My basic proposition in the pages that follow is that the psychological contract is much more than an interesting vehicle to understand organisations, rather it is a highly practical framework we can use to help organisations become both more effective and better places to work.

---

1   Conway, N. and Briner, R. (2005), *Understanding Psychological Contracts at Work* (Oxford, OUP)

PURPOSE OF THIS BOOK

Ten years ago the psychological contract only meant something to a small number of business psychologists and organisation-behaviour professionals. Since then it has become a topic of increasing interest, discussion and writing among a broader audience of human resource students, practitioners and, even, some business leaders. Much of the credit for the change in fortune of the psychological contract must go to the pioneering research and theory of Denise Rousseau.

Rousseau[2] defined the psychological contract at its core as:

> *The psychological contract encompasses the actions employees believe are expected of them and what response they expect in return from the employer.*

Since she published her seminal work[3] the volume of published papers and conference presentations on the psychological contract has increased significantly.

Despite the increased interest, much of the discussion of the psychological contract has been limited to two distinct arenas. Among the academic community, focus has been directed on research into narrow aspects of the psychological contract, particularly the effects of breach of the psychological contract on thinking and behaviour. Among human resource practitioners the focus has been on the use of the psychological contract to describe broad trends in the relationship between employees and employing organisations.

My purpose in writing this book is to encourage a very different type of discussion; I hope to encourage discussion about the application of the psychological contract as a vehicle for changing organisation behaviour and business performance. If, after reading this book, you have some better idea of how you might use the psychological contract to make the organisations in which you are involved more fulfilling and or more successful places to work, I will have achieved my purpose.

As a professional business psychologist I have an interest in ideas which help understand people's behaviour in organisations. As a consultant working with commercial and social businesses I have particular interest in ideas that make a difference and add value to the organisation. My experience in different organisations over the last five years has convinced me that the psychological

---

2   Rousseau, D. and Greller, M. (1994), 'Human Resource Practices: administrative contract makers', *Human Resources Management* 33:3, 385-401
3   Rousseau, D. (1995), *Psychological Contracts in Organisations* (California: Sage)

contract is one of the most powerful vehicles for improving the quality of life in business as well as enhancing the performance and success of organisations.

Coaching has become a very widely used vehicle for bringing about individual and organisation change. I firmly believe the psychological contract has similar potential to become an equally powerful vehicle for change.

My objectives in writing this book are three-fold:

OBJECTIVE 1: THINK OF THE PSYCHOLOGICAL CONTRACT MORE AS A 'PERSONAL DEAL' AT WORK

By using the term 'personal deal' I want to encourage focus on actual relationships between people at work, particularly between individual leaders and their people, which are open to change, and are accessible by everyone at work.

The term 'personal deal' emerged as a result of a comment by Colin Harris, Managing Director of Parkside Housing Group, that while he liked the idea, the term 'psychological contract' would mean nothing to his people. He and his colleagues applauded when we came up with 'personal deal'. Even though we completed our assignment with the organisation some three years ago – managers continue to have 'personal deal' discussions with their staff. We therefore take encouragement that the proposed change of focus can be easily understood by people with different interests and from diverse backgrounds, and that it has potential to contribute to the way an organisation works over time.

Emphasis on the personal deal signals a shift in focus away from viewing the psychological contract as something between an individual and the organisation. In this book we shall view the personal deal at work to refer to the relationship between one employee and another employee, between colleagues in a team, or between colleagues in different teams. I hope to show how the personal deal at work can be used and changed at an individual level, a team level or between teams to improve working relationships and performance.

One of the reasons the concept of the psychological contract has had limited practical value to date is because it has concentrated almost exclusively on the somewhat abstract relationship between an employee and their employing organisation. In practice our relationships with people are more powerful than our relationships with abstract things. The single most important personal deal at work for most people is their relationship with their team leader because it includes and embodies their relationship with the organisation.

To support the proposed approach four different models of the personal deal will be presented in the book. One describes the components of the personal deal (Chapter 3), the second provides a framework which illustrates how the personal deal operates dynamically over time between people (Chapter 5), the third describes different types of personal deals that are possible (Chapter 6) and a final model describes how the personal deal operates at a behavioural level (Chapter 12).

OBJECTIVE 2: PRESENT CASE STUDIES OF HOW THE PERSONAL DEAL HAS BEEN USED TO ENHANCE ORGANISATION PERFORMANCE

As a practising consultant the value I give to ideas and concepts is determined by the extent to which they can be used to influence and bring about organisation change – whether at an individual, team or organisation level.

There are many different approaches available for understanding individual interaction and behaviour. One of the approaches which emerged in the 1970s, transactional analysis, is now going through a revival in interest as it is still one of the few behaviour frameworks to provide a truly dynamic method for us to understand and then make choices about how to manage and change our relationships with others.

One of the objectives of this book is to provide practical case studies which show how the psychological contract when used as the personal deal can bring about change in different organisations. Descriptions will be provided of the types of interventions we implemented in organisations, as well as their perceived impact. In one case the impact has been systematically evaluated over time by an independent organisation.

When presenting the case studies my aim is to encourage you to think about how you can apply and use the idea of the personal deal in the organisations in which you are involved – whether you are an HR professional, an organisation consultant, a leader or a follower. In the final analysis you, the reader, have to decide if these case studies resonate with you and the organisations in which you work.

OBJECTIVE 3: PROVIDE SOME PRACTICAL TOOLS THAT YOU CAN PERSONALLY USE TO ENHANCE PERSONAL DEALS IN YOUR ORGANISATIONS

My third objective is to go beyond ideas and case studies, and provide some practical tools which you can adapt and use to enhance the psychological contracts or 'personal deals' in which you are personally involved.

At a high level personal deals are impacted by almost every piece of HR activity. My aim is to encourage HR practitioners to think about how the different actions they undertake – whether resourcing, implementation of new people processes and systems, learning and development, or working as a strategic business partner – impacts the psychological contract and in turn personal deals between people. Anticipating and taking into account how different HR practices can most positively impact personal deals is a practical step every HR professional can take to increase their value to the business.

The techniques we have used to enhance leadership effectiveness as well as change organisation culture may be of interest to organisation change consultants, whether working internally or externally. I hope they are also of interest to line managers leading major organisation change initiatives and projects.

Whatever role you fulfil in an organisation – I hope the tools and techniques provided in this book will be relevant at a personal level. Chapter 11 provides some practical 'how to' action steps which you can use to clarify and refine the personal deals you have with colleagues.

The most important feature of the personal deal is that it is not abstract but something tangible which we can all influence and change. We have a personal deal with everyone we have a relationship with and our enduring relationships are the ones where the personal deal works well for both parties. We have personal deals with our partner, our children, parents, friends, our boss, and our team members and colleagues. While the focus of this book is all about personal deals at work, there is no reason why you cannot have a personal deal discussion with anyone in your life. Chapter 11 shows you how.

WHY THE PSYCHOLOGICAL CONTRACT AND PERSONAL DEALS MATTER

Before I can invite you to do something about the psychological contracts in your life and in the organisations in which you are involved, I need to convince you that it is worth your while. Just because you may have read a book entitled *Managing the Psychological Contract* (and you haven't yet!) will not be sufficient reason for you to do anything. Convincing you will require me to provide some clear evidence that the approach will provide you with greater returns than the many alternative approaches and frameworks that are competing for your attention in your search for achieving personal and organisation success.

I believe there are three fundamental reasons why the psychological contract/personal deal can add value to people at work and to the prosperity of organisations. It helps us:

- understand and predict how people behave;

- engage people at work;

- align people better to customers and strategic business goals.

In the sections which follow each of these reasons will be explored with reference to some broader evidence. Understanding and predicting how people behave will be explored from two real examples. We will explore how the psychological contract helps to engage people in the context of ideas from some of the leading management gurus. Finally, we shall explore how the psychological contract helps better align people to customer and strategic business goals in the context of some world-class business organisations.

HOW THE PERSONAL DEAL AND PSYCHOLOGICAL CONTRACT HELPS US UNDERSTAND AND PREDICT HOW PEOPLE BEHAVE

The first benefit of the personal deal is that it can help to better understand people and their behaviour and predict how people will react in different situations. Academic studies suggest how the fulfilment or non-fulfilment of the psychological contract impacts behaviour, and this will be considered in Chapter 6. In this chapter I will limit myself to two practical examples of how the psychological contract or personal deal helps us understand and predict people's behaviour.

In summer 2005 a strike occurred among staff of British Airways at London Heathrow airport, which grounded all flights for some 48 hours and disrupted their international flight schedules for over seven days. The reason staff walked out was to do with the way colleagues in the catering company which provided in-flight meals, Gate Gourmet, handled its staff. On 10 August Gate Gourmet quite abruptly announced that it was dismissing some 670 staff. Allegedly many staff were informed about losing their jobs via phone text messages. The day after the dismissals were announced, some 1000 British Airways ground staff walked out in sympathy with those sacked by the catering firm, many of whom were relatives or friends.

British Airways was forced to cancel all flights from mid-afternoon the following day, throwing Heathrow airport into chaos at one of the busiest periods of the year and stranding more than 100 000 passengers, many of them holidaymakers. Overall, more than 700 flights were cancelled and the dispute was believed to have cost the airline up to £40 million. Other airlines also had their flights disrupted.

What Gate Gourmet did was to dramatically break the psychological contract and personal deals with its people. Top management in Gate Gourmet, when it sacked staff, overlooked the fact that many of those sacked had friends and families working for British Airways. The reaction from British Airways staff was abrupt and swift as they gave vent to their fury about the way their colleagues and friends had been treated. It cost the airline more than the total losses suffered by Gate Gourmet over 12 months, which was the original reason for the dismissals.

Understanding how the personal deal works – as described in Chapter 5 – could have saved Gate Gourmet what turned out to be very costly and totally unnecessary industrial action that totally disrupted the activities of its principal client British Airways.

To bring the personal deal to life in many of our personal lives we can use it to better understand why young people become rebellious towards their parents in their early teens. You may remember what you went through with your parents, or if you are a parent like me, recall your experiences with your teenage children.

As children develop they typically create a close relationship with their parents that essentially amounts to parents making decisions and children mostly going along with these. Suddenly when children become teenagers there is a huge upheaval as children rebel against parental authority. This is often attributed to adolescent hormones kicking in and is viewed as one of those biological things that parents just have to put up with.

Typically over a short space of time arguments arise in the home between parents and their children. New teenagers realise they can now make more decisions for themselves and seek to exercise more choice in their lives – what they do with their time, who they spend time with, when and how they do their homework. For their part, parents are bewildered and often push back to re-establish the way things were. It takes a few years until a new equilibrium emerges for the parent–child relationship.

Using the personal deal gives us a powerful perspective of what happens in the relationship between parents and children. Teenage children clearly demand a different type of personal deal with their parents. Many parents (including this author) find it quite difficult to have their established personal deal with their children suddenly turned upside down. Instead of the parents making most decisions, the teenager now wants to make an ever-increasing number of decisions for themselves and they push hard for this. Parents may not always respond to the demand for a new personal deal in a rational way and find themselves in arguments about all manner of decisions which become blown up out of proportion, some of which are important, while others are trivial.

Basically what is happening during early teenage years is a renegotiation of the personal deal. The teenager wants more freedom of choice, while parents, in some cases quite rightly, want to retain decision making and, in others inappropriately, may seek to hang on to the way things were. What happens to the relationship between parents and children depends significantly on how parents renegotiate the personal deal with their children.

Understanding how the personal deal operates gives us insight into the issues of the changing relationship between parents and children and provides a means to make the transition to a new personal deal a more positive experience.

The two real examples of what happened at Gate Gourmet and in teenage child rebellion do I believe give an idea of how understanding the personal deal can give us greater insight and understanding into our relationships. The personal deal can also provide a powerful vehicle for anticipating how others, whether friends, children, colleagues or our boss, may react and behave in specific situations.

WHY ENGAGEMENT IS REALLY IMPORTANT

There is very considerable evidence that engaged people are more fulfilled, more productive and more successful. Evidence from many internationally renowned experts put the case very clearly, we will consider three here:

Management Expert	Idea
Peter Drucker	Understanding our Strengths
Stephan Covey	Find your Voice
Richard Koch	The 80/20 Way

The legendary management guru Peter Drucker has some powerful ideas about the individual:[4]

> In a few hundred years, when the history of our time will be written from a long-term perspective, it is likely that the most important event historians will see is not technology, not the Internet, not e-commerce. It is an unprecedented change in the human condition. For the first time – literally – substantial and rapidly growing numbers of people have choices. For the first time, they will have to manage themselves. And society is totally unprepared for it....

> To succeed in this new world, we will have to learn, first, who we are. Few people, even highly successful people, can answer the question. Do you know what you're good at? Do you know what you need to learn so that you get the full benefit of your strengths? Few have even asked themselves these questions....

> Understanding our strengths, articulating our values, knowing where we belong – these are also essential to addressing one of the great challenges of organisations: improving the abysmally low productivity of knowledge workers.

Peter Drucker is very clear that one of the critical challenges in organisations in our twenty-first century is about helping people to get in touch with their talents and then focus these in ways which increase individual and organisation performance. That's what engagement is about.

Stephen Covey advocates broadly similar ideas to Drucker. In his book *The Eighth Habit*[5] Covey advocates the importance of our 'inner voice'. As he puts it:

> Between stimulus and response there is a space. In this space lies our freedom and power to choose our response. In those choices lie our growth and our happiness....

> Any individual who has had a profound influence on others, on institutions or on society and parents whose influence has been inter-generational, anyone who has really made a difference for good or evil possessed these three common attributes: vision, discipline and passion. I suggest that these three attributes have ruled the world from its beginning.

4   Drucker, P. (2000), 'Managing knowledge means managing oneself', *Leader to Leader* 16:Spring
5   Covey, S. (2004), *The Eighth Habit* (London: Simon Schuster)

Choosing the path of vision, discipline and passion is about expressing our inner voice, which in turn is the path of real engagement.

An essentially similar message is presented by Richard Koch to support his notion of the 80/20 Rule.[6] He goes beyond the conventional notion that in most companies 80 per cent of revenues and profit are derived from 20 per cent of customers. He advocates that this principle applies equally to how we devote our time – and that 80 per cent of our results are achieved by 20 per cent of our efforts and 20 per cent of our time. Effective application of the 80/20 rule requires focus:

> *Focus is the secret of all personal power, happiness and success. Focus means doing less, being less. Focus makes less more. Few people focus, yet focus is easy. Focus expands individuality, the essence of being human....*

> *Developing one's authentic self, the vital and best part of oneself, is not difficult or unnatural. In being true to yourself, you give up parts of you that are not genuine or natural. You stop acting. You stop pretending to be interested or excited in things that bore you. You stop worrying about what other people think of you....*

> *Life is easier after making a few big decisions: Who and what do you care most about? What kind of person are you and want to become? What are your strongest qualities, emotions, and abilities?*

The messages from Drucker, Covey and Koch have much in common. They each emphasise in their own way the importance of personal engagement for individual success.

How the psychological contract facilitates engagement

One of the core implications of the psychological contract is that the organisation lets people know, either directly or indirectly, what is expected of them. The heart of the personal deal as we said earlier is about mutual expectations between people.

Every organisation lets people know what it expects – the only question is what these expectations are and how well are they are communicated. A number of organisations I know have until quite recently let people know that they are paid to do as they are told by successive layers of senior managers. The role people essentially had was to keep busy and fulfil what they were told

---

6   Koch, R. (2004), *Living the 80/20 Way* (London: Nicholas Brealey)

– even if this at times added questionable value to the business or its customers. Typically people who asked many questions were sidelined and told not to challenge the system. The implicit message from such command and control organisations is that they do not want to engage people as people, but as robots who do as they are directed. This is not something that will encourage engagement of the type advocated by Drucker, Covey or Koch!

Another organisation I know encourages people to do their job in their own way. The message is we expect you to perform your job to the best of your ability. We will give you freedom to do this in your way – once we know we can trust you. Gaining this all important trust is not always straightforward but individuals who win it are allowed to get on with their job their way. As well as having an international reputation for quality in its field, this organisation is one of the Sunday Times[7] top 100 organisations to work for. By encouraging and expecting people to do their job to the best of their ability, their way, the organisation encourages real engagement.

The reason the psychological contract or personal deal is fundamental for engaging people is that it drives and shapes the extent to which people are allowed to be themselves and to harness their own unique talents in pursuit of the organisations' goals. Some organisations stifle people from becoming engaged – and treat them as machines - while others very much encourage this. The type of psychological contract and personal deal in an organisation conveys fundamental messages about the amount of engagement that people are expected to display. How the personal deal can be changed to encourage increased engagement is described in Chapters 8 and 9.

WHAT WORLD-CLASS ORGANISATIONS ACHIEVE THROUGH ALIGNMENT

Organisations in the twenty-first century have an amazing capability – a capability that could scarcely be imagined only a few years back. Two organisations illustrate this well – Toyota of Japan and the Eden Project of the UK.

While most other car manufacturers lacked serious interest in the environment, Toyota started development of its Prius petrol electric hybrid motor car in 1993. The Prius emerged from two goals Toyota set itself – to develop new production methods and to significantly improve fuel economy.

---

7   'The Top 100 Companies', *The Sunday Times*, March 2005 (Times Newspapers Ltd)

Even with top management support the Prius project ran into serious technical difficulties with prototype cars overheating, not working below 14°C, semiconductor failure and flat batteries. The success of the Prius could never have been achieved without dramatic changes in working practices. Toyota was known as a risk-averse, fast-follower company. Bringing the Prius to market involved breaking its own rules about consensus management – and implicitly also the traditional personal deal that went with this. Building on its initial launch success, Toyota now expects to sell over a million hybrid cars a year by the end of the decade.

The importance of the Prius is that it acknowledges in a very practical way the damaging impact of the internal combustion engine on our environment as well as the finite supply of oil. By producing a car that halves the amount of petrol used per mile the Prius provides a robust response to the environmental challenges we face on our planet. It is an approach that is being rapidly emulated by other motor manufacturers.

What the Eden Project achieved in the UK is in the same league as the success of Toyota. Between 1995 and 2000 a multi-talented team of enthusiasts led by Tim Smit transformed a derelict clay pit in Cornwall in the UK into what the press has described as the 'eighth wonder of the world'. Eden has three separate climate zones each of which is contained within separate giant conservatories or 'biomes'.

The Eden Project faced enormous challenges in construction and funding, and these challenges, against all the odds were all overcome by the dedicated construction team, uniquely made up of archaeologists, botanists, engineers and horticulturists. The miracle they created now houses 5000 different plant species and is visited by over two million people a year, and is Britain's fifth largest tourist attraction. Eden, most importantly, is a test bed for ideas – particularly for ideas about change and how to unlock and engage people's potential.

As Smit put it, Eden is a stage for change:

> *The Trust's interests lie in explaining how the natural world works seen through the lens of plants, exploring how people might best organise themselves in the face of this knowledge and thereby reach an understanding of what sustainability might mean and, through best practice of these principles, create an organisation that is sustainable to act as a model for others.*

On one level the achievements of these two organisations were technological – the Prius a unique combination of electric and petrol power, and the Biomes a marvel of construction and botany. At another level both successes are the result of inspired and dedicated leaders; respectively Hiroshi Okuda and Fujio Cho, and Tim Smit.

The two products are also the result of imagination, vision and determination in the face of adversity and challenge. The successes, while different, are underpinned by what became a shared willingness to challenge conventional thinking, intense collaboration between colleagues and determination to create something which did not previously exist. While their leaders' vision was important, the outcomes would not have moved beyond the dream stage without the alignment of people to make them a reality.

The achievements of Toyota and the Eden Project are awesome. They are powerful tributes to human endeavour and show in a very tangible way how world-class organisations have the capability not only to sustain their own future but to do things that add value to the way all of us in our global village think and live. Without alignment between people and the strategic goals of the organisation they could never have achieved so much.

How the psychological contract increases alignment

When people are aligned across an organisation, a few critical expectations required for success are shared by people across the organisation. This involves every person who is working towards the goal being focused on its achievement – for Toyota, creation of the Prius, and for the Eden Project, creation of the Biomes. The expectation was that everyone, whatever their personal role, whether senior or junior, professional or non-professional, female or male, would do their utmost to deliver the final goal.

If a chain of people in different teams or at different organisation levels have discussions about their personal deals, in particular their mutual expectations of one another, it becomes much easier to create new but consistent expectations across the different discussions. This is precisely what we did in our work with Royal Mail Sales when we introduced the concept of the 'culture touchstones' which became a component of every team deal in the business unit. Chapter 9 describes this in detail.

Alignment of expectations looks something like Figure 1.1. Team D might create a set of expectations between them and Team C. Team C in turn would create some common expectations between them and Team B. These same common expectations would be included in the personal deal agreed between Team B and Team A. By viewing the personal deal as expectations that exist between people, or teams of people, it becomes totally realistic to use the approach to align behaviour and performance across an organisation.

A wonderful illustration of alignment up and down an organisation occurred when the National Aeronautics and Space Administration (NASA) was working to put the first man on the moon. During this exciting time opinions and views were sought from among different NASA staff. There is an apocryphal tale of a supervisor of the toilets who when asked what his job was commented 'I am working to put a man on the moon'. What this man said (for purposes of the diagram below he might be in Team A) totally reflected the personal deal for people at the top of the organisation (Team D in the diagram).

The notion of the personal deal at work provides three powerful benefits for organisations. It provides an understanding of people and how they behave in organisations. It provides a mechanism for engaging people more in their work. Finally it can help align people to customers and the strategic goals of the business. These benefits are all achieved much more positively as a result of the shift away from the traditional psychological contracts focus on expectations between individuals and the organisation as a whole. Rather, the personal deal emphasises expectations between different individuals or between different teams. Subsequent chapters in this book show in more depth how the personal

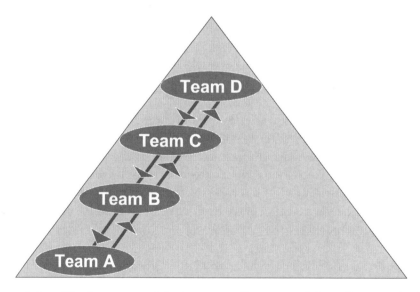

Figure 1.1   Aligning personal deal conversations up and down the organisation

deal can be used in a very practical way to achieve these three important benefits for business.

CHAPTER SUMMARY

- Almost none of the growing numbers of articles and books on the psychological contract focus on how to manage and change the psychological contract. The proposition of this book is that when viewed as a personal deal the psychological contract can add real value in helping organisations improve performance and be better places to work in.

- Most academic research into the psychological contract has focused on the impact of breach of the psychological contract on employee behaviour. Most HR practitioners use the psychological contract to describe broad trends in the relationship between employees and employing organisations.

- The three objectives of *Managing Psychological Contracts* are to:
  - view the psychological contract as the personal deal at work;
  - present case studies of how the personal deal has been used to enhance organisation performance;
  - provide some practical tools readers can personally use to enhance personal deals in their organisations.

- Personal deals are about the expectations people have of one another. We have a personal deal with everyone we have a relationship with – our partner, our children, parents, friends, our boss, and work team members and colleagues. A personal deal at work refers to the expectations one employee has of another employee, or one group of employees have of another group of employees. The personal deal with our team leader is particularly important as it also symbolises for many people their relationship with the organisation.

- The personal deal helps understand and predict how people behave. The disruption caused to British Airways flights by the Gate Gourmet strike in 2005 could almost certainly have been avoided if management in the company had understood the personal deal. The personal deal also provides a powerful vehicle for understanding the changes that occur in the relationship between children and their parents during teenage years.

- Many management experts, including Peter Drucker, Stephan Covey and Richard Koch agree that personal engagement is critical for personal success. The psychological contract and even more the personal deal are critical drivers of the extent to which people are allowed or prevented to become really engaged in their work.

- World-class companies have achieved awesome results through alignment. Outstanding examples include Toyota of Japan with the Prius and the Eden Project of the UK with the Biomes. The personal deal provides a framework for creating new forms of alignment between people across an organisation.

CHAPTER 2

Current Use of the Psychological Contract

BACKGROUND TO THE PSYCHOLOGICAL CONTRACT

The term 'psychological contract' is something of a contradiction. If we have a *contract* with someone, this refers to a precise and legally binding arrangement we have with a person or an organisation involving the exchange of money for an object or a service. Examples of this are when we contract to buy a house, fly with an airline or sign up for a new credit card. This is completely different from something *psychological* which relates to our mind and therefore is intangible – such as the picture we have in our heads about an experience or a forthcoming event, or the feelings we have towards another person.

The psychological contract essentially refers to the mutual expectations people have of one another in a relationship, and how these expectations change and impact our behaviour over time. The term is currently used mainly to describe the expectations an employee has of the organisation and the expectations the organisation has of the employee. But the idea could apply to any relationship; for example to a wife's expectations of her husband and a husband's expectations of his wife. We will look at the different academic definitions of the psychological contract later in this chapter.

Much greater interest is now being shown in the psychological contract as demonstrated by the increasing number of HR journal articles, including those published in the UK by the Chartered Institute of Personnel Development (CIPD). This chapter explores how the idea of the psychological contract has emerged, and the form it can take in practice. Specific examples will be given of psychological contracts in different business organisations. Later in the chapter we will explore the increasingly transient nature of psychological contracts as a result of pressures from both employees and organisations.

The origins of the psychological contract go back thousands of years to the major world religions. One of the most important prayers in the Jewish faith for example, the Amidah, refers to the mutual expectations, in essence the psychological contract, between God and the Jewish people.[1] More recently social and political philosophers such as Hobbes and Locke talked about a 'social contract' as an understanding between citizens and the state regarding reciprocal expectations, obligations and duties.

The notion of the social contract between the individual citizen and the state continues to be fundamental to our lives in society today. For most of us in knowledge economies, the social contract is something we largely take for granted. As citizens we expect the state to provide us with things like a democratic process for electing a government, an equitable judicial system, an army and police to protect the country both externally and internally, and social services such as education, public transport, healthcare and recreational spaces. To sustain protection by the state and other services we, for our part, have an obligation to pay taxes, abide by the laws of the land, and exercise some control over how we express our feelings and desires so that we can live in reasonable harmony with others in the community. When this arrangement breaks down, as it appears to have done in Iraq, and not so many years ago almost did in Northern Ireland, then the stability of society is threatened.

At its core the social contract is about mutual expectations; things that the individual can expect from the state and things the state expects from the individual. Some of these expectations may be written down and enshrined in law, such as respect for others' property, while others, such as expectations about the state's provision of recreation facilities, are mostly implied rather than laid down in statute. The implicit and typically unspoken nature of the social contract is a fundamental feature of the psychological contract.

One of the first writers to use the term psychological contract was Argyris[2] who defined it as the implicit understanding between a group of employees and their foreman. He described it as:

> A relationship may be hypothesised to evolve between the employees and the foremen which might be called the 'psychological work contract'. The employee will maintain high production, low grievances etc. if the foreman guarantees and respects the norms of the employee informal culture (i.e. let the employees alone, make certain they make adequate wages and have secure jobs).

---

1   'Forms of Prayer for Jewish Workshop', The Assembly of Rabbis of the Reform Synagogues of Great Britain, The Reform Synagogues of Great Britain, London 1998, P 145
2   Argyris, C. (1960), *Understanding Organisational Behaviour* (Homewood, Illinois: The Dorsey Press Inc)

This early view of the psychological contract, like the social contract before it, clearly refers to mutual expectations and obligations. It differs from the social contract as it specifically relates to the workplace and what the foreman expects of their team and what team members, in turn, expect from the foreman.

The psychological contract was refined by Schein[3] in his seminal work on organisational psychology in the form it is used today by many human resource practitioners. He describes it as:

> *The unwritten expectations operating at all times between every member of an organisation and the various managers and others in that organisation... Each employee has expectations about such things as salary or pay rate, working hours, benefits and privileges that go with a job... the organisation also has more implicit, subtle expectations that the employee will enhance the image of the organisation, will be loyal, will keep organisational secrets and will do his or her best.*

While Argyris refers to a specific understanding between the workgroup and the individual foreman or team leader, Schein's definition focuses on the high-level collective relationship, between the individual employee on the one hand, and management of the company on the other hand – in other words the organisation.

HOW SOME BUSINESS ORGANISATIONS DESCRIBE THEIR PSYCHOLOGICAL CONTRACTS

Many business organisations use Schein's approach to the psychological contract to seek to clarify understanding between employees and the company. A good example of this comes from the successful sandwich company Prêt à Manger. Their implied psychological contract, as shown in Table 2.1, is based on a summary of the jobs section of the website www.pret.com

The table shows the psychological contract for store employees in two components; 'this is what the company expects' and 'this is what you as an employee can expect'. The psychological contract is presented on the website in a much looser and less overt way – that is if you do this then this is what we will do for you – rather than as the set of up-front mutual understandings presented in the table overleaf. Reading the website does, however, allow the reader to identify each of the expectations shown in the table.

---

3   Schein, E. (1965), *Organisational Psychology* (Engelwood Cliffs, NJ: Prentice-Hall)

Table 2.1   Prêt à Manger's implied psychological contract

What Prêt à Manger expects from people	What people can expect from Prêt à Manger
Reasonably hard working	Get paid as much as we can afford (not as little as we can get away with)
Good sense of humour	Cosmopolitan atmosphere as a result of diverse employee backgrounds
Enjoy delicious food	Invest in people training and development (in-store trainer)
Start early and leave early	Most managers are promoted from within

The contents of the Prêt à Manger psychological contract describe important aspects of the relationship between the company and its people. While the company does not promise incredible rewards it does promise reasonable pay and a lively environment. It also places high emphasis on the provision of above average training and development compared to other retail organisations; retail is not renowned for its emphasis on training. However, the in-store trainer in each Prêt location appears to offer more than most companies. This has value for employees by helping them learn to do the job, fit in and develop themselves for the future. It also has value for the company in enabling new employees to achieve the required store performance standards faster.

By making a feature of diversity and employing people from different backgrounds Prêt à Manger is able to make its shops feel more interesting both for customers as well as employees. Prêt à Manger is therefore simultaneously fulfilling the two goals of being a socially responsible and equal-opportunity employer, while also creating a differentiator in its marketplace compared to other sandwich shops. One of the other features of working in Prêt à Manger is that, because sandwiches are freshly made on site on the day of sale, employees have to come to work early to make these: therefore the conventional 9.00 a.m. retail start is replaced in Prêt à Manger with a 6.00 or 6.30 a.m. start.

A very different psychological contract is provided by Ernst & Young, one of the 'big four' accounting organisations, based on its People First principles.[4] People First is based on the idea that the organisation can only create value and confidence for clients through outstanding solutions and services by giving the highest attention to people's growth and satisfaction. By showing its

---

4   People First – 2006, www.ey.com

commitment to people's careers Ernst & Young hopes people will stay longer with the organisation. Some ways the organisation seeks to do this is through:

- fostering leadership and innovation;

- stressing teamwork as a firm value;

- providing continuous learning opportunities and access to knowledge;

- listening and responding to people's ideas and concerns;

- developing lifelong relationships with people;

- ensuring Ernst & Young is an enjoyable place to work.

The Ernst & Young psychological contract with employees can therefore be summarised as in Table 2.2.

Table 2.2   Ernst & Young's implied psychological contract

What Ernst & Young expects from its people	What employees can expect from Ernst & Young
Do the right thing and succeed for clients	Recognise and reward individual's contribution
Energy, enthusiasm, stretch and excel yourself	Enjoyable place to work
Build relationships, teamwork and the courage to lead	Care, listen and respond to people's ideas and concerns
Take charge and personal responsibility for your career	Continuous learning opportunities, access to knowledge and support for personal and career growth, and achieving your potential

The above table implies a very different relationship between employees and the organisation compared to Prêt à Manger. Whereas Prêt à Manger refers to working hard, Ernst & Young instead emphasises success achieved by the individual. The implicit assumption here is that working hard on its own is not enough – and it is something that is taken for granted by Ernst & Young. What the organisation emphasises and expects is that people will achieve high-level business outputs and results.

Other clear differences occur with regard to career development and living the values of the organisation. While Prêt implies few expectations about employees having a desire for long-term careers or more demanding roles, Ernst & Young takes this for granted in its offer to provide 'continuous learning opportunities, access to knowledge and support for personal and career growth and achieving your potential'. The organisation expects its people to want to develop their careers; however, responsibility for this is clearly placed on the individual themselves. This differs significantly from the implied contract in more traditional organisations where the implicit assumption is often that the company will take on significant, if not total, responsibility for individuals' careers. What Ernst and Young does promise is that, as a result of working there, individuals will have an opportunity to achieve their potential.

Ernst & Young undertakes to reward and remunerate individuals according to their contribution – the more you achieve the more you will be rewarded. Prêt à Manger makes no promises about this – it simply states that it will reward people as much as it can afford. It does, however, offer a carrot for effective performance by stating that most promotions to management occur from within.

The psychological contract of a totally different organisation, a mining company, has some interesting similarities and contrasts with Ernst & Young and Prêt à Manger. In recent years the company has very consciously shifted from being supply led to become customer led. One of its strategies to stay the best is through developing diverse talent. The psychological contract between the mining company and its employees, as shown in Table 2.3.

Table 2.3   Mining Company's implied psychological contract

What the mining company expects	What people can expect from the mining company
Commits to company values and purpose	Jobs and careers that create the opportunity to add increasing value
Focus on delivery excellence	Clarity of purpose
Continuous self-improvement and self-mastery	Pursues a well-defined vision
Responsible for own career planning	Consistent learning opportunities
Networking and building effective relationships	Enables high performance

The mining company's psychological contract has a number of similarities to that of Ernst & Young. Individuals can expect to be developed by the company but are personally responsible for their careers. The mining company, like Ernst & Young, expects individuals to display passion for what the company does.

The mining company's psychological contract differs in a fundamental way from Ernst & Young and Prêt à Manger in that it makes no reference to financial rewards. This is somewhat of a surprise as money is an important reason why most of us go to work – even if it is not what excites people about their work. The implicit thinking presumably is that for the company to offer meaningful careers it must include at least competitive financial rewards, and therefore direct reference to financial reward is not required.

Another unique feature of the mining company's psychological contract is that it makes explicit reference to provide jobs that offer the opportunity to add increasing value. This could be interpreted to mean offering larger and more responsible roles – something which neither Ernst & Young nor Prêt à Manger offer as part of their explicit psychological contract.

The information contained in the tables has been pulled together from different documents created by these three organisations. In practice, however, the psychological contracts in each of these businesses are to the author's knowledge not presented in such an explicit tabular way to employees. Obviously, there may be an up-front discussion about two-way expectations between a new employee and their boss when they join one of these organisations. Because of this the psychological contract is very much as Schein said, subtly communicated, rather than stated explicitly.

The majority of organisations today typically make their psychological contracts less explicit than the three organisations considered. Instead organisations rely on hints that may be dropped at different stages of the recruitment and induction process, or discussions at performance review time, to shape mutual expectations and the psychological contract between the organisation and its people. The psychological contract therefore typically operates at an unconscious or at least semi-conscious level. People pick up informally what is expected from them and what they can expect from the company through discussions and the occasional direct comment, for example when an employee is given specific directions or when they receive critical performance feedback. An employee will learn what they can expect in return from the organisation from the responses to requests made of the company or, more generally, through the organisation's socialisation processes. The important point is that the psychological contract in the majority of organisations is rarely directly articulated or communicated.

A fundamental feature of all three psychological contracts referred to above is that they refer to employee effort and work; Prêt à Manger refers to being 'reasonably hard working'; Ernst & Young refers to 'succeeding for clients'; and the mining company refers to 'focusing on delivery excellence'. This reference to employee outputs is not surprising, as the primary reason any commercial organisation employs people is to get work done and produce results. Despite the reference to work effort it is interesting to note how each company frames its expectations about this somewhat differently.

Another common feature of all three organisations' psychological contracts is their reference to development. While each contract treats it slightly differently, they all refer to it. Prêt à Manger does not claim to offer long-term careers; it does however offer training and development for all, some of which goes beyond the requirements for job performance. Ernst & Young offers the opportunity to realise your fullest potential, which implies career development; and the mining company makes explicit reference to offering more responsible jobs and careers.

Having looked at the psychological contracts from three different organisations, the most obvious conclusion is how different they are, even with regard to common features all three contain – like work output and career development. Viewed in the context of the very different activities they are involved in – making and selling sandwiches, professional services, and mining – this may not be altogether surprising. These examples hopefully bring to life the very real differences in the psychological contract that can exist in different organisations both in terms of what they expect from their people, and also what people can expect from working for these organisations. These examples of the psychological contract also illustrate how Schein's definition of the psychological contract can be seen in practice by three very different organisations.

Useful as these three descriptions of the psychological contract are, they are not intended in themselves to actively change behaviour. It could therefore be argued that these applications are relatively passive in that they provide a description of mutual expectations rather than seek to actively change people's thinking, behaviour or performance. In the next section we will consider an example where a very different psychological contract exists and which appears to seek to drive behaviour and performance a bit more directly.

A DIFFERENT PSYCHOLOGICAL CONTRACT

The core proposition of this book is that the psychological contract can be used as a powerful vehicle to drive behaviour and, more importantly, business performance. The notion that the psychological contract can influence behaviour was proposed by Schein:

> *Though it remains unwritten the psychological contract is a powerful determiner of behaviour in organisations.*

Schein almost certainly made this comment based more on his personal observation and intuition than empirical data. Since then dozens of academic research studies have provided empirical data which support Schein's view about the impact of the psychological contract on behaviour and performance. Some of this research will be considered in more detail in Chapter 6.

While Schein acknowledged that the psychological contract can influence behaviour he did not anticipate how it could be leveraged to enhance performance. A small number of business organisations now implicitly use the psychological contract to influence and shape organisation behaviour and, in turn, business performance. One example of how a retail organisation uses the psychological contract to drive competitive advantage will be considered below, and other more detailed examples will be given in Chapter 7.

One of the best known UK retail organisations is John Lewis, which is also one of the country's most sustainable business success stories. A special feature of John Lewis is that instead of being owned by shareholders it is a partnership owned by all its long-service employees, Despite the recent crisis faced by the UK's other major high-street name Marks and Spencer, John Lewis continues to grow and increase its sales year on year.

Information on their implied psychological contract can be obtained from the company's web site[5] and suggests it looks something like Table 2.4.

John Lewis is unique on the high street in operating a psychological contract where all 63 000 permanent employees are themselves owners of the business. As it says on the John Lewis website:

> *Commitment of partners to the business at John Lewis is a unique source of competitive advantage which has fuelled 75 years of profitable growth and a reputation amongst customers and supporters unparalled in UK retail industry.*

---

5   www.johnlewispartnership.co.uk

Table 2.4   John Lewis's implied psychological contract

What John Lewis expects from partners	What partners can expect from John Lewis
Exceptional quality of customer service	Competitive pay, bonus based on business success and discounts for staff purchases
Collective Responsibility – treat colleagues fairly and with respect	Work as a co-owner of the business – with staff committees involved in key decisions
Propose new ideas and use skills and knowledge to assist the organisation	Fair and equal opportunities, and wherever practicable promote from within
Honesty and integrity towards colleagues and customers	Loyalty holiday and leisure facilities in Lake District, Poole Harbour, and so on

The implication of the partners owning John Lewis is that the psychological contract is not between employees and the business, as occurs with most other business organisations; rather, their psychological contract is between each individual partner and all the other partners. This therefore creates an altogether different quality of relationship than the one between an employee and their employer. It is manifested by the organisation's expectation of collective responsibility, treating colleagues with respect and behaving as a co-owner. This is a significant departure from the psychological contracts operated in most other commercial organisations.

Another feature of John Lewis's psychological contract is that partners (equivalent to employees) are expected to focus specifically on serving customers and they can expect to share in the success of the business which arises from this. The important feature of the psychological contracts operated by John Lewis is that there is a clear commitment to provide a payback to employees when their focus on the customer bears fruit.

While there is no concrete proof that the success of the businesses is based on its unique psychological contract, there is a strong belief among managers in John Lewis that the employee care and sharing of profit with employees as a result of their contribution to customer service make a real difference to business performance.

The author believes the John Lewis psychological contract is quite special and differs significantly from those in the vast majority of profit and not-for-profit organisations – even those few where the psychological contract has been made quite explicit.

There is now an increasing body of academic research which shows how the psychological contract can impact on behaviour and, in turn, performance of employees, and some of this will be considered later in Chapter 8. The evidence from this research viewed together with the results of companies such as John Lewis makes a convincing case about the importance of the psychological contract for influencing and driving business behaviour and performance.

REDEFINED VIEW OF THE PSYCHOLOGICAL CONTRACT

The definition of the psychological contract provided earlier by Schein, while clear, implies that the psychological contract is what management as a group expect from all individual employees. This approach raises many complex questions, including the definition of who is a manager, and how to take best account of the different views of different managers. Very importantly if the psychological contract is made up of all managers' views then how can a decision be made that the psychological contract has been fulfilled or broken? These and similar questions create a significant challenge about how we can measure and define the psychological contract that is prevalent in an organisation.

To address these and similar issues Denise Rousseau redefined the psychological contract as something which essentially exists in each individual's head. Rousseau defined the psychological contract as: [6]

> … *individual beliefs, shaped by the organisation, regarding terms of an exchange agreement between individuals and their organisation.*

A more straightforward way of saying this was formulated by Rousseau and Greller: [7]

> *In simple terms, the psychological contract encompasses the actions employees believe are expected of them and what response they expect in return from the employer.*

The importance of these revised definitions is that they refer to individual employees' expectations of the organisation and also what they believe the organisation's expectations are of them. In practice of course an individual's beliefs about what the organisation expects of them may or may not have much bearing on what their managers actually expect from them! An employee might for example believe that their manager really values quality – in practice the

---

6 Rousseau, D. (1995), *Psychological Contracts in Organisations* (California: Sage)
7 Rousseau, D. and Greller, M. (1994), 'Human Resource Practices: administrative contract makers', *Human Resources Management* 33:3, 385–401

manager might put far more emphasis on volume, and not care much about quality. Rousseau's definition focuses on what each individual perceives and believes in their head about their own and the organisation's expectations. Rousseau's definition has now become widely adopted by the majority of researchers into the cause–effect relationship between psychological contract, its violation and the impact of this on attitudes to work and organisation behaviour.

While two people involved in a work relationship will have expectations about each other, Rousseau's definition implies that there may be two entirely different psychological contracts in operation: one set of beliefs about the exchange agreement between them in the employee's head (Person One) and another and separate set of beliefs about the exchange agreement between them in the manager's head (Person Two). The manager and the employee each have a perception of their psychological contract, whether or not their perceptions refer to the same issues or are consistent.

Despite this multiplicity of psychological contracts Rousseau's definition does have the great benefit of making measurement more straightforward. Each individual's psychological contract can be measured, analysed and interpreted – the individual's expectations about the organisation, as well as the individual's beliefs about what management expect from them as employees. If the perceptions of employees are aggregated they then provide a picture of the state of psychological contracts in the organisation. This definition also avoids the need for a rigorous definition of what constitutes management – management is simply what people understand it to be!

The importance of Rousseau's individual-based definition of the psychological contract is demonstrated by the very considerable increase in academic research into the psychological contract that has occurred since it was published. Despite its appeal to academics, practitioners mostly prefer to use Schein's definition of the psychological contract as a broad single set of expectations between the organisation and its employees.

CHANGE AND THE PSYCHOLOGICAL CONTRACT

One of the fundamental issues raised by Schein in his writing about the psychological contract was that it inevitably changes over time. As Schein put it:

... the psychological contract changes over time as the organisation's needs and the employees' needs change... What the employee is looking for in a job at age 25 may be completely different from what the same employee is looking for at age 50. Similarly what the organisation expects of a person during a period of rapid growth may be completely different from what that same organisation expects when it has levelled off or is experiencing economic decline... As needs and the external forces change, so do these expectations making the psychological contract a dynamic one which must be constantly renegotiated.

Schein's view was that the expectations of employees gradually change as they progress through their life. At a very simple level, employees' needs from employment could be viewed as falling into three stages:

1. *Early work life*   During their 20s many people try out, experiment and explore alternative job and career options. This is done in an effort to seek and identify job and career options and paths which are most appealing and personally fulfilling, so that the individual can pursue the paths which are most in their future interests.

2. *Development*   This occurs once the individual has identified a positive path from a work content, lifestyle and reward perspective. It occurs after exploring alternatives, and they then decide to develop and increase their skills and expertise in the chosen area of work, and develop their careers in the area.

3. *Maturity*   Having found and developed their work niche, the individual typically seeks stability so that they can provide for their increased and continuing family responsibilities. The goal is essentially one of sustaining the chosen direction.

While this view of careers was valid in the latter part of the twentieth century there is now very considerable evidence that this perspective of an individual searching until they find a niche which they stay in for the duration of their career is no longer valid. Far-reaching changes in society, as well as the global economy, are creating dramatic changes in the psychological contracts in many business organisations.

One example of this comes from changes in society. As increasing numbers of people go through divorce their economic requirements change significantly. Many of those over 40 who divorce find that instead of moving into the maturity phase, they decide to return to the development phase to increase their income to regain the level of assets they had prior to breaking up with their partner. Similarly, many people who have passed the development phase find they are bored. Instead of passing into the maturity phase they return again into the early-work-life stage.

More significant still are employees who having found what they believed was their career niche – whether at management, professional or operator level – find that their future becomes totally insecure. This may be because the jobs or career path they pursued are no longer appropriate or even exist in the economy. Examples in the UK are jobs such as printer or coal miner: changing technology or fuel economics have eliminated these jobs, and in the second case even the organisations where these jobs existed have disappeared. The demise of Rover in 2005 as the last UK-owned mass car manufacturer has seen the elimination of what 40 years ago was a major employment sector in the UK.

Changes to the psychological contracts of hurricane proportions are arising as a result of business pressures. Dramatic changes in the global economy, including the development of low-cost, high-quality manufacturing and now also services in China and India, are accompanied by ever-faster changes in technology, liberalisation of markets and changing consumer expectations. As organisations are pushed to innovate, increase market and customer responsiveness and reduce costs, they are being forced to bring about equally dramatic changes in work practices and in turn employee behaviour. The impact and nature of the changes are described well by Hamel[8] when he says:

> We now stand on the threshold of a new age – the age of revolution. In our minds we know the new age has already arrived; in our bellies we're not sure we like it.... For change has changed. No longer is it additive. No longer does it move in straight lines. In the twenty-first century change is discontinuous, abrupt, seditious... Today we live in a world that is all punctuation and no equilibrium.

SHIFTS IN THE PREVAILING PSYCHOLOGICAL CONTRACT OVER TIME

The far-reaching changes in business are according to Rousseau (1995) bringing about major shifts in both organisations and the psychological contracts that exist in them. She believes that the psychological contract has evolved over three distinct stages:

- *Emerging phase*   This occurred in the late eighteenth century during early industrial production and was characterised by a

8   Hamel, G. (2000), *Leading the Revolution* (Boston, Mass.: Harvard Business School Press)

central workplace with high levels of manager/owner control. Organisations in the UK that have survived since that stage include Royal Doulton (china manufacturers) and Twinings (tea growers and importers).

- *Bureaucratic phase*   This emerged in the 1930s epitomised by Whyte's *The Organisation Man*[9] in companies such as Ford. It was characterised by an internal labour market, organisation hierarchies which controlled behaviour, with spare resources being allocated to allow for unpredictability. Organisation life was characterised by a paternalistic psychological contract where the company took care of its loyal servants and implied lifetime employment in return for employee loyalty.

- *Adhocracy phase*   This has emerged since the early 1990s, epitomised by companies such as Apple and the successful dotcom companies. These are boundary-less organisations which emphasise the use of knowledge and are characterised by horizontal career moves, with a diversity of employer–employee relations. Companies in the adhocracy phase typically operate a range of psychological contracts for different employee groups.

As a result of economic pressures the bureaucratic style of organisation with (almost) lifetime employment, defined career structures and pay increases for continuing to serve the organisation is rapidly becoming history. In its place we have to think of our psychological contracts as being almost in a constant state of flux, influenced by ever-evolving business strategies with current business management approaches including performance management, employability and performance-related pay.

An increasing number of people find that the career path they moved into earlier in life has either disappeared or the opportunities have far reduced. One very obvious recent example is the large numbers of clerical office roles which have been replaced by call-centre operators who talk to customers directly and input changes as they speak to customers directly into the company systems. The need for processing customer requirements based on paper documents is fast disappearing, as is the need to write letters as correspondence is now increasingly generated automatically by IT systems.

The concept of change has caused the psychological contract to shift significantly away from the bureaucratic to the new adhocracy which, in many

---

9   Whyte, W. (1956), *The Organisation Man* (Simon & Schuster)

countries, is now the most prevalent type. The changes in the psychological contract between the bureaucratic and adhocracy have been summarised by Kissler in Table 2.5.[10]

Table 2.5   Changes in the psychological contract

Old bureaucratic psychological contract	New adhocracy psychological contract
Organisation is 'parent' to employee 'child'	Organisation and employee are both 'adult'
Organisation defines employees worth and identity	Employee defines their own worth and identity
Those who stay are good and loyal, others are disloyal	Regular flow of people in and out of the organisation is healthy
Employees who do as they are told will work until they retire	Long-term employment is unlikely – expect and prepare for multiple employments
Promotion is the primary route for growth	Growth is through personal accomplishment

As we can see from the table, the difference between the two psychological contracts is quite fundamental. The changes place increasing responsibility for individual's lives in their own hands, rather than in the hands of the employer, as occurred in the bureaucratic psychological contract. (The terms 'parent', 'adult' and 'child' are used in transactional analysis, which is discussed in Chapter 12.)

Recent research by the UK Chartered Institute of Personnel Development[11] adds weight to the conclusion that broad changes are taking place in the psychological contracts operated across different organisations in the UK. At a headline level the research suggests that organisations are now more successful in delivering against the broad expectations they encourage employees to believe: they are fulfilling their side of the psychological contract more than before. CIPD concluded that employees today seek one of three types of psychological contracts with their employer:

- traditional – those who seek long-term tenure and work long hours;

- disengaged – those for whom work is not a central life interest and seek no emotional tie to their employer;

---

10   Kissler, G. (1994), 'The New Employment Contract', *Human Resource Management* 33, 335–352
11   Guest, D. and Conway, N. (2004), *Employee Well-Being and the Psychological Contract*, Research Report (London: CIPD)

- independent – those who are well qualified, and seek short tenure and high rewards.

The far-reaching changes in the psychological contracts that are taking place in organisations provide one of the important rationales for this book. When the psychological contract was relatively straightforward and stable, as in bureaucratic organisations, it was less important to understand others' expectations, as these became apparent over time and any misunderstanding could be dealt with gradually. With increasingly dramatic changes in psychological contracts, brought about by ever-faster and vigorous economic and social forces, the need to be clear about our psychological contracts becomes more and more important if we are to cope and thrive in business.

CHAPTER SUMMARY

- The psychological contract refers to the expectations, many of which are unspoken, between an employee and the organisation which employs them. The origins of the concept can be traced back thousands of years to major religions which refer to mutual expectations between members of the faith and God.

- The psychological contract is most commonly defined as 'unwritten expectations operating at all times between every member of an organisation and the various managers and others in that organisation'. Employee expectations may include obvious things such as pay, as well as softer issues such as personal support or development. Organisation expectations may refer to working hard or results, as well as more subtle expectations such as loyalty or enhancing the reputation of the organisation.

- Many organisations articulate their psychological contracts indirectly through their websites, recruitment literature and so on which describe what they expect from an employee, and what the employee can expect from them. Prêt à Manger's website suggests that the company expects its people to be reasonably hard working, have a good sense of humour, enjoy delicious food and start and leave work early. Employees for their part get paid as much as the company can afford, join a cosmopolitan atmosphere, receive training and development, and internal promotion opportunities.

- The psychological contracts of many organisations typically make reference to the efforts/results employees are expected to deliver, and also to the way the organisation will contribute to their development. Importantly even these common components of the psychological contract are treated subtly but quite differently by different organisations.

- John Lewis' one of the UK's most successful organisations' has a psychological contract which focuses employees on serving customers, it also promises a share in the success arising from this. Because employees own the company, this psychological contract unusually is between employees and other employees, rather than with the organisation.

- The psychological contract was redefined by Rousseau to refer to an individual's beliefs about what is expected of them and what they can expect from their employer. Therefore each employee will have their own perceptions of their psychological contract, and their manager will have their own perceptions of what it involves. Their views of the psychological contract may not be the same or even compatible. Rousseau's individual-based definition of the psychological contract has encouraged a major increase in research in the psychological contract.

- Individual employees and organisations are under enormous pressures to change their expectations of people and in turn their psychological contracts. As individuals move through life their personal needs from work change. While people in their 20s typically seek to experiment and try out new things, those in their 50s typically seek continuity and security. Simultaneously changes arising from new technology and competition from the rapidly growing economies of China and India are putting pressures on large corporations to implement psychological contracts which emphasise greater individual output, flexibility and customer responsiveness.

- The prevailing psychological contracts in organisations have shifted from the emerging, through bureaucratic towards one characterised by adhocracy. This involves both the individual and the organisation being 'adult', and where employees define their own worth and identity through accomplishment. People regularly flow in and out of the organisation and long-term employment becomes less likely.

CHAPTER 3

Viewing the Psychological Contract as a Personal Deal

In Chapter 2 we explored how the psychological contract has evolved and examples of the form it can take in different organisations. This chapter will present a framework for understanding how the psychological contract works in practice as a type of deal – what we will call the 'personal deal at work'. It embodies similar features to other deals we make in life, but with important differences, which is why we have called it the 'personal deal'.

BUSINESS DEALS AND PERSONAL DEALS

When we talk about a business deal we mean an understanding about an exchange: something you give me, and something I give you in return. When we buy flight tickets at easyJet we pay a sum of money and in exchange receive an entitlement to fly from one destination to another. When we buy a car we hand over a sum of money in exchange for our new vehicle. Almost all conventional deals we make involve an exchange of money for goods, services or assets. In some cases we are the purchaser (for example when we go to the shops, physically or on the web), and in others we might be the vendor (for example when we sell our house, sell stuff in a car boot sale or over eBay).

Many of the deals we make when exchanging money for goods or services involve a legal agreement. When we buy or sell a house we sign a long contract. There is a two-page contract when we apply to use a new credit card. When we buy or sell shares we will almost certainly have signed a legal agreement with our bank or stockbroker beforehand. Even the purchase of easyJet tickets over the web requires us to 'check this box to confirm you have read, understood and accept easyJet's conditions of carriage'.

The importance of the legal agreement is that it stipulates what happens if things do not go according to plan. If I do not show for my easyJet flight at the designated time for example I forfeit my right to fly. If I fail to vacate my house on the appointed date for the completed sale in the UK there will be financial and other penalties, and so on.

At its heart the psychological contract is a personal deal. It involves an exchange of what I will give you, and what you will give me. The previous chapter described the psychological contracts in different business organisations. We saw that the amount of employee effort expected in some organisations is different from the amount expected in others. There are also differences in what employees get back. Some organisations for example commit to play a much more active part in their people's development than others.

A second and related similarity between a business deal and the personal deal is that they both involve expectations. If you buy a new apartment for £400 000 you will have expectations about it – that the fittings you saw when you viewed are still there, that essential services work normally, that it is safely constructed and so on. Similarly we will have a series of expectations about our personal deals at work. Our employing organisation will have a whole series of expectations about how we as employees will perform not just the core job, but also things such as how we behave towards colleagues and customers, the way they dress and so on.

Another similarity between the personal deal and the business deal is that there are consequences if one party breaks their commitments. If the new stereo you buy goes wrong two weeks after you get it home you typically have recourse to the manufacturer's warranty, and if that does not help you could seek to use the legal system to redress your problem. It is similar with the personal deal, but may be less formal. If an employee consistently underperforms against their company's expectations they are likely eventually to get fired. Equally if a company consistently fails to deliver against what employees expect they will sooner or later quit, assuming that there are alternative jobs available – and sometimes there are not. Just as some employees find they have few alternative employment options, some organisations find they have some employees who have mentally quit because the organisation has failed to fulfil their expectations – but remain in employment. We shall explore this issue in Chapter 4 'Making and Breaking Personal Deals'.

A fourth similarity between a business deal and a personal deal is that both are usually entered into voluntarily. If you decide to book a holiday, buy food at the supermarket, buy shares from your broker, or sell stuff on eBay you will almost certainly do this voluntarily. If we have a personal deal with a business which employs us, we most likely will have entered it voluntarily. There are exceptions – like a prisoner's relationship with the guards – but, fortunately, for most of us these types of personal deals are rare.

While there are similarities between a business deal and a personal deal there are also two important differences between them. One of the differences concerns money or financial considerations. Almost all business deals involve an exchange involving money – the amount you pay for a house, the cost of flight tickets, the cost of a new PC and so on. Personal deals typically involve expectations about a broad range of intangible behavioural and emotional components. Many personal deals are fulfilled or broken without any reference to money. If the personal deal with an employee implies variety of work, but the job in practice is mainly routine, the personal deal is likely to have been broken. Equally, if my employer assumes that I will be polite to all customers but, in practice, I decide to be abrupt and argumentative with customers I do not personally like, I am likely to have broken the personal deal. A personal deal may therefore not have a financial component.

The second important difference between a business deal and a personal deal is that many, if not most of the expectations each party has of the other in a personal deal may never be articulated or talked about. Typically many expectations only emerge when things go wrong. An organisation may, for example, have a regular and demanding performance management system which involves defined targets, time periods when performance will be reviewed, and so on, and these may be explained in the pre-employment discussion. The manager may however not mention to an employee before they join that they expect to have a weekly one-to-one discussion with each team member, and that they are expected to take action on every single thing raised by the next weekly meeting.

Equally, an employee may have expectations about the amount of personal interest they expect the boss to take in them as an individual, and not raise this before joining. In practice your manager may express far less interest in you personally than you expect. Alternatively, you may be surprised by the very high interest they express in your personal life. Our expectations in a personal deal may cover a very broad range of things, which involve many different states – emotional, intellectual, behavioural, physical, as well as financial. We carry these expectations in our heads and frequently never articulate them unless we feel the personal deal has been frustrated.

At one level the personal deal is similar to any other deal, it involves an exchange of things we give to another person, and expectations of what we want from the other person. Both are usually entered voluntarily, and both parties bring a set of expectations about what these involve. The personal deal differs from a conventional deal in that it may not always involve money and involves components which are never talked about or articulated. These differences make the personal deal subtly and importantly different from a conventional deal. Hence we will refer to it from now onwards as the 'personal deal' as opposed to any other business deal.

There are situations where a business deal is combined with a personal deal. A good example of this is with a maintenance contract. The business deal about the maintenance contract may be laid out in writing – however we as consumers are likely to have a series of expectations about the provision of maintenance which is more of a personal deal and goes far beyond what is stipulated in the contract. We may well have expectations about how our request for maintenance is handled by the supplier, and how the maintenance person conducts themselves when on our premises, and how they communicate and interact with us personally. A feature of many services, including business services, is that they involve a combination of both a business deal as well as a personal deal.

ALL OUR RELATIONSHIPS INVOLVE A PERSONAL DEAL

The psychological contract is conventionally seen to operate exclusively in the workplace, but the personal deal applies as much out of work as in work. While the focus of this book is on personal deals at work, it might be helpful to explore the concept first in a broader context. This will provide a broader social perspective to the personal deal, and demonstrate its power as something which permeates all our relationships in life.

All relationships we have, whether with an individual, group or organisation involve four components:

- *Awareness*   We have a picture in our head about other people or organisations. A relationship with a person we have never seen or met face to face involves some awareness about them – even if it involves a picture we have created in our heads. We typically have a visual image of colleagues in our work area that we interact with frequently. We also have an image of a colleague or associate on the other side of the globe who we never have met but only talked to over the phone or exchanged emails with. This image will come from their voice over the phone or even from the style in which they write emails.

- *Activity*   Every relationship we have involves some activity or behaviour. This may be simply talking or writing. An exchange of words or emails involves an activity. The activity might involve walking past someone in the corridor – such as when we pass the security guard en route to do other things. All the relationships we have involve some form of activity – even the superficial ones we have with people we pass in the office and give a nod in greeting. The passing and nodding are an activity.

- *Feelings*   These may be intense – for example admiration towards a colleague we really like, or anger towards a boss we dislike. With some relationships our feelings may be much more low key – such as towards the security guard who we only see occasionally. We will nevertheless have some feelings towards them, even if these are less intense – we may admire their physique, or perhaps not particularly like their hairstyle.

- *Reciprocity*   In other words we give something to the other person, and they give something towards us in return. If the person is a colleague we work with closely we may give each other information or ideas for getting our jobs done. There will be other people with whom we exchange very little – perhaps nothing more than a look of acknowledgement or simple greeting as we enter and leave the building.

Some of our relationships may involve all four components intensely – for example when we dance closely with someone we love, or when we work closely with a colleague we value and respect to solve a complex business problem. Other relationships may involve one or two of these components, such as the relationship with our squash partner, who we only see on the squash court, but never spend time with outside the clubhouse. In this case the activity component will be particularly prominent. There are some people we work with to solve problems infrequently. An example is when our IT system crashes and we then work intensively with the IT helpdesk personnel to restore connectivity, but do not interact much apart from then. Finally there are the many people with whom we interact and relate in only a superficial way – examples include a neighbour a few houses along from where we live, the cashier across the bank counter, the receptionist in our offices or the security guard at the office.

EXPECTATIONS LIE AT THE HEART OF THE PERSONAL DEAL

Whatever the nature of our relationship with another person, it will give rise to a set of expectations covering the four components of a relationship – our awareness of the individual, some actions and behaviour, feelings and reciprocity. We have expectations about a close colleague, about the IT helpdesk colleague, about our manager, colleagues in our team, as well as about the receptionist and the security guard. If I asked you to describe what your expectations are about any of these or similar people you could probably do so quite easily.

These expectations matter because they are one of the most important drivers of our behaviour in the many and varied situations we encounter at work and throughout life. If you expect the office cleaner to influence your promotion to the next job you may behave differently towards them. Equally if you believe your boss can never assist you in your work you may not bother to ask for their input and ideas.

We all have specific expectations of the different people we know. For example, we may know from experience that one of our colleagues has a great sense of humour, and can provide a lift if we are feeling low. We may therefore seek them out if we are feeling down. We may know someone who has a wealth of knowledge about technology, and if we want ideas or advice when making decisions about the use of technology we ask for their advice – rather than anyone else. Someone else we know may have a great brain and be able to slice through facts and data when there is a difficult problem to solve. We may go to them when we cannot decide between alternative decisions or approaches.

Take a few minutes to reflect on some of the expectations you have of your partner, your children, your parents and a close friend. Also get in touch with the expectations you have towards specific colleagues? These expectations lie at the root of your personal deals with each of these different people.

The importance of the personal deal is illustrated when you think about what happens if your expectations of someone close to you are not fulfilled. How would you feel and react if a friend you think of as having great expertise in technology turns round and says they have no interest in the technology issue you are trying to solve? What would you think if the colleague with a great brain is unable to solve the complex problem on which you seek their ideas and input? How would you react if the friend with a normally great sense of humour and lots of empathy tells you they are too busy to talk to you? You may just shrug the incident off if it is a one-off – but if this occurs repeatedly you may well decide to change your future behaviour towards them.

Just as we have expectations of people we know, all these different people – our friends, our partner, our colleagues and manager – will have expectations of us. What do you think your boss or close work colleague expect from you? Do you think they anticipate you to be supportive, helpful, and constructive? Are they likely to expect you to be difficult, or as someone who readily engages in their ideas?

A CLOSER LOOK AT A PERSONAL DEAL

To explore mutual expectations involved in a personal deal we will consider a situation we have all experienced – with a waiter or waitress when we visit a restaurant. The reason for choosing this situation and relationship is that while it is typically less intense, it provides a powerful illustration of how expectations and the personal deal operate in a very practical and tangible way. Importantly, I hope it illustrates how fulfilment of our personal deal can result in entirely different behaviours by us when our personal deal is frustrated. This example also illustrates the power of the personal deal in customer service, something which concerns many of us in business.

Look at the list of things given in Table 3.1 and rate how important each of these is for you when you visit a restaurant. Place a number between 1 and 5 against each item to indicate its importance for you, 5 being very important and 1 being unimportant.

Table 3.1   Your expectations in a restaurant

Things you expect from a waiter or waitress in a favourite restaurant	*Importance rating 1–5*
The table you booked is available as soon as you arrive	
You are greeted positively and with enthusiasm	
The waiter is courteous and makes pleasant small talk	
The waiter can talk knowledgably about food on the menu and how it is cooked	
The waiter can advise about the different wines available	
The waiter is unobtrusive while you are eating	
The waiter brings the correct food to each person	
The food is placed in front of you with great dignity	
The food is cooked from high-quality ingredients	
The waiter is entertaining, cracks jokes and is fun	
You are not pressurised to leave as soon as you stop eating	
The waiter attends you quickly if you call or catch their eye	
The bill is correctly added up	
Other	

There could be other things you want and expect from a restaurant which are quite personal to you – and a blank space is provided for you to add these.

By rating what you expect from a restaurant you will have looked at one part of your personal deal with the restaurant.

The second part of the personal deal is made up of what the waiter or waitress in the restaurant expects from you. Possible things that they may expect could include the things listed in Table 3.2. Now rate what you believe is the importance given by a waiter or waitress in one of your favourite restaurants to each item shown below.

Table 3.2   Waiter/waitresses' expectations of you

What does a waiter or waitress in a favourite restaurant expect from you?	Importance rating 1–5
You arrive at the restaurant at the time you reserved	
You are dressed in a way typical of other clients	
You are polite and courteous	
You and your guests order a starter and a main course	
You are in a frame of mind to enjoy your food	
Your party does not disrupt other diners	
You respond to their conversation and humour	
You do not steal the cutlery	
You do not request lots of extras for example free tap water, etc	
You are relaxed if the waiter makes a mistake	
You pay your bill without a hassle	
You leave at least the recommended service charge	
Other	

One of the key features of the personal deal is that it is unique to each person, and unique for each and every relationship we are involved in. What you expect in a restaurant may be somewhat different from the expectation of some people you know, and may be very different from others. Equally the expectations waiters and waitresses have of customers in a particular restaurant may all be somewhat different; and their expectations may be very different to those held by waiters and waitresses in other establishments.

You may find it interesting to rate the expectations you believe waiters and waitresses in different restaurants have of you. I was quite amazed during a recent trip to Italy when a smart restaurant owner was totally relaxed when my family and I did not order a main course, after our appetites were satisfied by the first course. I cannot imagine many owners of smart restaurants in England reacting in quite such an easy-going way!

Discuss your expectations about a restaurant with a friend and find out whether your expectations are similar – and where you differ. While the degree to which you expect the waiter or waitress to be entertaining and fun may be unimportant to you, does it matter more to your friend?

The importance of our expectations about the waiter or waitress, and their expectations about us is that together they form our personal deal in the way we will refer to it throughout this book. We define the 'personal deal' as:

The personal deal refers to the mutual and often unexpressed expectations that operate at all times between people (individuals and teams) who interact and communicate with one another. The extent to which others exceed or fall short of our expectations underpins the way we respond, relate and behave towards them. Personal deals apply to our relationships with family, friends, colleagues, customers, community organisations, employers and service providers.

Our expectations and those of others will be influenced by many things, including our personality and national culture. For example, your concept of what is polite is likely to be determined by the culture in which you live. To the Japanese, for example, politeness will often involve bowing the head and not looking at you directly. If you are American however the expectation of politeness may involve looking you directly in the eye.

A warm person may have an expectation that supportiveness will be demonstrated by another person smiling and gently touching your arm. To someone who is more distant and less expressive an expectation about supportiveness may simply involve paying attention while you are talking. You will almost certainly have your own unique ideas about the type and forms of behaviour involved for you to consider someone supportive.

In the same way that we have a personal deal with a restaurant waiter, we have personal deals with the many people we interact with, including our partner, children, parents, friends and people we know in the community. We also have personal deals with colleagues at work, our boss, our team members, people in other departments, associates outside the organisation, with customers, suppliers – even competitors. Our focus in this book is on personal deals at work; nevertheless the concept of personal deals is equally relevant in all the different domains of our life.

VISUALISING THE PERSONAL DEAL

So far we have seen two components of the personal deal with a restaurant – 'What I expect from the waiter', and 'What the waiter expects from me'. There are two other key components of the personal deal we need to add to understand how it operates. One is 'What the other person gives you' relative to your expectations, and the other is 'What you give the other person' relative to their expectations of you.

These four components of the personal deal are shown in Figure 3.1 as they apply when we visit a restaurant.

The importance ratings you gave to each of the 13 items shown in the earlier list of 'Things you expect from a waiter or waitress in a favourite restaurant' make up the box shown in the diagram of 'What I expect from the waiter'. The ratings you gave to the 13 items shown in the earlier list of 'What does a waiter or waitress in a favourite restaurant expect from you?' makes up the box shown in the diagram of 'What the waiter expects from me'.

To understand what happened to your personal deal in a recent restaurant visit you now need to complete the two additional boxes concerning 'What the waiter gives me' and 'What I give the waiter'. Before reading further

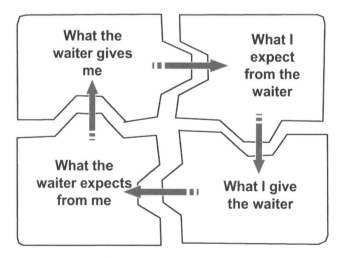

Figure 3.1   Components of our personal deal with a restaurant

you may want to reflect on what actually happened in a recent visit to the restaurant for which you made the ratings. To what extent did the waiter fulfil your expectations? To what extent do you believe you fulfilled the waiter's expectations about you? The answers to these two questions will determine the state of your personal deal.

Arrows link the four boxes in the diagram above. The two horizontal arrows connect the boxes of what is given by one party to what the other party expects to receive from them. An important feature of the personal deal is that it takes account of the comparisons we make between what we expect to receive and what we actually receive from the other person. Undoubtedly you will be able to recall times when your expectations in a restaurant were fulfilled, and surpassed. If your experiences are anything like mine, you may also have had your share of experiences where your expectations remained unfulfilled.

HOW WELL WAS YOUR PERSONAL DEAL WITH THE RESTAURANT FULFILLED?

If your expectations about the restaurant were fulfilled or exceeded it is likely you will have enjoyed the meal, and this may have impacted your feelings towards the waiter and the restaurant, as well as your frame of mind while eating and perhaps during the rest of the evening. You may have felt more positive towards your dining companions, and perhaps this impacted how you felt and behaved after leaving the restaurant. Your good mood may well have rubbed off on your companions and in turn influenced their feelings about the evening.

If your expectations were exceeded by what you received from the waiter in the restaurant you may have decided to thank them very positively before leaving, been very friendly towards them, perhaps you decided to leave more than the usual non-discretionary 12.5 per cent tip. After the evening you may have decided to become a regular customer of the restaurant. You may have recommended the establishment to your friends, or suggested that a large group of you dine there.

We all make comparisons between what the other person/people in our personal deal actually give us and what we expect from them – hence the arrow in the diagram. If our expectations are fulfilled or exceeded this will have a completely different impact on how we subsequently behave towards the waiter than if our expectations were not fulfilled – hence the horizontal arrow from 'What I give the waiter' to 'What the waiter expects from me'.

The comparison process between 'What the waiter gives me' and 'What I expect from the waiter' is largely a subjective process, and gives rise to feelings. Our feelings might be pleasure, happiness or well-being that our expectations were exceeded. Alternatively our feelings might be irritation, annoyance, frustration, perhaps even anger, if our expectations were not fulfilled. These feelings and their intensity will in turn impact 'What I give the waiter'. So if I feel mildly positive about the treatment I received from the waiter I may behave differently than if I feel intensely pleased and happy about the way I was treated. The feelings that arise from my perceived match between 'What the waiter gives me' and 'What I expect from the waiter' will therefore determine my decisions about 'What I give the waiter'.

If your expectations were not fulfilled the situation would probably be entirely different. This might have been caused by any of a number of reasons. Perhaps your table was not ready when you arrived, or the waiter or waitress was unable to answer your questions about the food. Perhaps the waiter was intrusive when you expected to be left alone with your dining partner – or the bill was inaccurately added up. If any of these, or similar things happened, your reactions both towards the waiter when you left, and towards the restaurant subsequently might have been very different. The result in the diagram would be that your decision about 'What I give the waiter' would be entirely different than if your expectations had been fulfilled.

From the restaurant's perspective fulfilment of your expectations will have critical business consequences. If the restaurant regularly exceeds your and other customers' expectations they are likely to gain a good reputation – resulting in more people wanting to dine there. Revenues are therefore likely to increase and the restaurant is likely to become more successful and more profitable. Because of the high demand for tables the restaurant management may subsequently be able to raise their prices as people will be willing to pay these and the restaurant will in turn become more profitable and successful.

If your expectations about the restaurant were not fulfilled you may have felt dissatisfied with the restaurant and it could have adversely affected your mood for the evening. If this was a first dinner with a new hot date or a birthday dinner with your partner it may impact the atmosphere between you. If it was a first dinner with a hot date they might have questioned your judgement, and whether you are right for them because of your poor choice of restaurant!

After the evening was over you may well have decided to take the restaurant off your list of places to go, and searched for other places for future evenings out. You may have asked friends for names of other places to eat, and told them about how dissatisfied you were with the restaurant. Your unfulfilled expectations may have adversely affected your feelings after you left the premises, and adversely affected your mood for the rest of the evening.

Your unfulfilled expectations might prove to be an expensive mistake by the restaurant. The immediate impact might be that you do not personally visit again, and therefore they have lost revenue from you. However if you also tell a number of people about your poor experience you may put them off dining there. If other people had similar experiences to you it would not take long for the reputation of the restaurant to go down. Before long the establishment would lose customers and this would have a direct impact on its revenues and profitability. Eventually if enough customers feel their personal deal has been frustrated it is likely the restaurant will go out of business.

The downward vertical arrow in the right of the diagram shows how the extent to which your expectations about the restaurant were fulfilled influenced your subsequent behaviour. In the case of the restaurant your fulfilled expectations would have resulted in dramatically different behaviours towards the restaurant than if your expectations were not fulfilled.

HOW WELL DID YOU FULFIL THE EXPECTATIONS OF THE WAITER/WAITRESS?

So far we have only considered the personal deal from your point of view; we can now consider how well you fulfilled the waiter's expectations of you, and in turn how this might have influenced how they behaved towards you. There is no doubt that your waiter's behaviour towards you during the evening will have been influenced by the extent to which you fulfilled their expectations. If, for example, you turned up 40 minutes after you booked the table it is quite possible that your table might have been given to someone else. If you ignored the waiter's conversation, or made more demands than the waiter expects from a typical customer it is quite possible that this will impact how they reacted and behaved towards you. They may have decided to ignore your requests for attention, they may have decided to serve food to another table before they served yours, or they may have decided to go out of their way to be difficult or less positive towards you.

Alternatively if the waiter thought you were patient about the slight delay in preparing your table, friendly and did not look down on them, they are likely to behave differently towards you. Instead of getting their standard treatment they may have gone out of their way to be positive towards you. They may have been more talkative towards you, told you to avoid one of the specials that were a bit off, responded quickly when you wanted their attention. The waiter may also have decided to bring your food out quicker from the kitchen in preference to the food for another table which was also ready. There are many different ways the waiter or waitress in a restaurant could behave more positively towards you if they felt you were a good customer.

The importance of the two vertical arrows in the personal deal diagram is that they show how our subsequent decisions about how we will behave towards another person are significantly influenced by the extent to which our expectations were fulfilled by them.

PERSONAL DEALS AT WORK

The mutual expectations we have with a waiter in a restaurant and how we fulfil these expectations provide an example of how the personal deal operates in practice. In our work we are likely to have a myriad of personal deals and mutual expectations with the different people with whom we work. These are likely to be particularly important for our relationships with our manager and people who report to us, but will also be significant for our relationships with colleagues, associates, customers and suppliers.

At work we may have many different expectations about our manager and the organisation we work with. Equally our manager is likely to have a series of expectations about us. These two sets of expectations together make up our 'personal deal at work' with our manager.

Table 3.3 contains 22 separate items which fall under 11 separate expectations headings. These have been derived from an analysis of work of different organisation-behaviour experts, including Denise Rousseau,[1] Marcus Buckingham,[2] and Edgar Schein.[3] While the list attempts to cover things that could matter to many different people the list cannot include every possible expectation. Some people will have expectations that are unique to them. Nevertheless, the 11 expectations probably cover the most common things that employees expect from their manager and employer.

---

[1]   Rousseau, D. (2000), *Psychological Contract Inventory – Technical Report* (Heinz School of Public Policy and Graduate School of Industrial Administration, Carnegie Mellon University)

[2]   Buckingham, M. and Coffman, C. (1999), *First Break all the Rules* (New York: Simon Schuster)

[3]   Schein, E. (1990), *Career Anchors: Discovering Your Real Values* (San Diego: University Associates)

In practice the emphasis that each person places on each of the eleven expectations will be unique. Some items will matter more to some people and less to others. Even people who share broadly similar expectations at work are likely to place different emphasis on the things that matter to them. The list below should therefore be treated as a framework of the most common expectations and not as a definitive list which applies to everyone.

Table 3.3   Employee expectations of the personal deal at work

Factor	Examples
Environment	Provide the materials and equipment I need to do my work
	Pleasant physical workplace and environment
Direction	Clarity about what is expected of me at work
	Understand how job contributes to team/company strategy
Well-being	Concern for me as a person and my welfare
	Respect for personal life, and work/life balance
Challenge	Able to use many skills and talents at work
	Opportunity to tackle more demanding goals and objectives
Development	Encouragement to learn through feedback, coaching, training and so on
	Opportunities to take on increased responsibility and advance
Creativity	The opportunity to come up with new ideas and approaches
	Requirement to implement new solutions and practices at work
Influence	Someone listens to my ideas and opinions
	Opportunity to influence and lead people
Equity	Receive fair pay and conditions for work undertaken
	Transparent criteria for pay and reward changes
Relationships	Work with congenial/friendly people
	Engaged and committed colleagues
Recognition	Recognition and praise for doing good work
	Support to address problems and issues at work
Security	Reasonable predictability that company and job continue
	Change is implemented in a caring way

The emphasis each of us gives to different items will vary according to what kind of a person we are, and our stage in life. A single person in their 20s is more likely to place emphasis on challenge and development, while a person in their late 50s with an established partner and family responsibilities is more likely to place emphasis on equity and security.

The importance we attach to the different factors is also likely to be influenced by our personality. Someone who is highly ambitious is, for example, likely to place more emphasis on challenge and development. In contrast someone who is unambitious and simply views work as something instrumental in providing them with the means to do the other more important things in life is likely to place more emphasis on well-being and equity.

The employee perspective of the personal deal at work only provides half of the picture, in the same way that customer expectations about the restaurant only provided half the view of the personal deal at the restaurant. The other half of the personal deal at work involves what the organisation expects of the individual. The list presented in Table 3.4 is based on the work of Huiskamp and Schalk[4]. The same caution applies to this list as to the list of individual expectations – it is intended as a framework to cover the most common things that matter to managers and organisations. Each organisation and manager will in practice have their own unique combination of expectations about people. The table shows the more common things that managers in an organisation might expect from their employees.

The examples of the psychological contract given in Chapter 2 show in a very clear way how each organisation has unique requirements for their personal deal with people. An organisation involved in handling money or precious metals such as a bank or a jeweller is likely to place high emphasis on protection. A new dotcom organisation is likely to place considerable emphasis on flexibility. A professional service organisation is likely to place particularly high value on learning and ambassador expectations, while a hospital or care home may put high emphasis on care. The business sector and marketplace in which an organisation operates is likely to be one of the most important drivers of the organisation's expectations of its people.

As well as differences between organisations there are likely to be important differences between the personal deal for different jobs and departments. If we visit the IT departments in many large organisations it is likely that people will be dressed more casually than those involved in face-to-face sales where more emphasis is placed on the ambassadorial and conformance aspects of the role. IT departments typically place low emphasis on conformance to dress standards,

---

4   Huiskamp, R. and Schalk, R. (2002), 'Psychologische contracten in arbeidsrelaties: De stand van zaken in Nederland', *Gedrag en Organisatie* 15, 370–85

Table 3.4   Manager and organisation expectations of the personal deal at work

Factor	Examples
Performance	Fulfil levels and quantity of outputs that are expected Quality of work fulfils/exceeds standards
Flexibility	Adapt work times to suit changed business needs Undertake additional activities for benefit of the organisation
Learning	Develop own skills, knowledge and expertise Build new skills in anticipation of future organisation needs
Collaboration	Interact and work with colleagues to get work done efficiently Support and encourage individuals, team and unit to achieve
Conformance	Implement and adhere to broader procedures and work systems Understand and live team and company values and culture
Knowledge	Share knowledge with colleagues to maximise performance Develop the skills and capabilities of colleagues
Improvement	Come up with new ideas and approaches to improve performance Champion change initiatives which add to the business
Ambassador	Promote the reputation of the organisation in the marketplace Increase network and external visibility for the organisation
Care	Listen and show empathy towards others Show care and consideration for customers' personal needs
Commitment	Remain with the organisation for a reasonable period of time Displays enthusiasm towards the business and its goals
Protection	Reduce exposure and risks to acceptable levels for the organisation Protect the confidentiality of company information and plans

while people in sales typically place much more emphasis on this. People in research or development roles however place high emphasis on improvement.

From this brief overview of the personal deal we can see that different people will emphasise different aspects of the employee personal deal. Also different organisations, departments and managers will place different emphasis on the organisation components of the personal deal.

The fact that different organisations and different employees want different types of personal deals at work means that there are an incredibly diverse range of personal deals in existence. This becomes apparent when we change organisation and notice that what is valued in our last company is not in our new one. Equally, we become aware that there are some practices that are tolerated in our new company that were not in our previous organisation, and vice versa. There are some organisations which have low expectations about performance, but where conformance is everything – for example some traditional government departments. In these organisations being seen to do the right thing is everything. In other organisations performance and flexibility as demonstrated by the value you brought to the business last quarter is all that counts; results here, such as in fast growing entrepreneurial organisations, are everything.

Within every organisation there will be individual departments where the requirements differ from those which prevail in most other parts of the organisation – for example IT and development where there are often unique requirements for success. Chief executives and general managers are often quite surprised to see the diversity of personal deals that exist within their organisation. The challenge at that level is to decide which components of the personal deal need to be consistent across the organisation, and which can be variable according to function, product or geography. This will be explored further in Chapter 8 on leadership.

Within any one team working for the same manager there will be some people who seek recognition above all else, while other people doing the same job may put challenge or development top of their agenda. The range and

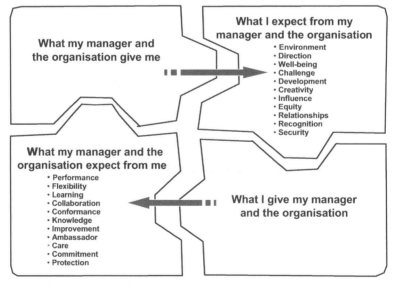

Figure 3.2   Components of the personal deal at work

variety of personal deals in organisations is almost infinite. A diagram showing the components of the personal deal is shown in Figure 3.2.

We have been able to identify eleven different things that an employee may want to include in their personal deal with an organisation and eleven different things that a manager and the organisation may want to include in its deal with an employee. In practice, the personal deal between any one individual and their manager is unique, and will involve not only different emphasis on each of the eleven organisation and employee components of the personal deal, but different interpretation of what each means. Also in practice most managers and employees will only want to emphasise four or five of the items in the list of expectations.

DIFFERENCE BETWEEN THE PERSONAL DEAL AT WORK AND THE PSYCHOLOGICAL CONTRACT

From this chapter you may be aware of a fundamental difference between the personal deal at work and the psychological contract. The psychological contract, whether we use Schein's or Rousseau's definitions (see Chapter 2), is about expectations between an individual and their employing organisation. The way we describe the personal deal at work here is as expectations between individuals, particularly between a manager and their team members, rather than between an individual and the whole organisation.

This different approach to the personal deal at work compared to the psychological contract is fundamental for the practical focus we adopt in this book. The value of the personal deal at work approach is that it takes account of the actual issues and needs of individual managers and individual employees. The notion that one psychological contract operates consistently across an entire organisation is in any case unrealistic; we all know that employment arrangements for senior managers are different than for junior staff, and that in many organisations there are very real differences between functional and geographic units or departments. To maintain that there is one single prevailing psychological contract does not accord with the reality of organisation life. What I have seen, and the evidence provided in Chapter 2 I hope supports, is that it is possible to think of some broad high-level expectations which apply with a degree of consistency across an organisation – for example with Prêt à Manger, Ernst & Young, the mining company and John Lewis. These are the psychological contract or the 'organisation deal'.

What happens in practice is that while there may be a predominant psychological contract, this is incorporated to varying degrees in the actual personal deals at work that individuals have with one another. In some cases the psychological contract may be strongly incorporated in the individual personal deal between an individual manager and his or her team members. In other teams and departments the organisation deal may be incorporated to a lesser extent, and may have other completely different components.

The evidence from our practical work in organisations is that seeking to work with and change the psychological contract on its own is very difficult, and in most cases will be mission impossible. However seeking to change individual personal deals at work can bring about a significant shift in the psychological contract. The business value of the personal deal at work is that it provides a practical vehicle for change which can then change the overall psychological contract. By focusing on the personal deal at work we create an opportunity for change which could not occur using the psychological contract on its own.

CHAPTER SUMMARY

- Every relationship we have with another person involves a personal deal. At their core both personal deals and business deals involve expectations about what we will get from the other person and what they will get from us. Personal deals have many similarities to conventional business deals when we buy or sell something, as they involve reciprocity, exchange, and implications if one or the other party fails to fulfil the other's expectations.

- Personal deals differ from business deals because they always have a significant non-financial component. Also our expectations in a personal deal are frequently not communicated or articulated to the other person until the personal deal is broken.

- People have very different expectations and personal deals about similar situations. Each of us has unique expectations about how we would like a waiter in a restaurant to behave towards us. Even if we do not know much about them, a waiter in a restaurant will have their own personal set of expectations about us as customers.

- The personal deal at work is the practical manifestation of the psychological contract. The personal deal refers to the mutual and often unexpressed expectations that operate at all times between people (individuals and teams) who interact and communicate with one another. The extent to which others exceed or fall short of our expectations underpins the way we respond, relate and behave towards them. Personal deals apply to our relationships with family, friends, colleagues, customers, community organisations, employers and service providers.

- Fulfilment of personal deals with customers has a direct impact on business performance. Fulfilment of customer expectations in a restaurant can lead to an enjoyable evening, return visits and recommendations to our friends, which is likely to result in increased restaurant revenues. If however our expectations of a restaurant are unfulfilled, the consequences could go beyond our changing mood that evening, resulting in us advising others to avoid the establishment, ultimately bringing about reduced revenues and profit.

The personal deal at work has four components:

- what I expect from my manager and the organisation;

- what I give my manager and the organisation;

- what my manager and the organisation expect from me;

- what the organisation gives me.

- While the psychological contract focuses on expectations between an individual and their employing organisation the personal deal at work focuses on the actual relationship between people at work – with our boss, our team members, colleagues. Focusing on the personal deal at work provides a practical vehicle for change which is not provided by the psychological contract.

- Employee expectations of the personal deal at work may refer to any of 11 possible categories – environmental, direction, well-being, challenge, development, creativity, influence, equity, relationships, recognition and security.

- Manager and organisations expectations of the personal deal with employees may refer to: performance, flexibility, learning, collaboration, conformance, knowledge, improvement, ambassador, care, commitment and protection.

CHAPTER 4

Making and Breaking Personal Deals

From here the book focuses on how the personal deal operates in practice. Most academic research on the psychological contract has focused on the effects when the psychological contract is broken or, as it is often referred to, 'breached'. This chapter will explore first how our personal deals are created, and then what happens when they are broken.

The contents of this chapter area derive from academic research into the psychological contract. The following two chapters will build on this academic research to provide what I hope are some practical ideas and frameworks which can help us manage how the personal deal operates in practice from day to day in organisations.

PRE-EMPLOYMENT STEPS IN CREATING PERSONAL DEALS

Our personal deal with an organisation that employs us can be viewed in four basic stages; pre-employment, recruitment, initial socialisation and later experiences.[1] The pre-employment stage starts with our initial awareness of the organisation – it might come from reports in the media, publicity or the web. We may hear about the organisation from views expressed by friends, associates, careers advisors and so on. Organisations develop reputations in their markets – it may be for their overall business performance, their innovative products and services, brand reputation or their reputation as employers. This employment reputation, and it is not always a favourable one, has a direct impact on the beliefs, expectations and potential personal deals of potential new employees.

One of the most recent high-profile evaluations of UK companies personal deals has been 'The Sunday Times 100 Best Companies to Work For'.[2] The annual competition by the Sunday Times seeks to identify the 100 organisations

---

1   Rousseau, D. (2001), 'Schema, promise and mutuality: The building blocks of the psychological contract', *Journal of Occupational & Organizational Psychology* 74:4, 511–541
2   'The Sunday Times 100 Best Companies to Work For', http://business.timesonline.co.uk/section/0,12190,00.html, last accessed 6 October 2006

most applauded by their employees for providing a supportive environment where they feel rewarded, appreciated and encouraged to develop. The results since 2001 have been based on the opinions of more than 130 000 employees from all over the UK to find out which ones truly are the best. Not surprisingly, many of the companies listed in the top 100, report that recruitment becomes easier as a result of their standing and reputation. Being one of the top '100 Best Companies to Work For' will also have an impact on employees' perceptions about the anticipated personal deal involved in working for one of these companies.

In the same way that some companies will develop a positive reputation from a listing in the '100 Best Companies to Work For' or similar evaluations, other companies may acquire a less favourable reputation, for example when employee tribunal cases make the news headlines, or when there is an announcement about a downturn in performance or large-scale redundancies. The business standing of an organisation as being successful, disappointing or highly entrepreneurial is likely to influence how potential future employees perceive any future personal deal if they were to work there. It is, for example, quite likely that an organisation that is perceived to be resilient and tough with its competitors may also be seen to be tough with its own people. An organisations reputation can create pre-employment expectations for potential future employees.

RECRUITMENT STEPS IN CREATING PERSONAL DEALS

Involvement in recruitment activity starts to provide a prospective employee with more complete information about the future personal deal offered by an organisation. Interaction and discussions with recruitment consultants, HR and line managers all provide potential future employees with a rich source of information about the organisation, how it works and how it treats people. This enables them to anticipate what it is really like to work in the organisation and the types of personal deal they can expect to create within it.

During recruitment much information of an objective kind will be passed on to potential employees, for example about hours of work, how the company treats people who come up with good ideas, what the promotion prospects are and so on. Much of this information is intentionally presented in a favourable light to encourage prospective employees to adopt a good impression about what it is like to work in the organisation.

In Chapter 2 we provided information about the potential personal deals from a number of organisations, based on comments made in their websites. In the same way any potential employee will gain impressions about the anticipated personal deal they might expect from other company websites they visit. Much of this will come from dedicated recruitment sections, as well as statements about employee values, community involvement and so on. Not surprisingly these are intended to create a positive impression about the organisation and this is epitomised by the website and company literature that organisations provide for potential new graduates as part of the race to attract the best young talent from the graduate marketplace. This information is aimed at selling the company by creating positive expectations the individual should have if they join the organisation. Topics covered in company website pages for graduates include how friendly people are, the way people are treated by colleagues, how people are given greater responsibilities, the training opportunities that are available and promotion paths to top management.

There is a danger, as many organisations have found to their cost, that the website and other literature produced by the organisation may create unrealistic expectations among prospective employees – for example about the rate at which a new graduate might expect to get promoted, obtain overseas assignments and the amount of training and development that is provided. If a business over-promotes itself in recruitment presentations, literature and websites there is a real possibility that new employees arrive with unrealistic personal deals, which can never be fulfilled.

As well as hard factual information provided at the recruitment stage, many subtle and non-verbal messages are also given to employees about the personal deal they might expect from the organisation. The way people answer the phone, the timing of responses to job applications and the interpersonal skills of those involved in talking with potential recruits are but some examples of the things which signal what it is like to work in the company, and how an individual can expect to be treated once they join. A wide range of communication and personal interaction experiences are likely to provide prospective employees with such signals as how much you are respected as an individual, the extent to which your opinions will be listened to, the degree of compliance the company expects from you and the amount of personal empathy and support you are likely to receive.

It is well known for example that one of the best ways to increase the take-up of external job offers to new candidates is to speed up the decision time and communication of the offers. Phoning them the evening after they attend for interview and telling them you want them to join is much more likely to get a new candidate to accept a job offer than waiting two weeks to convey the same information through a formal letter. The obvious benefit is that it puts your organisation ahead of others who may want to make job offers to the same individual. The other and more subtle benefit of quick candidate decision making and communication is that it sends a subtle message that the organisation wants you personally – not just anyone.

Something which may easily be forgotten is the value of giving clear information to candidates whose application has been unsuccessful. It may not always be appropriate to give rejected candidates the reasons for not offering a job. However, if the selection process involves advanced assessment methods such as an assessment centre or psychometrics it is known that candidates value feedback from this as it provides information they can use to assist their development. Letting candidates know they have been unsuccessful, and where appropriate why, is more than a courtesy as it contributes to the organisation's reputation in the marketplace. It is particularly important if you expect the unsuccessful candidates to be in contact with others who you may want to apply for jobs with the company in the future.

CREATION OF PERSONAL DEALS DURING NEW JOB SOCIALISATION

As has been put so eloquently, 'Recruitment and selection only provides the raw materials: the new employee. What transpires once the employee enters the new organisation should greatly influence that employee's tenure and performance.'[3] Once we join an organisation an intensive period of socialisation starts. This covers many diverse experiences, and has a powerful impact both on what the individual eventually contributes as well as how fulfilled they feel from their work in the organisation. It has been suggested that the socialisation of new members is one of the most vital processes an organisation can influence.[4]

Socialisation involves four distinct components, initiation to the:

- *Group*   This is the core group of people the individual will interact regularly with as part of their job. It covers how individuals will

3   Liden, R., Bauer, T. and Erdogan, B. (2005), 'The Role of Leader-Member Exchange in the Dynamic Relationship Between Employer and Employee', in Jacqueline Coyle-Shapiro et al., *The Employment Relationship* (Oxford: OUP)

4   Cascio, W. (1991), *Managing Human Resources* (New York: McGraw-Hill)

need to work together and what are the social rules and informal behaviours of colleagues. The expectation increasingly is that individuals will quickly create their own personal network across a new organisation after joining. The network will be relied on if the individual is to become an effective performer and someone who gets things done with and through others. The key issue is how can the new employee build relationships so they feel accepted and trusted by their new colleagues while working and involved in social interaction related to work – for example over lunch.

- *Task and role*   This covers the tasks and activities involved in work, what the new employee is expected to do, what they should do together with colleagues and what they should leave well alone and avoid. The key issue here is how the new employee can come to feel fully competent and accepted as a work partner. A key part of this involves receiving feedback and recognition for performance and being motivated to want to achieve goals that are salient to the group and the organisation. Communicating about the role and tasks is one of the major responsibilities of line managers of new recruits and makes a real contribution to how effectively the individual subsequently performs their role.

- *Culture*   This is the learned, shared and tacit assumptions on which people base their daily behaviour. This refers to the shared norms and rules which underpin the way people interact and work across the organisation. This extends beyond the immediate work group and refers to the prevailing ethos and values held and expressed by people across the organisation. Different frameworks are available for describing culture, including the four types formulated by Cameron and Quinn: adhocracy, market, hierarchy and clan.[5] These are described later in Chapter 9, together with the notion that personal deals in an organisation are heavily influenced by its culture.

- *Shared evaluations*   This refers to the extent to which the new joiner adopts shared standards and a mindset in the way they perceive and evaluate issues and outcomes in the workplace. Examples of this include views about what quality looks like, what success or adding value look like. It will also include more subtle things such as what doing someone a favour looks like. One of the important

5   Cameron, K. and Quinn, R, (1999), *Diagnosing and Changing Organizational Culture* (Reading, Massachusetts: Addison Wesley Longman)

requirements for success is that the new joiner, their leader and colleagues create shared evaluations about things that are important in the workplace. Without this common understanding it becomes difficult to achieve harmony, consensus or even effectiveness.

The socialisation process is likely to be most intensive with a newcomer's immediate team, and particularly their leader. Discussions with colleagues will start right away and in many cases will have started prior to joining. All company recruitment processes known to the author involve contact between the prospective new employee and their leader, and an increasing number of organisations also involve potential colleagues and peers in the recruitment and selection process.

For most people their immediate leader is the most influential individual who determines how they are socialised into the organisation. As the principal provider of resources and personal support the leader fulfils a critical role in socialising the new joiner and in helping them create appropriate personal deals, both directly with them and also with other new colleagues. Research shows that leaders who become personally involved with their new people rather than those who are distant and adhere purely to the employment contract result in the new joiner perceiving the organisation as more supportive.[6] Employees who are personally engaged by their leaders also tend to become more committed to the organisation and engage in behaviours that are beneficial to the business, and we suggest this is largely because this helps align the newcomers' and the leaders' personal deals.

Effective leaders fulfil the role of mentor to new joiners: they provide information as well as advice about how to allocate priorities, how to tackle work and who to talk to about what, in the new joiner's initial time with the organisation. A key part of this involves helping the new employee understand their obligations towards the organisation across a diverse range of things including the amount of work they are expected to undertake, the quality standards used by people in the organisation to determine effectiveness and what makes an effective employee.

One of the responsibilities of the leader is to show higher levels of consideration and support to the new joiner to help them become established. Whereas established employees are likely to have a clear view of their own personal worth and contribution to the organisation, the newcomer initially

---

6   Wayne, S., Shore, L. and Liden, R. (1997), 'Perceived Organizational Support and Leader-Member Exchange: A Social Exchange Perspective', *Academy of Management Journal* 40, 82–111

will not. At times the leader will simply provide factual information and answer questions about things established employees already know. At other times the leader will need to shape by using praise, personal support and recognition – things that would normally not be addressed with a more experienced employee. The leader therefore needs to pay more attention to the recent joiner, reviewing their performance, asking how they are getting on, encouraging and commenting positively on what they deliver.

The example given later in Chapter 5 describes how Anna, a new employee, reacts to certain events and situations. One of these concerns her negative reaction when she was asked to complete a form to support her suggestion to improve the way customer complaints are handled. Her leader noticed her reluctance to complete the appropriate form and decided to sit down and complete it with her. The result was that she was asked to present her ideas to a committee and her recommendations for change were subsequently implemented. The intervention of her leader helped prevent an initial negative reaction about filling in a form turning into a permanently negative view about the organisation's willingness to implement employees' ideas and suggestions.

One of the roles of the leader is to help new employees adjust to discrepancies they may perceive about the job or the organisation with business realities. An employee may join with the idea that they are able to make changes in the ways of working without reference to colleagues. In an organisation where such changes are made by consensus the leader may need to advise the recent joiner of the need to consult and gain input from other colleagues, including those in other departments. The implicit personal deal here is that before implementing changes in working practices that impact others, it is important to gain their input and ideas. The new joiner needs to modify their expectation that if they come up with a new idea for improvement they can just implement it on their own. A more realistic expectation would be that a new employee who has an idea for change will be given an opportunity to influence and persuade colleagues who are involved with the procedure that the idea is indeed an improved way of working before it can be implemented.

During the initial socialisation phase the leader will be advising, supporting, and facilitating the new joiner about appropriate behaviour across a broad area of organisation functioning at both a formal and informal level. While one new employee may need a lot of coaching about the details of their new job, another new joiner may need mentoring about how best to establish relationships within the team. Yet another individual may need help in working cross-functionally with colleagues in other departments. Every organisation has its own unique ways of getting things done and the challenge facing the leader is how best to assist and support the newcomer to understand and relate to colleagues and work itself.

VALUE OF THE PERSONAL DEAL IN INDUCTION AND SOCIALISATION

The value of the personal deal for understanding induction and socialisation is that it provides a framework within which the new joiner can understand their new world of work. The personal deal focuses on mutual fulfilment of expectations and this is the core challenge faced by the newcomer – to identify what others' expectations are about them and what realistic expectations they can have about the organisation and people in it. When we take up a new position the challenge is to find what expectations others have of us and, in particular, the behaviours and activities that are valued and rewarded by colleagues as opposed to those which create indifference or a negative reaction.

In some teams spending the first few minutes at the beginning of every day just talking casually is considered the right way to start the day. In other teams and organisations the appropriate behaviour is to get into work mode right away by just coming in and logging on to one's PC. Talking to others casually may occur only later – perhaps at 10.30 after everyone has made a start on their work – or it may only occur on a one-off basis with people at the end of a concentrated piece of work.

In teams where the personal deal is to talk casually first thing in the morning before getting down to work, someone who just gets straight on with their stuff without talking to others might be considered unfriendly or aloof. In a team where it is the done thing to get straight down to work and only talk later in the morning, the individual who comes in first thing and starts talking about what they did the previous night might be considered casual or a timewaster. This is because they will have broken the team personal deal of coming in and getting on with work until morning coffee time.

Personal deals about social conversation are only a small part of the story. One of the most important aspects of the personal deal is how we undertake and deliver work. In one internationally known American organisation with which the author worked, the personal deal appeared to involve a high degree of compliance with one's immediate leader. The personal deal for many appeared to involve an expectation that even those in senior professional or middle management positions would not use their initiative to clarify direction. The personal deal or norm is to wait until someone in top management has decided direction and the goals that need to be achieved. Once the top manager has pronounced, then individuals are expected to work extremely hard to implement or execute decisions. This contrasts markedly with other organisations where the personal deal is all about using your initiative to clarify direction and get results, and not wait until someone at the top has made a decision.

The personal deal provides a framework for setting mutual expectations between the new joiner and their leader. As well as focusing the expectations that the leader and colleagues have of the new joiner, the personal deal highlights the importance of the new joiner's own expectations. One of the vital contributions the leader can make is to check out the new joiner's expectations about work and work relationships. In many instances their expectations may be based on their personal needs – for example to be a high achiever, or to relate and communicate with many and varied people. In practice, however, the way an individual manifests and expresses their personal needs (for example to achieve or to communicate) will be influenced by the personal deals they have experienced elsewhere, particularly previous organisations in which they have worked.

An extrovert individual may, for example, expect from experience in previous companies that the right thing to do is to engage in personal conversation with colleagues for the first ten minutes of the working day before getting down to work. This would go some way towards fulfilling their personal extrovert preferences. However in a company where getting down to work first thing is part of the team personal deal, that would be considered inappropriate. If the team personal deal did however allow for casual personal conversations at coffee break time it would be very helpful for the newcomer to be told that it is OK to engage in conversations then – but that it is frowned on first thing in the morning. By telling the new joiner about this informal rule the leader will assist the individual in creating the most appropriate personal deal which best fulfils their own personal needs while, at the same time, fulfilling the team personal deal regarding personal conversation.

A very different personal deal situation might occur with regard to achievement of results. A highly ambitious and determined individual might have an expectation that it is appropriate for them to identify goals and then pursue these on their own and with little reference to colleagues. The leader may value highly the individual's determination but realise that on its own it might cause unnecessary problems for them and others in the organisation.

The leader may therefore decide to counsel the new joiner that before going into action they need first to discuss and clarify their goals with the leader and, on occasions, with others as well, before moving to implementation. A new joiner is likely to find it helpful if their leader mentions that ideas for change need to be discussed and agreed before they can be implemented.

By counselling the new joiner the leader will in effect be creating a personal deal which looks something like Table 4.1.

Table 4.1   Personal deal expectations

What the leader expects from the new joiner	What the new joiner expects from the leader and organisation
Come up with ideas for change and discuss these with me and relevant colleagues first before implementation	You will make time and listen to my new ideas for getting things done and for change
You need to take account of the issues and ideas colleagues put forward regarding your ideas for delivering results and change, and how they should be implemented	You will support my ideas for action and change wherever practical, and advise me about organisation enablers and barriers that I need to take account of
You will enthusiastically pursue the goals and targets we have discussed, with minimum interference or involvement from me	You will give me the freedom and space to go ahead, make things happen and deliver results
You will deliver high-quality results that add value to the business	You will recognise praise and reward my efforts and result

The challenge facing the leader is how best to channel the personal strengths and capabilities of the new joiner in ways which add most value and also support the organisation's formal and informal ways of working. The key to this is I believe to make the personal deal more explicit between both the employee and the leader. A healthy match and alignment between what the employee expects and what the leader expects is predicted to provide the most effective long-term relationship.[7] To date there is only one actual research study known to the author which supports this important proposition and, while this occurred between leaders and new employees, it comes from a study of nannies and their employers rather than from a commercial organisation[8]. This lack of more detailed empirical data is unfortunate, and prevents us knowing

---

7   Kotter, J. (1973), 'The Psychological Contract: Managing the Joining Up Process', *California Management Review* 15, 91–99
8   Millward, P. and Cropley, M. (2003), 'Psychological Contracting: Processes of Contract Formation During Interviews Between Nannies and Their Employers', *Journal of Occupational and Organizational Psychology*, 76, 213-241

as much as we would like about how the psychological contract or personal deals are formed. Some of the feedback from our practical work in supporting the implementation of personal deals does however very much support the validity of making personal deals more explicit.

Creating appropriate explicit personal deals with new joiners will help develop their understanding which in turn will make it more possible for the individual to fulfil their aspirations as well as achieve the goals of leaders and the business.

The value of the personal deal in induction and socialisation is that it focuses on the creation of shared and aligned expectations between the new joiners on the one hand, and the leader, colleagues and the organisation on the other. It acknowledges the real need for mutuality between the new joiner and others in the organisation. Effective leaders known to the author as a matter of course have discussions with their new joiners about their individual interests and expectations. That way, expectations are created which as far as practical support fulfilment of business goals and also the needs of the individual employee.

Managing expectations during induction or on joining can make a real impact on the individual's performance and indeed their commitment to the organisation. If employees' perceptions and expectations are consciously attuned to the realities of the new organisation during the first three to six months the individual is more likely to become effective and stay. If the labour turnover of organisations is studied for different levels a peak typically occurs some six to 18 months after joining. The reason for this is that individuals after six months are over their honeymoon in the new job; the organisation expects them to deliver, and the individual will also have become exposed to the realities of the job and the organisation. If mutual expectations are effectively shaped and managed during induction fewer new joiners will leave, and unnecessary recruitment costs can be significantly reduced. Managing the personal deal with new employees as well as being helpful to the individual has been shown to make a real contribution to the organisation's bottom line.

The personal deals that are set up shortly after an individual joins an organisation are critical for the subsequent success and happiness of a new employee. They set the pattern for what happens subsequently, and point the way for the individual's employment relationship with the organisation.

FREQUENCY OF BROKEN PERSONAL DEALS AFTER INITIAL SOCIALISATION

One of the interesting questions about the personal deal concerns the frequency with which it is breached or broken after initial formation. All the evidence suggests that personal deals once created are, in the eyes of employees, frequently broken.

A major piece of work in a UK local government survey suggested that over 80 per cent of people surveyed reported that their psychological contracts had been broken.[9] A different but much more intensive study of individuals over a ten-day period in their working lives based on personal diaries suggested that different types of employees feel that breach of the psychological contract occurs as a regular part of most people's working lives. On average it was reported that each person who kept a diary felt that one promise per week was broken and also that two promises were exceeded in each three-week period.

The evidence shows that breaking personal deals is quite common. While, some of the breaches of expectations were relatively minor – for example failure to greet an individual – they were nevertheless sufficient to be noticed by the individual. The importance of the research findings is that many of us are quite sensitive to even small breaches of our personal deals. An example of the personal deal creation and breach is given in Chapter 5 which describes the type of situation that occurs in real life for many people. While there are many and frequent breaches of the personal deal that are noticed by individuals, many are isolated and relatively insignificant. The important thing is that they do register on individuals' radars and are noticed, even if many of these breaches do not result in changes in employees' behaviour or performance.

The research into frequency of breach of personal deals is important on two counts. First, it indicates that the idea of a personal deal is implicitly perceived by people. Secondly and of greater significance, the sheer numbers of perceived breaches of personal deals show the value and importance of the concept for understanding the relationship between employer and employee. The idea of the personal deal is not just something of theoretical interest: it is part of the reality of all our lives at work.

---

9   Coyle-Shapiro, J. and Kessler, I. (2000), 'Consequences of the Psychological Contract for the Employment Relationship; A Large Scale Survey', *Journal of Management Studies* 37, 7

Other investigations into personal deal breach suggest that the causes of these vary according to the employee group to which we belong.[10] Some evidence suggests that among international business executives breach is perceived by them to most frequently concern training and support from their leader. Among bank employees however perceived breach was most often perceived to be due to lack of job security and lack of decision-making authority – the latter finding accords with what one would expect in the light of cut-backs that are being made across many different branch banking networks.

To explore the issue of breach in more detail you may want to reflect on someone in your place of work with whom you have felt frustrated or annoyed in recent weeks. What was it the person did or did not do? How did you expect them to behave and perform differently? Did you share your annoyance or frustration with them, or did you keep it to yourself? Did the other person get any idea of your feelings from any other source – for example from your non-verbal behaviour, or perhaps from someone else who knows how you felt? How often do you feel some slight frustration with this or other people at work? Is it because they have, in your eyes, broken the personal deal they had with you?

Fortunately the picture about broken personal deals is not all negative. The evidence from the research indicated that many people also perceived instances when their personal deals were exceeded. This again suggests that people do really notice what happens to their personal deals – and it is not just one-sided.

The perceptions people have about both exceeded and unfulfilled expectations all give support and credibility to the model of the personal deal which is provided in Chapter 5. What appears to happen in life is exactly as indicated in the personal deal model, and shown in the Figure 5.2 'How the deal works' on page 84.

IMPACT OF PERSONAL DEAL BREACH ON EMPLOYEE ATTITUDES

There is considerable evidence concerning the impact of personal deal breach or violation on employee attitudes. The two most likely changes in attitude as a result of personal deal breach are that individuals feel reduced job satisfaction and also that they report greater intentions of leaving their jobs. This finding is

10 Turnley, W. and Feldman, D. (2000), 'Re-Examining the Effects of Psychological Contract Violation; Unmet Expectations and Job Dissatisfaction as Mediators', *Journal of Organisational Behaviour* 21, 25–42

supported by work in the UK and the US.[11] Conversely, research on the effect of exceeding the personal deal suggests that it results in greater feelings of self-worth.[12]

The findings very much match things I have heard during my coaching of senior executives. One case concerned a senior individual I have been coaching over a period of years. I first met this robust and resilient individual a number of years back, when he held a middle manager role. At that time I recall him setting his ambitions on achieving a role as chief executive. Earlier this year he was appointed to a chief operating officer role in another organisation and I recall how excited he felt about the challenges and opportunities to achieve that this new role promised.

Earlier in 2005 the individual was taken aside by the chairman and told that he would very shortly be appointed as chief executive, the existing job holder would leave the organisation and that a formal announcement would be made in a few days. The individual was elated by the news. Over a number of weeks however no further announcements were made and it appeared that the existing chief executive was re-asserting himself and his intention to remain in the organisation. This really challenged my client, who had expected to be appointed chief executive at any moment. It challenged his normally robust self-confidence considerably and he wondered whether he should continue in the organisation. What was interesting was that when I asked my client why he thought there had been a delay in being appointed he gave many different reasons for this. He asked me if he should think about seeking alternative employment because the promise of appointment to chief executive had been reneged on. I counselled that while the situation was unsatisfactory and challenging that my client should keep calm, maintain his current course of action in the organisation and not even think about the possibility of leaving for a few months, until the possible reasons for the delay in their appointment had been carefully discussed. I also counselled that my client talk again to his chairman and ask for updates on what was happening.

Very shortly afterwards the chairman gave some reassuring comments to my client and within three weeks of the discussion my client's despair turned to elation as his appointment to chief executive was confirmed publicly.

---

11 Bunderson, J. (2001), 'How Work Ideologies Shape Psychological Contracts of Professional Employees: Doctors' Responses to Perceived Breach', *Journal of Organizational Behaviour* 22, 717–41

12 Conway, N. and Briner, R. (2002), 'A Daily Diary Study of Affective Responses to Psychological Contract Breach and Exceeded Promises', *Journal of Organizational Behaviour* 23, 287–302

The experience of my client, his brief breakdown in self-belief and thoughts about quitting are exactly what the research findings on breach of personal deals would predict. What my client went through in fact was a strong feeling that his personal deal had been breached after being told by the chairman that he would be appointed interim chief executive. The fact that nothing happened for a few weeks led my client to believe that the promised appointment was now being reneged. His brief breakdown in self-confidence about the situation occurred even though my client had correctly guessed the reasons for the delay.

It shows that people really do notice when their expectations about what they will receive from their work are not fulfilled. Breaches and violations of personal deals really do have an impact on our feelings of self-worth, our job satisfaction and on our intentions to quit.

IMPACT OF PERSONAL DEAL BREACH ON EMPLOYEE BEHAVIOUR

There is some evidence that breach of personal deals does have an impact on employees' actual behaviour and not just their attitudes. Despite the large number of academic research studies in this area only a small proportion provide meaningful evidence of the existence of a cause–effect connection between personal deal breach and what people do at work.

One study of employees and their supervisors over a period of time showed that when breaches of personal deals did occur there were statistically significantly more reported incidents of deviant work behaviour.[13] Deviant work behaviour detracts from business performance and examples include taking more frequent breaks, leaving work early, talking excessively with colleagues and not supporting colleagues.

Another piece of research found a positive relationship between personal deal fulfilment and supportive behaviour. In other words people whose personal deals were fulfilled behaved in a more supportive way towards colleagues than those for whom personal deals were less fulfilled.[14]

---

13 Kikul, J. (2001), 'When Organisations Break Their Promises: Employee Reactions to Unfair Processes and Treatment', *Journal of Business Ethics* 29, 289–307
14 Turnley, W. et al., (2003), 'The Impact of Psychological Contract Fulfilment on the Performance of In-Role and Organisational Citizenship Behaviours', *Journal of Management* 29

These and other case studies present evidence which suggests there is a link between personal deal fulfilment and behaviour by people in the organisation. From a rigorous academic perspective this link is not as well proven as we would like. Nevertheless reactions my colleagues and I have encountered in our coaching work in organisations make us confident that breach of the psychological contract has a distinct impact on employee thinking and behaviour.

In Parkside Housing Group we undertook an intervention which involved training all managers to have discussions about their personal deals with their people in 2003. The training involved input followed by practice in one-to-one coaching and planning, and undertaking discussions about the personal deal between each manager and their team members. To support the discussions the author and his colleagues also provided what we called a 'personal deal toolkit' which helped leaders to structure the discussion with their colleagues.

During the six-month period after the training we understand that some 60 per cent of leaders undertook personal discussions with their team members. Feedback from individuals across the organisation suggested that these discussions were considered very worthwhile and that they helped to increase openness and understanding between leaders and their teams.

A survey conducted by the organisation compared views about communications with responses from employees 12 months prior to the intervention. Responses to the question 'My manager encourages me to give my views' improved from 20 per cent positive to 60 per cent positive. Responses to the question 'I understand how my job contributes to objectives of the organisation' improved from 40 per cent positive to 60 per cent positive.

The results we obtained at Parkside Housing Group suggest that improved understanding between people about their personal deals result in improved perceptions by people about their roles and the wider organisation.

The evidence we have from our work in coaching as well as organisation change assignments make the author very confident that breach and fulfilment of the psychological contract does have a very real impact on employee attitudes and feelings and in turn on actual behaviour and performance in the workplace.

CHAPTER SUMMARY

- The personal deal an employee has with their manager and the organisation is created in four sequential stages: pre-employment, recruitment, new job socialisation, and later socialisation. It is easy to forget the power of experiences an employee goes through before they even join the organisation in the pre-employment and recruitment stages which determine their expectations and personal deal after they join.

- The value of the personal deal during induction and early socialisation of new employees is to provide a framework and method for planning and then shaping the expectations of the new joiner, thus creating a platform for their subsequent commitment. Early clarification of the personal deal will assist the newcomer to understand how they can best fulfil their own needs – for example social or achievement needs – while simultaneously also fulfilling the needs of colleagues and the new team they are joining.

- During the induction stage the leader can discuss and counsel a unique personal deal with the new joiner which takes specific account of the individual's personal needs as well as informal rules about how people behave and interact together. In contrast to the psychological contract the personal deal can help to make the understanding between the new joiner and their leader personal and explicit, and something to which they can both relate and commit.

- There is considerable evidence that the majority of employees experience breach of their psychological contracts. One study suggests that people are aware of small breaches, on a regular weekly basis. The causes of contract breach vary, and there may be specific causes for employees in different sectors. While a study of international managers found that breach was mostly about training and support from their manager, a study of bank employees found that there were many significant breaches about employment security.

- There are considerable research findings that breach of the psychological contract are noticed and may cause powerful and intense feelings among people. Breach of the personal deal can cause normally highly competent and robust individuals to question their self-worth and confidence. Evidence to support these findings can be found frequently in one-to-one personal coaching.

- Evidence from academic research shows that the psychological contract not only impacts attitudes and feelings but also actual behaviour at work. The data suggests that breach of the psychological contract can cause people to invest less in their work, and undertake more of what is referred to as 'deviant work behaviour' – leaving work early, taking more and longer breaks, talking for longer with colleagues. The author's consulting work with a social business suggests that fulfilment of the psychological contract leads to improved communications and relationships and improved organisation effectiveness.

CHAPTER 5

The Personal Deal Process

THE DYNAMIC NATURE OF PERSONAL DEALS

In Chapter 3 we introduced a model of the personal deal. In this chapter we build on this model, taking account of the research findings described in Chapter 4, and propose a process and model of how the personal deal operates in practice. The model takes account of the continual change and development of relationships which are a reality of our working lives. The model can be used from the initial pre-recruitment contact between an organisation and potential employees, their entry into the organisation, transition through different and evolving roles, to the individual's eventual departure from the organisation.

The business value of the personal deal for managers and HR practitioners is that it provides a highly dynamic and practical perspective for understanding and managing relationships between an organisation and its people over the short, medium and longer term. The personal deal provides a method for changing the way employees relate to their line manager and through them to the organisation.

Recent academic research and theory into the psychological contract views it as a series of stand-alone transactions between an individual and their employing organisation.[1] While this focus has provided useful insights, its narrowness fails to do justice to the reality of life in organisations.

The fundamental challenge facing leaders and managers in the workplace is how to enhance and develop relationships with their people in ways that take account of changes in customer needs, the organisation's goals and strategies, as well as people's evolving and changing needs, wants and aspirations.

Fulfilment of new customer expectations frequently requires shifts in ways of working to implement changes in delivered services and products. This may involve changing the composition of teams, the allocation of work between people, as well as changes in work processes and flow. New technology adds to the opportunities for change in the way work gets done. Balanced against these demands are changing employee personal needs and preferences.

---

1   Conway, N. and Briner, R. (2005), *Understanding the Psychological Contracts at Work* (Oxford: OUP)

When an individual has children their personal priorities for leaving work on time change, employee needs may also change due to circumstances such as employee or family illness, divorce, a home move, embarking on further education and so on. An individual may also after a period of time become bored with their job and decide they want to do something different, and this also creates pressures for change. Quite simply the drivers for implementing change in work are almost endless.

To face up to these challenges leaders require tools and methods which help them manage changes in the way work gets done, and respond to individual employee demands. The personal deal potentially can make a real contribution here as it takes account both of the needs of the business as well as the needs of the employee. Because of this it holds a promise of adding value when change needs to be implemented. To live up to this promise the framework of the personal deal needs to become more dynamic than the psychological contract, and relationships between the organisation and the individual viewed as a continually evolving process. As Conway and Briner say:

> As long as the psychological contract literature neglects tackling process issues, it will we believe fail to capture the essence of the psychological contract and thus put a halt on future development in our understanding.

Most literature on the psychological contract views it as a non-dynamic relationship between employees and the organisation. While this has provided interesting insights, I believe it is insufficient for the line manager and HR professional to use as a robust vehicle for managing their actual relationships with employees.

PERSONAL DEALS OCCUR BETWEEN EACH LEADER AND THEIR PEOPLE

For practical purposes it is very important that the definition of the personal deal at work should focus on the relationship between the individual employee or small team of employees, and their manager. There are a number of important reasons for adopting this approach:

- There is evidence that while there may be some consistency of personal deals across the business, there are compelling reasons which suggests that considerable variation occurs between the personal deals that different people have within the organisation.

Much of this variation is due to the unique impact of individual managers and leaders. While one team leader may place very high emphasis on quality, another team leader may instead emphasise punctuality. While marketing departments may value innovation and creativity, accounting teams may place more emphasis on consistency and reliability.

- My experience in different organisations suggests that the most important personal deal for most individual employees is primarily with their line manager. The manager represents and embodies the organisation for many people. The power of this notion is nicely captured by the often-used phrase that 'individuals join companies but leave managers'. In other words people leave a company when their personal deal is broken by their manager.

- Viewing the personal deal between individual leaders and their people will encourage each leader to become aware that they personally can and do manage the personal deals with each of their people. Once leaders recognise they personally have responsibility for the personal deals with their people they can be expected to rise to the challenge, rather than ignoring it or passing it to senior management or to people in HR! We have evidence from organisations where we have introduced the personal deal concept to leaders that they easily become enthusiastic to take up this new responsibility.

- Viewing the personal deal between a leader and their people is the starting point for much of the practical work on culture and leadership change the author has undertaken. (Refer to Chapters 8 and 9). One of the reasons why application of the psychological contract has not become more widely used is because it is viewed as something which people see operating across the total organisation, or at least large units in it. Because the personal deal is viewed as something between individual leaders and their people it becomes something realistic for them to use to plan and effect change.

- This personal deal perspective encourages HR processes such as induction, performance management, grievance and disciplinary procedures, performance-related pay and so on to be viewed as enablers which can be used by individual leaders to develop and shape what people do in the workplace. This in turn will give further encouragement to the view of the HR function as a creator of business value through the support it provides leaders in managing their personal deals with their people.

Figure 5.1 compares the proposed view of the personal deal with the more conventional way in which the psychological contract is talked and written about. Rather than think of a psychological contract which spans the whole organisation or large sections of it, it is more appropriate to think of a very much larger number of personal deals that operate at an individual or team level in the organisation.

The practical implication of the approach proposed is that every organisation will have a multitude of personal deals. The exact shape of each of these deals will be dictated by the nature of the work in individual jobs, the style and approach of the individual leader and the personality and other preferences of individual employees. When thinking about application of the personal deal at work it therefore is important to do so as a unique arrangement for each team and or each individual and his manager in the organisation.

The degree of consistency among all individual and team personal deals across the organisation will provide a measure of the consistency of the psychological contract. Organisations with a clearly defined psychological contract will display high consistency across some components of the personal deals which exist in the organisation. Organisations with a less well-defined psychological contract would be expected to have a lower level of consistency across personal deals. For example, an organisation with a consistently bureaucratic psychological contract culture would be expected to have personal

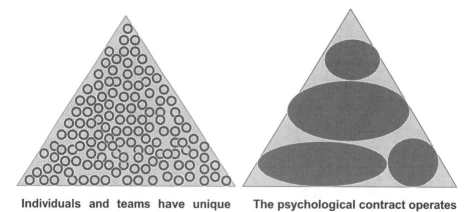

Individuals and teams have unique personal deals with their leader

The psychological contract operates for all people in larger groups or across the total organisation

Figure 5.1   Different perspectives of the personal deal and the psychological contract

deals between individual managers and leaders and their people which emphasise rules and procedures, and which place less emphasis on personal creativity.

The important advantage of this approach to the personal deal is that it recognises that each of our relationships is unique: the relationship we have with one person will be different from the relationship we have with someone else; also our relationship with one person will be different from the relationships they have with others. Our relationships will be a function of many different things including our personalities, our mindsets as shaped by our experiences, and our different beliefs about the other individual. Importantly, each of our personal deals will also be a function of the interplay of our different personality types. The way different personalities relate is illustrated by frameworks such as the Myers-Briggs Type Indicator.[2] The prevailing view is that individuals who have some things in common as well as some differences will get on best in the long term. Our personal deals will be significantly influenced by the combination of our and the other person's personalities and how they interact.

The value of the personal deal is that it focuses and takes account of what happens in real life between individuals and teams – namely that we each expect different things from different people and different people in turn expect different things from us. A leader might have demanding expectations about reporting back from an employee who they view as difficult – but may be much more easygoing and have more relaxed expectations about someone they trust or personally like. Equally, an employee may have more demanding expectations of a manager with whom they do not have a close relationship, but be more tolerant of someone they personally like working with.

HOW THE DEAL OPERATES IN PRACTICE

Before describing a framework of how the personal deal operates it might be useful to consider what typically happens in the course of an employment relationship. To bring this to life the paragraphs below describe the changes that might occur over time in an essentially positive employment relationship. While the description below is fictional, it is a composite story based on many real-life situations encountered by the author.

---

2 Briggs Myers, I., revised by Kirby, L.K. and Myers, K.D. (2000), *Introduction to Type – A Guide to Understanding Your Results on the Myers-Briggs Type Indicator'*, (PaloAlto, California: Consulting Psychologists Press)

Anna reads an advertisement about a vacancy which catches her eye because it indicates that the company values people who use their initiative. This is particularly important for Anna because she feels her present boss stifles her initiative. Whenever she puts forward ideas for improving how things get done her boss listens but never implements her ideas.

Anna decides to go for an interview and is pleasantly surprised when the interviewer asks about what she has done to improve the ways of working in her present job and organisation. The interviewer seems most interested when she describes some of her ideas which were not taken up, and comments positively about this. As a result she begins to believe that this is a company where she could use her initiative. This impression is strengthened when she attends further interviews, where her ideas for change are listened to with interest. Anna is further encouraged when she hears about the way the company put people through different development programmes to encourage them to make decisions for themselves.

Shortly afterwards Anna is offered the job and is delighted to accept. On her first day at the new organisation she feels welcomed and is pleased she made the move. In the afternoon she meets a member of HR who again says that this is a company that values people with new ideas and initiative. On her way home she feels really excited about her new job and resolves to put more effort and energy to make a success of this new job than she did with her previous company.

Things go well and Anna feels comfortable with the other people in the office. In her third week she learns about a particular procedure for handling customer complaints and realises that this is unnecessarily complicated and inefficient. At the end of the day she talks to her manager about what she has seen and asks what she needs to do to get the process simplified. He says that she needs to complete a two-page electronic form which she has to email to a colleague for the proposal to be evaluated. Anna gets apprehensive about this, and asks her boss why, if he understands what she is suggesting, he cannot just make the change. He comments that this is the way they do things in the company and he simply asks her to copy him when submitting the form.

In her previous company Anna remembers how suggestions for changes and improvements had to be emailed and how the whole thing just became a bureaucratic procedure which resulted in very little of value. She feels disillusioned that, despite the earlier talk about encouraging initiative, this company like her last one may not really value it. Anna feels somewhat frustrated and she forgets about the idea. Her natural enthusiasm feels dampened.

A week later Anna's manager asks her if she has completed the two-page form for her new idea for handling changes to customer complaints. She says she cannot stand filling in forms. On hearing this, her manager suggests that they take ten minutes then and there to fill in the form together. Anna is pleasantly surprised at that suggestion and the two of them sit down at her workstation, complete the form and submit it.

Three days later a manager from another part of the organisation calls Anna and asks her to come to a meeting to discuss her ideas about changes in handling customer complaints. She is told that there will be a number of people at the meeting who together have responsibility for managing the way customer complaints are handled. She feels pleased to be invited to present her ideas and is thrilled to hear a few days after attending the meeting that her suggestion is being implemented. Anna's manager congratulates her on her idea and getting it implemented. Anna feels really proud that her ideas have been put into practice across the whole of Europe. She feels that she really wants to find more opportunities for putting forward new ideas for change.

Things go well in Anna's new job until six months later when she submits her third idea for change, this time concerning the way customer orders are processed. Anna submits the usual form but when she presents her ideas she hears a number of challenges to her proposals. A member of the group explains why Anna's ideas would not work, but she is not really convinced. She feels disappointed and dejected and her mood over the next few days becomes quieter and she displays less enthusiasm at work.

Fortunately Anna's manager notices that she is less positive and asks her if anything is wrong. Anna describes what happened at the meeting and he asks her to describe the reasons her ideas were turned down. She is not very clear about this and her manager discusses the issues and eventually asks Anna what it was she did not understand about the explanation given for turning down her ideas. Her manager reminds her that she and the company value the initiative she has demonstrated so far, but that she should realise that she may not always be in a position to understand the impact of her ideas on other people and other things going on in the company. Anna feels somewhat reassured by this discussion with her manager and her mood at work lightens up.

At her performance discussion after eight months Anna's manager gives her positive feedback. He tells her that her overall rating is 'fully effective' but it falls short of the highest rating of 'excellent' she had hoped for. Anna feels disappointed about this and challenges her manager. Her manager listens and comments that while Anna is hardworking, collaborates well with her and the team and has come up with good ideas, her overall work so far falls short of being excellent. Anna feels quite let down by this feedback. While she has felt appreciated by her manager and the company up to now, she wonders if this is the company for her long-term future. She puts a brave face on the feedback but believes that she has given her best and feels that she warrants an excellent rating. In her heart Anna wonders whether this is the company where she can really grow and develop if her contribution is not fully appreciated.

Over the next month things go reasonably well on the surface, but in her heart Anna still believes that her manager has let her down. For his part, her manager knows that Anna found the 'fully effective' rating difficult to accept and has decided that it is important that he explains to Anna what excellent performance looks like so that Anna can target her efforts to achieve her desired rating. Over a few weeks her manager takes time to point out to Anna in a few separate five-minute conversations when he has seen excellent performance, so that Anna can really understand what this looks like for someone doing her job. As a result of these conversations Anna begins to understand why her present performance falls short of excellent, and she realises her recent doubts about staying in the company have been inappropriate.

This tale is typical of the emotional changes that take place during the course of what is a positive personal deal. There are quite a few highs, and some lows. The main highs and lows are:

- The initial job advertisement and pre-employment interview emphasise the value the company place on individual initiative, and the induction discussion with HR reinforces Anna's impression that her initiative will be appreciated and valued. She accepts the job offered to her enthusiastically.

- A brief low occurs when Anna is asked to fill in the electronic form about her proposed change in handling customer complaints, and her reaction is that this appears to be a similar practice to that experienced in her previous company.

- Anna is quickly taken out of what could become a downward cycle by her manager who fills in the forms with her, and things become really positive when she presents her proposals for change.

- Anna feels really encouraged by her recommendation for change being implemented, and this motivates her to perform her job well.

- After six months a dip occurs when a suggestion she makes is turned down, and Anna becomes dejected.

- Fortunately Anna's manager helps her see things more positively and she feels reassured.

- Anna experiences a distinct low when she is awarded a 'fully effective' rating at performance review time – as she feels that she warrants a much higher rating. Anna feels let down about this, even though she says little. As a result she wonders if this is the company for her to stay with long term.

- Anna gradually feels more positive when her manager points out and explains what 'excellent' looks like. She feels reassured, and this helps her feel positive again about her job and her boss.

These highs and lows are part of the normal tapestry of life at work, and something we all go through in our own personal and different ways. The value of the personal deal is that it helps the leader to better understand what is taking place and also to make decisions and take actions to address the employees' issues, even though in the overall scheme of things the ones described may not appear critical.

USING THE PERSONAL DEAL TO UNDERSTAND AND MANAGE OURSELVES AND OUR PEOPLE

In Chapter 3 we identified the four basic building blocks of the personal deal; 'What I expect from the organisation', 'What I give the organisation', 'What the organisation gives me', and 'What the organisation expects from me'. In this section we will expand this model further and use it to show what Anna went through in her new job.

Following the revised definition of the 'personal deal at work' as involving the mutual expectations between the individual leader and their people the four components involved now become:

- What I expect from my leader.

- What I give my leader.

- What my leader expects from me.

- What my leader gives me.

These four components are shown in Figure 5.2. The starting point could be in any box – but for now will be taken as the box 'What my leader gives me' which is received/perceived by the employee, and compared to the contents of the box 'What I expect from my leader'. As a result of this match the employee will then decide 'What I give my leader'. The leader, in turn, will compare 'What I give my leader' against the contents of their box 'What my leader expects from me'.

Depending on the match between these the leader will make decisions on what to include in their box 'What my leader gives me'. The flow between the boxes will continue in this fashion repeatedly over time. The flow between the four boxes as perceived by each of the parties is one of the most important factors which influence decisions about what each party to the personal deal decides to give the other. Therefore the contents of the box 'What I give my leader' will be influenced by how I perceive 'What my leader gives me' matches 'What I expect from my leader'. There is considerable evidence that

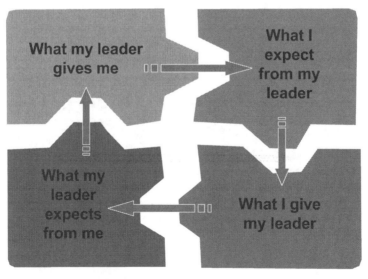

Figure 5.2   How the personal deal works (A)

if employees feel that what they receive exceeds their expectations they in turn will decide to increase 'What I give my leader'. However if 'What my leader gives me' falls significantly short of 'What I expect from my leader', then I may well decide to reduce what I decide to include in the box 'What I give my leader'.

In the same way that the individual employee will make decisions about 'What I give my leader', so also the leader will make decisions about 'What my leader gives me'. The leader's decisions about 'What my leader gives me' will be significantly influenced by their perceptions of 'What I give my leader' and whether this is perceived to match, exceed or fall short of 'What my leader expects from me'.

As well as decisions about what to give the other party in the personal deal both parties will also change and refine their expectations about what they will receive from the other party. Therefore, over time, the leader will refine 'What my leader expects from me' and this may increase, decrease or change. In the same way the individual employee will refine 'What I expect from my leader'.

What each party expects from the other will be influenced by things outside their relationship. Leaders' expectations will be influenced by business goals and strategies, market and customer pressures, and what others in leadership roles, including directors and senior managers, expect from their people. Equally, employees' expectations about what they want to receive from their leader will be influenced by things outside the relationship – for example what

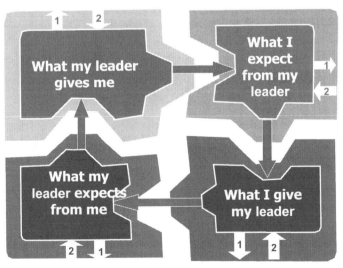

Figure 5.3   How the personal deal works (B)

they hear from other employees in the organisation and what they hear from others who work in different organisations.

This dynamic flow between the employee and the leader is shown in Figure 5.3. The arrows within the four larger boxes show how the amounts may increase or decrease over time. Arrows with the number 1 indicate an increase in the amount given or expected, while arrows with the number 2 indicate a reduced amount given or decreased expectation.

The important feature of this diagram is that it illustrates the dynamic process involved in the way the personal deal operates. Over the period of time from when an individual is recruited into an organisation through to the time they leave, there will be a whole series of changes in all four boxes of the personal deal. There will be times when one party gives more, and this may be followed by the other party giving more; and there will be times when the amount both parties give each other remains constant. There will also be times when one or the other party reduces the amount it gives the other party; and for a time the other party continues to give the same amount. Then, at some later point in time, the other party may decide to reduce the amount it gives the other. This may occur, for instance, when a leader takes on additional responsibilities and is unable to give so much attention to their existing team members. It might occur equally when an employee's needs outside work impact their ability to work – for example illness in the family, a new baby, divorce and so on. The final option is when one or other of the parties decides to terminate the relationship. The employee may choose to leave and work for another organisation; alternatively the leader may decide to terminate the employee.

Having introduced the flow model of what each party gives to and expects from the other party we can now return to Anna's personal deal with her leader and see how her experiences can be described on the model.

USING THE MODEL TO UNDERSTAND ANNA'S PERSONAL DEAL

Anna's experiences, the fictional employee described earlier, can be understood and interpreted using the personal deal. Table 5.1 shows the impact of each of her different experiences on her personal deal with her leader.

The value of the analysis using the personal deal is that it helps understand and explain what is happening between Anna and her leader. Most importantly,

Table 5.1   Impact of Anna's experiences

No.	Anna's experience	Impact on personal deal (+ or -)
1	The initial job advertisement, employment interview and induction discussion with HR create Anna's expectation that she can use her initiative in the company	+ 'What I expect from my leader' and + 'What I give my leader'
2	A brief low occurs when Anna is asked to fill in the electronic form about her proposed change in handling customer complaints, and her reaction is that this seems like her previous company	- 'What I receive from my leader'
3	Anna is quickly taken out of what could become a downward cycle by her leader who fills in the change forms with her	+ 'What I receive from my leader'
4	Anna feels really encouraged by her recommendation for change being implemented, and this motivates her to perform her job well	+ 'What I receive from my leader', and in turn + 'What I give my leader'
5	After 6 months a dip occurs when a suggestion she makes is turned down, and Anna becomes dejected	- 'What I receive from my leader' and - 'What I give my leader'
6	Fortunately Anna's manager helps her see things more positively, and she feels reassured	+ 'What I receive from my leader'
7	Anna experiences a distinct low when she is awarded a 'fully effective' rating at performance review time, as she feels that she warrants a much higher rating. Anna feels let down about this, even though she says little. As a result she wonders if this is the company to stay with in the long term	- 'What I receive from my leader' and - 'What I give my leader'
8	Anna gradually feels more positive when her manager points out and explains what 'excellent' looks like. She feels reassured, and this helps her feel positive again about her job and her boss	+ 'What I receive from my leader' and + 'What I give my leader'

the analysis provides a framework for understanding what is going on between any leader and their team member over a period of time and how different events have an impact on their relationship.

While the story of Anna is fictional we believe the model of the personal deal can be used in a proactive way by leaders to better understand what their people are experiencing. It can also help an employee understand their reactions towards the organisation and their manager.

PREDICTIONS ABOUT THE PERSONAL DEAL PROCESS

The ultimate test of the usefulness of the personal deal model proposed is whether it can help make predictions about how the different parties will behave towards one another. Much academic research has focused on the impact of breach or violation of the psychological contract on how employees feel and, in turn, behave and perform in their jobs. The conclusions from this research were considered in the previous chapter. In this section we will focus on two important features of the personal deal – the issue of 'reciprocation' and 'job creep'.

The concept of reciprocation is based on the idea of social exchange between people and suggests that if you do something I want, then I will feel obliged to do something you want. The conclusion from the research[3] is that employees perceive that their organisations have obligations towards them, for example regarding payment, job interest, involvement and so on (refer to Chapter 3 for the full list). The idea is that if employees perceive that the obligations of others towards them are fulfilled then they, in turn, will feel obliged to reciprocate and fulfil their obligations towards the organisation. This conclusion accords with common sense and is based on a number of research studies.

The typical way reciprocation will occur is that if one party reduces what it gives the other, the other in turn is likely to reduce what it gives back. So if a leader reduces the amount of support and encouragement they give team members, then the team members in turn may reduce the amount of effort they put into work. The same can be expected if an employee puts in less effort or simply produces fewer outputs. The leader may decide to give them less – for example involve them less in decision making, give them less interesting work and so on.

One of the interesting practical implications of this research is that making the provision of employee rewards contingent on performance may

---

3   Levinson, H. (1965), 'Reciprocation: The Relationship between Man and Organization', *Administrative Science Quarterly* 9, 370–90

not necessarily be the only positive way of motivating people. Traditional motivation theory suggests that rewards should only be offered when an individual achieves their goals. Therefore the traditional prediction is that if an employee is given a target of say 1000 units they should be told that they will be rewarded when they deliver the 1000 units. (The units might refer to sales, quality standards, numbers of customer calls answered, fulfilment of management strategic priorities and so on.) Many organisations reward schemes are based on this approach. The approach is frequently labelled 'carrot and stick' motivation – that is if you do X, then I will deliver Y to you (where X refers to things the company wants, and Y refers to things the employee wants). This approach underpins the bonus schemes operated by many City of London financial institutions.

The predictions from exchange theory[4] contrast with the carrot-and-stick motivation. The suggestion from this approach is that if the organisation wants to achieve ambitious goals, then it first needs to fulfil the needs of employees. Once employees receive the rewards they expect, (reasonable salary, personal care and respect and so on), they will feel obliged to reciprocate and take steps to deliver what the company expects from them.

The validity of this approach is supported by the results of a small but growing number of sales organisations. In these sales forces rewards are not driven by individual or team targets, but by what seems reasonable. In such organisations, including John Lewis shops, sales assistants are not rewarded by commission but simply receive a fixed salary. The assumption underpinning this approach is that if employees are reasonably rewarded they will feel obliged to do their bit for the organisation and will therefore rise to the challenge of fulfilling their sales and other targets.

The findings from both research and different companies' results is that a way of achieving high levels of employee output is to give rewards that employees want. The organisation and in particular leaders can then communicate to employees that as the organisation is fulfilling its part of the personal deal to them it now expects employees to fulfil their part of the personal deal to the organisation.

In the context of the personal deal model described earlier the prediction from reciprocation would be that if a company seeks greater output and performance from its people, action should first be taken to increase 'What my leader gives me'. Once this has occurred leaders should then communicate that

---

4   Gouldner, A. (1960), 'The Norm of Reciprocity', *American Sociological Review* 25, 161–78

this has occurred and at the same time emphasise what the company is seeking from its employees in the form of contents they can provide in the box 'What I give my leader'. Interestingly, this differs almost diametrically from the more typical approach used in many large corporations. What happens typically is that leaders and managers first demand that employees increase their outputs in the 'What I give my leader' box of the model and, only when they have achieved the required results, will the organisation increase what it provides employees in terms of contents of the 'What my leader gives me' box.

A very different approach for understanding and predicting employee behaviour and performance is based on the concept of 'job creep'.[5] Job creep involves ongoing pressure on employees to deliver more than the normal requirements of their jobs. This is a situation where the norm of reciprocity which has evolved over time no longer applies. Instead the employer is gradually increasing their requirements from employees. Behaviour and performance that was previously discretionary now becomes increasingly expected or is taken for granted by the employer.

Viewed in the personal deal framework this means that the 'What my leader expects from me' box keeps increasing. Therefore to fulfil the expectations of the leader the employee has to keep increasing their behaviour and performance in the box 'What I give my leader' box. A simple example of this might be when a large piece of work comes into an organisation, employees might not automatically be expected to work overtime to ensure that this work is completed on time. In the past the leader might have specifically asked the employee to work longer hours, and not left it to their discretion. When job creep occurs however the leader might start by asking employees to stay late and complete the work. As time goes on the leader might take it as a matter of course that employees will work longer hours to complete the piece of work – without any additional reward. Working extra hours therefore becomes the norm.

It has been suggested that the initial reaction of many employees to job creep may be positive, because their work is considered so important that they are requested to undertake additional work or work longer. Eventually however employees are expected to want to restore balance. Instead of continuing to fulfil the additional workload (by increasing the box 'What I Give My Leader') they will decide to pull back on the additional work. They may do this directly

---

5   Van Dyne, L. and Ellis, J. (2004), 'Job Creep: A Reactance Theory Perspective on Organisational Citizenship Behaviour as Overfulfillment of Obligations', in J. A-M. Coyle-Shapiro et al., *The Employment Relationship* (Oxford: OUP)

by refusing to undertake the additional overtime workload, or by taking longer work breaks, working slower and so on.

The importance of the concept of job creep is that it is occurring increasingly in organisations as a reaction to competitive and other business challenges. At one level, there is a commercial logic to this. However, at an emotional level, there is a very real possibility that it could result in negative reaction from employees unless they are convinced of the emotional logic of the need for job creep.

CHAPTER SUMMARY

- One of the major shortcomings of the psychological contract is that it views the relationship between employee and the organisation as a series of stand-alone transactions over time. This does not do justice to the reality of business life where relationships between the organisation and people continually evolve to reflect the changing needs of business – for example in response to changing market demands – as well as the personal needs of employees themselves, which change as a result of societal pressures and as employees go through different stages of the employee life cycle.

- Viewing the personal deal as a relationship between the individual employee and their leader has important advantages: it makes it possible to take account of specific individual differences between people, and also encourages leaders to take personal responsibility for the personal deal with their people. Experience in working with organisations to change personal deals indicates that managers and employees find this a helpful and positive perspective which they can use to improve performance. The personal deal is therefore much more practical than the psychological contract.

- Viewing the personal deal as taking place between the individual employee and their leader means that there will be a multitude of different personal deals in existence in an organisation. This accords with our experience of organisations which show that the way people and teams operate will be different, to reflect the needs of different personalities as well as the requirements of different jobs and teams, such as marketing, operations sales and so on, all of which have their own unique requirements for success.

- Over time our emotional feelings about work wax and wane to reflect the series of small fluctuations that naturally take place as a result of our personal successes and setbacks at work, colleagues, behaviour, and changes in the process and systems within which we operate. These are entirely natural and reflect what actually happens in work. Over the course of time a multitude of small changes will take place in our personal deals at work.

- The original model of the personal deal provided in Chapter 3 was made up of four building blocks; 'What I expect from the organisation', 'What I give the organisation', 'What the organisation gives me', and 'What the organisation expects from me'. This model is enhanced to show how each of these components continually shift in size to reflect the differences in what the parties expect and give each other as a result of external pressures and their different interactions.

- The dynamic interplay in the personal deal can be better understood by the idea of 'reciprocation' which means that if you do something for me I will typically feel obliged to do something for you in return. This contrasts with the traditional carrot-and-stick motivation which prevails in many large organisations and where increased rewards are only provided after the employee has achieved their goals. The success of sales organisations which reward people with a fixed level of pay suggests that the concept of reciprocation does work.

- Another important factor which impacts operation of the personal deal is job creep, which involves ongoing pressure on employees to deliver more than the normal requirements of their jobs. As competitive pressures increase there will be an increasing tendency for leaders to expect employees to give more to their jobs, and for things that were previously considered discretionary to become the norm.

CHAPTER 6

Types of Personal Deal

So far we have explored what is meant by the term the psychological contract, and viewed it as a personal deal. This chapter explores the types of personal deals that have evolved in organisations. In particular we will explore how the personal deal has evolved from an essentially static and unitary notion to something which today takes different and diverse forms and continues to evolve. These changes are significantly driven by the shift in the global economy from a predominantly industrial base to an increasingly knowledge base. A related reason for the increase in diversity of personal deals is the global trend for labour laws and trade unions to have less impact on the shape and content of employment relationships.[1] The final part of the chapter proposes a framework for understanding the different types of personal deals and also the behaviour that is most associated with each.

RELATIONSHIP PERSONAL DEALS

The original notions of the personal deal focused on a long-term relationship, which involved the master providing shelter, protection and welfare and, in return, the servant provided loyalty and promised to give their labour to fulfil the master's bidding.

One of the earliest and most powerful examples of this personal deal is provided in the Old Testament.[2] The personal deal between God and the Jews is presented in Table 6.1 in the same format as the examples of specific company personal deals in Chapter 2.

The summary overleaf of the deal between the Jewish people and God is quite clear. God is expected to provide fertile land and food, enable the Jewish people to flourish, protect them from enemies and take care of the disadvantaged. The Jews for their part are expected to worship God and obey his commandments, love and serve God, not worship other gods, and love strangers. It is a very long-term personal deal which at its core trades security of the Jewish people for loyalty to God. This personal deal has endured for many generations, and

---

1   Schalk, R. (2004), 'Changes in the Employment Relationship Across Time', in J. A-M. Coyle-Shapiro et al., *The Employment Relationship* (Oxford: OUP).
2   *The Good News Bible*, 2nd edition (1994), Old Testament, Deuteronomy, Chapter 10 and 11 (UK: The Bible Societies/Harper Collins Publishers)

Table 6.1   Personal deal between God and the Jews

God provides the Jews	The Jews provide God
With the rich and fertile land I gave your fathers	Worship God
Provide rain so that there is corn, wine, olive oil and all the food you need	Obey the (Ten) Commandments and laws
Make you flourish	Love the Lord thy God
Protect you from more powerful enemies	Serve the Lord with all thy heart and stop being stubborn
Treat orphans and widows fairly	Do not serve or worship other gods
Love strangers who live with you	Show love for strangers

is anticipated to endure for many more. In contrast to other deals we shall be referring to in this book, it is a personal deal which transcends generations and provides an almost perfect example of the pure relationship personal deal.

More recent relationship personal deals – if spiritually less intensive and worldlier but at their core similar – were made between men in the Middle Ages in Europe. The lord of the manor expected his serfs to provide a proportion of their produce (later replaced by money), provide labour on his own land and bear arms when required. One of the more outrageous obligations of serfs in some communities was that women were expected to spend the first night of their marriage with the lord of the manor, a custom known as 'droit de seigneur'. Serfs were also obliged to seek the Lord's permission if they wanted to move away to another village – something which was rarely given.

For his part the lord of the manor provided the serfs with land on which to live and grow crops, and protection from invasion and violence from other parties. They were also expected to oversee the provision of justice, and allow use of common land for the grazing of cattle. Undoubtedly this is a less spiritual personal deal than that between God and the Jews but, nevertheless, one which bound lord and serf together across generations in the Middle Ages and based on essentially the same principle of an exchange of loyalty for security.

As industrialisation evolved in the late eighteenth and nineteenth centuries, new forms of relationship personal deals emerged between owners and workers, involving a trade of security for loyalty. It was implied that the personal deal was lifelong (or at least working lifelong) and involved a set of obligations by workers to provide their time and loyalty in return for both wages and a degree of caring and welfare – the amount of caring depended on the owners' greed or compassion!

EMERGENCE OF TRANSACTIONAL PERSONAL DEALS

The significant change introduced by industrialisation was that the personal deal in the new factories brought workers together under one roof and allowed closer supervision and control. It also involved, as many workers found to their cost, a more transient relationship. If workers did not produce at the standards of quality or quantity required, or were seen to behave in inappropriate ways towards the supervisor, they were dismissed. The relationship was changing to something more transitory – in which one party (most often the managers and owners) could dispense with the services of workers.

In the nineteenth century the personal deal shifted again with the emergence of mass-production hierarchical organisations. These bureaucratic organisations, as they were known, made enormous increases in efficiency possible and were led by career managers who devoted their lives to the company. This is described well by Whyte, and includes the implicit personal deal between the company and career managers who were promised long-term employment with increasing responsibilities in return for their obedience and commitment.[3] While long-term personal deals which traded security for loyalty were in operation in many corporations in the twentieth century, an altogether different personal deal operated simultaneously for most junior employees.

This personal deal was much more short term and has been described by Rousseau[4] as a 'transactional' psychological contract. The transactional psychological contract or personal deal involves a much shorter-term relationship of an instrumental nature in which the employee remains with an organisation for only as long as it suits them and/or the organisation. This transactional personal deal was a refinement of what existed earlier in the mines, steel foundries, mills and pottery works of the early Industrial Revolution.

The transactional personal deal involves the company employing the individual as long as there is a need, and the employee remains with the organisation only as long as it suits them. If lower customer demand for products reduces the business's needs for labour, or new equipment is introduced which

---

3   Whyte, W. (1956), *The Organization Man* (Simon and Schuster)
4   Rousseau, D. (1989), 'Psychological and Implied Contracts in Organisations', *The Employee Responsibilities and Rights Journal* 2, 11–139

increases efficiency and reduces labour requirements, then the employee will be sacked or, as they euphemistically say in the United States, 'let go'. On the employee's side if wages and conditions are considered satisfactory the employee will remain with the company. However, if they can get more money or better conditions at another organisation they leave and go there. The core of the transactional personal deal is an exchange involving money for labour – quite different to security for loyalty which characterises the relationship personal deal.

An important feature of the transactional personal deal is that at its extreme there are no expectations beyond an exchange of money for labour. Present-day examples are casual labourers on building sites who are employed for the day, for example, to lay bricks or carry building materials. The individual is paid at the end of the working day, and there is no obligation for either the contractor or the labourer to turn up the next day. A similar personal deal exists between farm owners and seasonal agricultural workers who turn up to bring in the harvest. Once the harvest is gathered in there is no further commitment by the farmer or the labourer. Similar personal deals apply to casual workers across different sectors – and particularly to migrant workers who are illegally in the country. In their case the personal deal goes something along the following lines;

- The employer knows you should not be in the country and that you will find it difficult to get work. They therefore agree to employ the illegal migrant for a lower-than-market wage, and agree not to disclose this to the authorities. The employer may also choose to omit other statutory employment rights enjoyed by other legal workers.

- The employee for their part accepts a lower-than-market rate for the job, because they acknowledge that they are not legally entitled to work, and therefore have fewer rights than others. They will also not disclose that the employer is not providing legal terms of employment because they themselves are not legally allowed to be in the country.

In the UK in 2004 there was a tragic case where hundreds of illegal immigrant workers from China were employed to pick cockles (a type of shellfish) from Morecambe Bay, an area of volatile coastal tide movements on the North West coast of the UK. On a particular day the tide moved more unpredictably than usual and some 30 workers were drowned as the tide rushed into the bay. The incident did much to highlight the plight of illegal immigrants, including their unsafe conditions of work, low wages and unsatisfactory personal deal.

In many ways the personal deal of illegal immigrants is a very pure example of a transactional personal deal, in the same way that the relationship between God and Jews is an example of a pure relationship personal deal.

The transactional personal deal can be viewed at the opposite end of a continuum from the relationship personal deal. While the relationship personal deal emphasises an enduring longer-term relationship, the transactional personal deal involves an instrumental material exchange between the two parties. While the relationship personal deal includes mutual personal care of the other, the transactional personal deal in its pure form omits any sentiment or caring.

In practice any particular personal deal is rarely purely of one type, but will contain elements of both types of personal deal. Figure 6.1 shows how the continuum of relationship and transactional personal deals operates in practice.

Even in the case of migrant workers, the supervisor may strike up a conversation with an individual with whom he has a transactional personal deal and view this person as personable and pleasant to talk with. As a result the supervisor may decide that this individual should be given priority to work over others. This is an example of how personal rapport has given rise to elements of a relationship personal deal in what is essentially a transactional personal deal.

Involves a short-term relationship trade
of extrinsic rewards and money for labour

Transactional personal deal

Relationship personal deal

Involves a long-term relationship
trade of personal security for loyalty

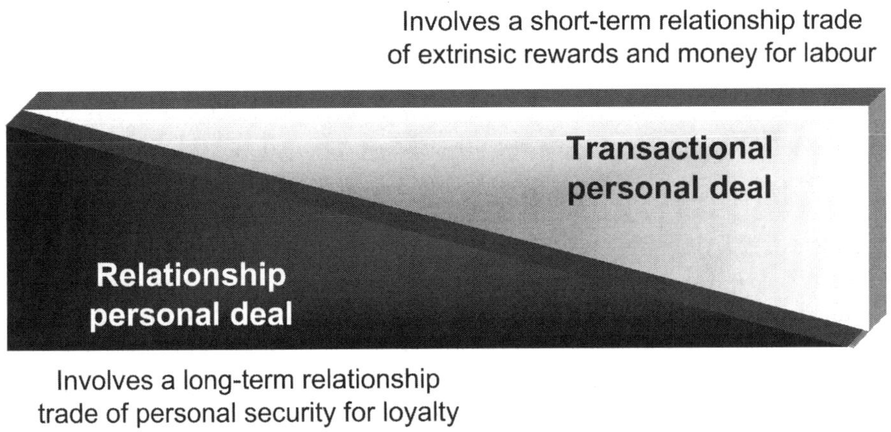

Figure 6.1   Relationship and transactional personal deal continuum

At the opposite end of the continuum, workers who have a largely relationship personal deal are also expected to deliver results. Even though an individual may have worked for 20 or more years in an organisation they are still expected to perform effectively and achieve results for the organisation. Cases are quite often reported in the media where long-serving and established employees are dismissed from employment because their performance is not deemed to keep pace with the increasing requirements of the organisation. In such cases what may have become a predominantly relationship personal deal is seen by employers to be secondary to the transactional component of the personal deal, which still involves a clear expectation that the employee will work in certain ways, or achieve required results.

The view of many observers of international employment trends is that the personal deal across different jobs and business organisations is shifting away from the relationship type, and moving increasingly towards a transactional type. While clearly supporting this principle, it has been observed that the emphasis given to transactional personal deals varies in different countries.[5] In Japan they found that personal deals place relatively more emphasis on relationships. These contrast with personal deals in New Zealand which they found tended to lie at the opposite end of the spectrum, and place more emphasis on the transactional and performance aspects of the personal deal.

Before exploring the content of personal deals in more detail it might be appropriate to consider some of the pressures which are bringing this overall shift towards transactional personal deals.

BUSINESS PRESSURES FOR INCREASED TRANSACTIONAL PERSONAL DEALS

Significant economic pressures have emerged over the last ten years which are having a profound impact on the global economy and particularly on the established economies of the Western world.

One of the most profound economic pressures is the growth of China and India. While the West experienced competitive pressures from Japan and Korea in the 1980s, these were relatively minor compared to the impact of current Chinese expansion and growth. While Chinese manufacturing was largely limited to toys until only a few years ago, China today is fast moving to become the most powerful industrial nation – and this is demonstrated by the forecast

---

5   Rousseau, D. and Schalk, R. (2000), *Psychological Contracts in Employment* (California: Sage)

that it will become the third largest national manufacturer of automobiles by 2010.[6] Similarly, India, until only a few years ago regarded as a developing nation, is today regarded as a significant provider of information technology and call-centre services to Western countries. The question is not if, but when will India emerge as one of the top-five international service providers across many sectors including insurance, banking and so on. So far awareness about India's competitive threat to the UK and the US has focused on call centres and IT services. How long will it take before the million new graduates each year in India increase their impact on global business activities?

The impact of China and India, as well as countries such as Vietnam, Poland, the Philippines, on prices of manufactured goods and services has only just begun. Established industrial nations especially the US and Europe are coming under increasing pressure from these many lower-cost suppliers and face a real threat to their supremacy. While businesses have long been used to the impact of manufacturers who undercut them by 10–20 per cent, the challenge increasingly will be to compete with suppliers who undercut their prices by 50 per cent. Chinese automotive manufacturers are currently planning an assault of this magnitude on car prices. The impact of this challenge will make the threat posed by the Japanese manufacturing of the 1980s seem gentle.

As well as direct competitive threats, the economies of China and India will put increasing pressures on raw materials and resources. The high oil prices experienced in 2005 are, in part, due to the significant demands for oil from China – a demand which is expected to increase by 30 per cent per annum in each year over the next few years. The same pressures will apply to other raw materials, which are now beginning to show a consistent increase in prices compared to only a few years ago.

Three other arenas are posing serious challenges to the personal deals provided by business organisations in the West. One is climate change – even in 2005 the signs from hurricane disasters in New Orleans and elsewhere suggest that the climate is indeed changing and that the atmosphere and sea levels are starting to shift. Another change is terrorism, which has and continues to make a significant impact on security practices and, in turn, costs incurred by airlines and other business organisations.

The final area which is creating organisation pressures for changes in the personal deal comes from technology. In recent years we have witnessed exponential developments in technology, ranging from the mobile phone, iPod

---

6   China Automotive Industry Association, Beijing, December 2004

and laptop, through to global changes in business communications, company information processing and so on. More was said about these changes in technology in Chapter 1.

These economic pressures are having a real impact on the nature of employment relationships in organisations. In the 1950s and 1960s to be an employee meant you worked full time with the tacit understanding that you were an employee for life. Since then, the nature of employment relationships have become increasingly divergent, and now commonly involve temporary workers, part-time employees, fixed-term contractors, consultants and interim workers. This variety of 'contingent' employment relationships, as they are referred to, today make up an increasing proportion of employees in many business organisations.

PERSISTENCE OF RELATIONSHIP PERSONAL DEALS

Our expectation from the greater competitive pressures is that both employer and employee will increasingly focus on transactional personal deals. Evidence from a study of 27 firms in Holland suggests however that the picture is not so straightforward.[7] The results found that employees felt a high obligation to deliver high quality and quantity of work, and felt few obligations not to switch jobs or to work additional hours to get the work done. This very much supports the notion of a transactional personal deal. The transactional focus is further reinforced by employees' lower expectations of their employer with regard to job security and challenging work, but higher expectations for open communications and fair treatment.

The data regarding what employers were perceived to provide their employees paints a less transactional picture however. It appears that some relationship aspects of the personal deal (for example job and income security and training) were better fulfilled than softer issues such as open and direct communication. The researcher concluded that, as of now, the new psychological contract or personal deal is not fully recognisable or visible. Employees fulfil obligations of the old personal deal but receive relatively fewer outcomes of the new personal deal.

---

7   Schalk, R. 'Changes in the Employment Relation Across Time' in J. A-M Coyle-Shapiro et al, *'The Employment Relationship'*, 2004, Oxford & New York.

As the researcher states: 'The research does not support the notion that the new personal deal has replaced the old personal deal in the Netherlands.' Some components of the relationship personal deal are considered important and timeless such as fairness, communication and respect, and seem related to basic human values, and appear important irrespective of the prevailing economic forces encouraging a more transactional personal deal.

In the opinion of the author, viewing personal deals along the relationship and transactional continuum does not do justice to the reality of what occurs in most organisations. Rather, a more flexible approach is required to describe the increasing variety of emerging personal deals.

REQUIREMENTS FOR A PERSONAL DEALS FRAMEWORK

Many people involved in managing relationships with employees – including line managers, people in HR, and corporate leaders will find it useful to have a framework which describes the different types of personal deals that can be developed and created with employees. To be effective a framework for the personal deal needs to meet a number of different criteria:

- *Organisation diversity*   The framework needs to be usable in different kinds of organisations. In particular it needs to be equally relevant to large and small businesses, those which are newly created and long established. It also needs to be applicable to organisations which operate in different business sectors and not-for-profit and public sectors.

- *Job diversity*   The framework needs to be applicable for a wide range of jobs. It must be usable to describe relationships between an organisation and jobs as different as shop-floor team leader, call-centre operator, marketing executive or chief executive.

- *Employee diversity*   The framework needs to be applicable to employees of very different types. Employees come in very different types – those who are well educated, others who are not, individuals who have high aspirations and ambitions, as well as those who live only for today. It needs to be applicable to people who are at different life stages – from the recent school leaver to the employee who is in their final few years of working life.

- *Social and culture diversity*   The framework needs to take account of the different social realities of organisations and people. While some organisations are autocratic others make decisions by consensus. Some organisations display high levels of ethics and integrity – while others focus purely on profit and returns to shareholders. It is important the framework can be used in organisations which operate in different national cultures.

- *Time flexibility*   The framework needs to be applicable to personal deals which endure for different time periods. Some employment relationships endure for many years. One of the UK's largest banks for example has an average length of service in the UK of 19 years. The framework also needs to be applicable to those on temporary and short-term contracts.

To fulfil these demanding requirements the personal deal framework will need to be based around factors which are fundamental to the behaviour of people and organisations.

FOUR TYPES OF PERSONAL DEAL

A large number of possible factors or dimensions are available for describing behaviour at work, including personal deals. Two dimensions seem to fit this requirement:

- Dimension 1 – Rational v Intuitive

- Dimension 2 – Stability v Change.

The first dimension of rational v intuitive is quite close to the dimensions used in the work of the Swiss psychologist Carl Jung, and are reflected in two of the four personality factors in the Myers-Briggs Type Indicator which is based on his work.[8] The second dimension of stability v change resembles the dimension used in Cameron and Quinn's model of organisation culture.[9] The dimension is intuitively appealing: we all at times experience things changing in our lives, while at other times experience continuity and stability. This dimension is also supported by its use to underpin other behavioural frameworks – for example in the area of leadership.[10]

---

8   Briggs Myers, I., revised by Kirby, L. K. and Myers, K. D. (2000), *Introduction to Type – A Guide to Understanding Your Results on the Myers-Briggs Type Indicator* (Palo Alto, CA: Consulting Psychologists Press)

9   Cameron, K. and Quinn, R. (1999), *Diagnosing and Changing Organizational Culture* (Reading, Mass.: Addison Wesley Longman)

10   Olivier, R. (2001), *Inspirational Leadership* (London: The Industrial Society)

Using these two dimensions provides us with four different types of personal deal: traditional, mercenary relationship, and developmental.

TRADITIONAL PERSONAL DEALS

This type of personal deal is *rational* and *stable*. Traditional personal deals are governed by clearly defined rules and procedures and implied if not explicitly stated principles of justice and fairness. Emphasis is given not so much to the amount of pay or work that is required but to the mechanisms and processes used to determine what is required and what is appropriate. This type of personal deal is highly prevalent in long-established stable bureaucratic organisations such as national and local government, Royal Mail, the National Health Service and so on. Some long-established manufacturing and financial services organisations, for example high street banks, may also have traditional personal deals. The traditional personal deal very much complements large bureaucratic organisations which have hierarchies of jobs, each with detailed role responsibilities and duties which determine who does what and how.

Personal deals of this type are often long enduring, and quite formal and impersonal. Despite their formality personal deals of this type will usually include caring for individuals who become incapacitated through illness and so on, because they include fairness as part of the rules. While there are a myriad of rules governing the employment relationship there will be many implicit but unwritten rules or norms which govern how people behave towards each other in traditional personal deals. The process of selection for being offered a role with a traditional personal deal will typically involve formal assessment procedures and the use of predetermined assessment criteria.

The value of traditional personal deals is that everyone is treated the same, and that principles of justice and fairness are usually built into the deal, even though it is quite impersonal in nature. The traditional personal deal is therefore likely to involve equality of opportunity and treatment – irrespective of the individual and their personal situation. It has the advantage of creating predictable and human, if somewhat inflexible, ways of working and relating together.

MERCENARY PERSONAL DEALS

This personal deal is *rational* and *change* oriented. Mercenary personal deals are governed by the exchange of extrinsic rewards between the parties. Emphasis is given on the amount of pay provided, and the amount and quality of work undertaken. The processes by which pay and work loads are determined are less important than the actual amounts involved. This type of personal deal is particularly prevalent among many sales roles and trading roles in investment banks and trading floors. It is also found among temporary- and short-contract employees – for example temporary secretaries from Kelly, agency nurses, contract programmers and IT professionals.

Mercenary personal deals are typically short term, but could endure for the medium-term relationships for permanent positions in organisations, especially in sales. This type of personal deal is quite tough minded and usually will not include any or much caring of employees whose performance deteriorates or falls short of what is expected. Quite simply if you do not turn up and perform, for example you do not achieve your sales quotas, you do not get paid and are likely to be dismissed fairly soon if this continues. Because of the high emphasis on extrinsic outcomes by both parties the relationship is likely to be terminated or modified if either party can obtain superior outcomes elsewhere. If a sales person can get more bonus pay from another employer they will leave and go there; equally if an employer decides to reduce the amount of work that it needs to get done the individual is terminated. The process for selection of individuals for mercenary personal deals may be quite basic or quite rigorous – but will be primarily governed by expediency.

The mercenary personal deal is similar in many respects to the transactional personal deal discussed earlier. It has the advantage of focusing on what the organisation and marketplace requires, and allows changes to be made quickly to what is delivered. It has the downside of being quite uncaring and promotes behaviour which is self-centred – as many sales people find. The mercenary personal deal does however have the advantage of encouraging people to be independent and take care of themselves and their needs, rather than rely on others.

RELATIONSHIP PERSONAL DEALS

This personal deal is *stable* and also *intuitive*. Relationship personal deals are governed by mutual feelings and affection. Emphasis is given to individuals' personal agendas and the quality of personal interaction, more than tangible outputs and results. This type of personal deal is becoming less common in the workplace. Relationship personal deals are found in some family firms where, once an employee has proved their worth, they are accepted almost as a member of the family through thick and thin – almost irrespective of what they deliver and the changing needs of the business. The relationship personal deal also operates in some long-established professional service firms such as law and accounting firms, particularly among partners. It may also be encountered in personal service, where a long-standing member of staff is tolerated even when they go off the boil.

The author knows of one highly entrepreneurial business which is tough and demanding of employees, most of whom are subject to mercenary personal deals. Once an employee has proved their worth over many years though, the personal deal subtly changes to a relationship type, as the proprietor recognises that an individual has given much of their working life to serve the business. If someone becomes ill, or the needs of the business requirements for people change, the individual who has proved their worth is accommodated along the lines of a relationship personal deal.

Relationship personal deals are long term, and could endure for life – for example until a business partner or employee retires. This can be the most personally tolerant caring deal between the parties. The expectation on both sides is that if problems are encountered by either party the other will take care of them, if necessary taking on additional work and personal care beyond the expectations of work. It is the opposite of the mercenary personal deal: if there are health reasons why one party cannot deliver their part of the normal deal, this will be entirely understood. If one or the other party decides to terminate the relationship this can often be a shock to the other party, who will usually take it as a personal affront, and view the other as reneging on their special relationship.

The relationship personal deal here is essentially the same as the one described earlier in the chapter. It has the positive advantage of binding the two parties closely together and takes account of each party's personal needs and motives. The downside of the relationship personal deal is that it can be quite restrictive on both parties at times of change and increased competitive pressures. The relationship personal deal might endure far longer than can be justified by economic grounds. It is therefore likely to be replaced by other personal deals in the face of new business and environmental conditions.

DEVELOPMENTAL PERSONAL DEALS

This personal deal is *change* oriented and *intuitive*. Developmental personal deals are future focused and centre on the acquisition and use of knowledge and expertise. Emphasis in the developmental personal deal focuses on how individuals take on, share and apply knowledge in their work to serve the organisation's goals. The knowledge may come from outside the organisation, such as an established profession or may come internally from knowledge gained by the organisation from its business activities over time.

The developmental personal deal is becoming increasingly important as the knowledge economy evolves, and organisations rely increasingly on the use of expertise and knowledge for their competitive advantage. Developmental personal deals have historically been part of most professional service firms' ways of working, but are now increasingly forming the basis for employee–employer relationships in more and more organisations. The development personal deal will be important in organisations such as IT, pharmaceutical and biotech, engineering services, and other technology-based organisations.

Developmental personal deals will usually be medium term, but can be long term. The heart of the developmental personal deal is that it implies that the employee will continually develop and update their expertise and knowledge and apply it in new ways. This personal deal will last as long as the individual is able to develop and apply expertise in pursuit of the organisation's goals. However once the individual ceases to acquire and apply new knowledge their potential usefulness becomes limited, and their days begin to be numbered. An inherent feature of the developmental personal deal is that the individual is valued and rewarded both for the current knowledge they apply, but also for their potential to continue to acquire and apply knowledge in future.

A classic example of the developmental personal deal is the employment of recent graduates. Many organisations which employ new graduates do so not because of their contribution in the first year of employment, which typically costs more than the value they bring to the organisation. The reason for employing new graduates is rather because of their potential future contribution in their second and subsequent years of employment.

The great value of the developmental personal deal is that it increasingly lies at the heart of how knowledge organisations work and how they relate to their people. It clarifies the importance of knowledge acquisition and application as one of the organisation's core processes. It also helps explain the challenge faced by many large professional service firms who find they have plateaued knowledge professionals at manager and senior manager levels who do not have the skills to make partner. Many professional service firms find it difficult to manage and motivate people at this level who are longer-serving employees. The downside of the developmental personal deal is that it may only focus on one of the things, albeit an important one, which contributes to the organisation's success.

Figure 6.2 illustrates the four types of personal deal that can exist in an organisation.

PERSONAL DEAL COMBINATIONS

The four personal deal types will in practice occur only very rarely in their pure forms in an organisation. The two earlier examples of the relationship personal deal between God and the Jews, and the mercenary personal deal between illegal migrants and an employer are examples of almost pure personal deals. In practice most personal deals between an individual and their employer will involve a mix of the four types described above.

An interesting example is the personal deal with knowledge workers in a professional services firm. The personal deal for professionals such as lawyers, accountants and architects is likely to centre predominantly on the developmental personal deal. The organisation will expect the individual to be an expert in their field and the issues involved in implementation, and use this knowledge to provide sound advice to clients in return for a stream of fee income. The personal deal in most professional service firms is likely also to have a clear mercenary component introduced by both the employer and employee. If an individual feels underpaid compared to rates of pay for comparable jobs in other firms they may decide to leave and join a firm which pays them more for the same work. Equally the firm will have expectations about the amount and quality of work the individual will deliver to clients, and if this falls consistently below the standard, the individual will eventually be terminated by the organisation. There is also likely to be a relationship component of the individual's personal deal, influenced by the quality of relationships between the individual and their managers and colleagues. It is

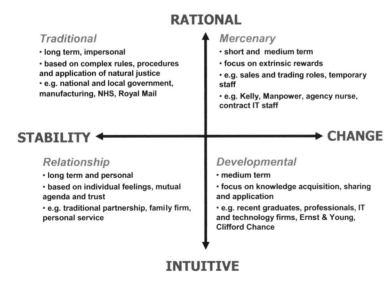

Figure 6.2   Types of personal deal

well known that someone who is liked is likely to get away with more than someone who is not liked. Equally someone who is universally found to be difficult and uncooperative by colleagues will find their contribution more under scrutiny than someone who is not. Finally the organisation will have a set of rules and procedures regarding the way it operates and these will form part of the traditional personal deal. An employee who consistently fails to comply with the procedures for recording chargeable time is likely to find themselves under pressure.

From these examples we can see that the actual personal deal an organisation has with its people is very likely to involve a combination of all four types of personal deal. In the professional service firm the personal deal may for example be 40 per cent developmental, 30 per cent mercenary, 15 per cent traditional and 15 per cent relationship. In a large bureaucracy such as a government department the personal deal may be rather different and involve say 40 per cent traditional, 30 per cent relationship, 20 per cent mercenary and 10 per cent developmental.

The important conclusion from these examples is that in practice the personal deals in any organisation or for any particular job are highly unlikely to be solely from one of the four types. Instead it will involve a combination of all four. This is shown by the dotted line in Figure 6.3, which shows high emphasis on the traditional, and rather less emphasis on the mercenary, relationship and developmental components. Typically we would expect one or two of the types of personal deal to be most prominent, and receive most attention from both employees and the organisation.

The challenge facing many organisations is what kind of personal deals do they have currently and what kind of personal deals do they want to have with their people in future? A way of looking at this question is shown in Figure 6.3, by comparing the dotted line shape with the continuous line shape.

The figure shows a prevailing personal deal at work which is highly traditional and relatively low on developmental or relationship focus. In contrast the required or aspirational personal deal shows a shift towards the mercenary and developmental components. This diagram describes the implicit change goals of one of the culture change programmes the author and his colleagues recently worked on. The objective essentially is to shift employment relationships and the personal deals between individual managers and their team members to emphasise business results and knowledge more, and place rather less emphasis on the traditional relationship with its emphasis on

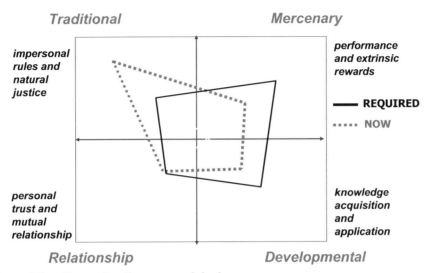

Figure 6.3   Measuring the personal deal

complex rules and procedures which prove to be an increasing handicap as the organisation is exposed to greater competitive pressures.

In this chapter we have explored how the personal deal has evolved from only one type – the relationship personal deal – to an appreciation that an almost infinite number of different personal deal types can be used. The options can be accommodated and described by the four personal deal types: traditional, mercenary, relationship and developmental. The challenge facing human resource professionals and line managers is to understand which type of personal deals they have now within their teams and organisation, and which types they need to create to best achieve their business and organisation goals.

CHAPTER SUMMARY

- The first psychological contracts or personal deals which emerged were of a relationship type. This involved a long-term exchange between one party which provided security to the other party, which in return provided loyalty. The classic example of this occurred in the Middle Ages between the lord of the manor and the serfs who worked his land. There are still organisations where a predominantly relationship personal deal prevails, such as social services departments in local authorities.

- As industrialisation got under way the relationship personal deal began to be replaced by the transactional personal deal. This involves a highly instrumental relationship in which one party only engages with the other so long as this serves their immediate interests. If lower customer demand reduces the requirement for labour, workers are laid off or let go. Equally if the employee can obtain a higher wage rate elsewhere they would leave for the other employer. In its pure form the transactional personal deal is no more than an exchange of money for labour.

- Transactional and relationship personal deals can be viewed as opposites on a continuum. In practice there are very few pure personal deals which are only one or the other form. Typically most personal deals today will involve some mix of the two. Many predominantly relationship personal deals will involve an element of the transactional personal deal and vice versa.

- An overall shift has been observed away from relationship towards more transactional personal deals in recent years. This is due largely to competitive pressures especially from China and India, as well as pressures on resources, climate change, security and technology.

- Despite the shift towards more transactional personal deals some research evidence suggests that people continue to prefer elements of the relationship personal deal. This is because some components of the relationship personal deal continue to be considered important for reasons of fairness, communication and respect for human values.

- A model with four different personal deals is proposed:

  - *traditional deals*, which are governed by defined rules and fairness;

  - *mercenary deals*, which are rational, short term and results focused;

  - *relationship deals*, which focus on feelings and personal agendas;

  - *developmental deals*, which are intuitive, future and knowledge focused.

- The personal deal most people have in practice with their manager will involve some elements of each of the four personal deal types.

The type of personal deal we have can be plotted as a shape on a two dimensional axis which shows the four personal deal types.

- The value of being able to measure and rate the personal deal is that this makes it feasible to evaluate the actual personal deal a person has today with their manager and the organisation, and compare this to the desired personal deal that is most appropriate for the organisation as well as the individual.

CHAPTER 7

How Three Companies Use the Psychological Contract

The focus now shifts to how the personal deal can be used to enhance the performance of organisations. In this chapter we will concentrate on how three business organisations, Arup, CMS Cameron McKenna and Richer Sounds, use the psychological contract to add value to their business performance.

These three organisations have been chosen for closer discussion for a number of reasons. Firstly, each comes from a different sector – Arup is primarily in engineering design, CMS Cameron McKenna is in legal services and Richer Sounds is in retail. A second reason is that each organisation has been independently evaluated to be a great place to work, from recent ratings in 'The Sunday Times Best 100 Places to Work' survey.[1] A third reason is that the author knows something about these three organisations and has contacts with them.

Each organisation will be described, followed by a description of its psychological contract provided by a senior individual in the organisation. The value and benefit each organisation believes it gains from its prevailing psychological contract will be considered, as well as some of the implications and challenges each company faces because of it.

The description of each organisation's psychological contract in this chapter is based on indepth conversations with at least one senior manager in each business. While the descriptions are not based on robust empirical research, the performance of each of these organisations in their respective marketplaces is beyond reproach, with regard to people practices and financial performance.

ARUP

Arup is an international design and engineering firm which employs just over 3000 staff in the UK and a further 4000 internationally. Operating out of 70 international offices, Arup typically has over 10 000 engineering

---

1   '100 Best Companies to Work For', *The Sunday Times*, March 2006 (London: Times Newspapers)

projects running concurrently. Projects typically focus on design solutions, predominantly in the building environment.

People in Arup pride themselves on being the creative force behind many of the world's most innovative and sustainable designs. Global landmarks to which Arup has made a significant contribution include the Sydney Opera House, the Channel Tunnel Rail Link, Seattle Library, Stonecutters Bridge in Hong Kong and the Water Cube for the Beijing Olympics.

Arup has three main global business areas: building, infrastructure and consulting. However, it adopts a multi-disciplinary approach which means that any given project may involve people from any or all of the sectors or regions in which the firm operates. Arup's fundamental aim is to bring together the best professionals to meet its clients' needs.

Arup was founded in 1946 by Sir Ove Arup, a powerful visionary, not only for what the firm stands for and what it delivers but also its ownership. Sir Ove and his partners handed over the business to be held in trust for the benefit of its employees and their dependants. Without external investors, the firm is at liberty to make long-term investment decisions unhampered by short-term pressures.

Arup has grown organically over 60 years to become an international consulting firm with exceptional scope. The skills base within Arup has grown considerably beyond its original core of structural and civil engineering. It now counts master-planning, economics, environmental and project management, alongside business and management consulting skills. The ethos of the firm emphasises the importance of technical excellence and continuing development.

THE ARUP PSYCHOLOGICAL CONTRACT

The psychological contract in Arup originates with Sir Ove Arup's vision and ideals, not just for innovative design, but for life. The Arup values are enshrined in a document known as the 'Key Speech' which he gave on 9 July 1970 to the partners, about the future of their business. The Key Speech describes the core values of the firm, the six aims of the business and how they can be practically brought to life in the way Arup does business.

The aims of the firm are:

- quality of work

- total architecture (integration of different functions and disciplines)

- humane organisation

- straight and honourable dealings

- social usefulness

- reasonable prosperity for members.

The Key Speech contrasted the Arup approach to life with that of Henry Ford. While Henry Ford regarded 'work as a necessary evil', Ove Arup considered work as 'something which can be made interesting and rewarding'. The Key Speech continues to be required reading for everyone who joins, and is still discussed with passion and enthusiasm. When I ran a workshop in winter 2005, one of the delegates challenged the issues under discussion in the context of the principles enshrined in the Key Speech.

Arup has an interesting psychological contract which was described by HR Director Stella Littlewood as involving the expectations from the firm and its people shown in Table 7.1.

Table 7.1   Arup's psychological contract

What Arup expects from employees	*What employees expect from Arup*
High performance from everyone, whatever they do	Freedom to express their individuality and not be stifled by bureaucracy and process
Take responsibility for whatever needs to be done	Have their voice heard as individuals, by providing forums for people to express their ideas and be given information
Failure to be allowed when innovating and trying out new ideas, but only once	Honesty and transparency: people expect leaders and peers to be open and honest with each other
Ask for the development they want, and demonstrate personal skills that stand out	A long-term career, not just a job
Have their own lives and manage their work/life balance as well as their career	A humane and caring employer which also nurtures and supports people in the outside world

An example of the firm giving 'freedom to express individuality' occurred a few years ago in Milan, where new offices were set up. When the founder of the Milan office expressed to colleagues his desire to set up new offices, he was quickly given a small amount of money, told to go and win some business there and go ahead. Apparently, the case for the Milan office did not have to be justified with a long and complex business plan, nor did it have to get signed off by different committees or senior managers. The founder, Gabriele Del Mese, simply made his case to a number of colleagues and then received funding. As a trusted employee, he was told to make it happen quickly, which he did, and the office now has 40 employees.

An example of people taking responsibility was after the tsunami hit in 2004, when Arup sent a group of employees to undertake redevelopment work on behalf of the firm. The engineers heard that a nearby orphanage building had been totally destroyed. In addition to their standard rescue role, the engineers took it upon themselves to put in their own money to help rebuild the orphanage. Since then, other employees and the firm have donated more money, enabling the orphanage building to be completely rebuilt for 75 boys and girls.

One of the important results of Arup's psychological contract is that in 2006, the firm achieved 74th position in *The Sunday Times* 100 Best Companies to Work For survey. Importantly, Arup achieved this ranking despite having 7000 employees, while most of the other top 100 organisations have fewer than 1000. The factors which enabled Arup to achieve this position also encourages 75 per cent of graduates who join, to remain with the company for ten years.

CHALLENGES ARISING FROM THE ARUP PSYCHOLOGICAL CONTRACT

Despite the very real benefits from its psychological contract, three challenges have emerged from it, in the areas of leadership, performance management and insularity.

The challenge in leadership is how to exercise the psychological contract in ways which encourage and enable people to perform effectively, while also allowing high levels of freedom to act. The implication is that leaders need to be highly inspirational role models who reinforce the culture and walk the talk. Leaders in Arup communicate significantly in different face-to-face forums and networks. They are expected to develop their people's skills and their own leadership skills. Finally, leaders are expected to have a strong self-image and personal values, which is a challenging requirement.

The second and related challenge was highlighted in recent employee opinion feedback, which indicated a widely held view that the firm does not always handle underperformance as well as it might. This is seen as a wake-up call for leaders to deal more robustly with poor performance. While this is a challenge faced by many organisations, it is typically something which top management advocates, rather than more junior employees, as with the Arup survey results.

A final, possible long-term challenge identified by the HR Director is that, because of its success, Arup could be in danger of becoming isolated by not bringing in external ideas from the world outside. Because the firm has so many advanced practices, people could be in danger of long-term complacency and as a result lose touch with the latest innovations in the external world.

Notwithstanding the challenges, the psychological contract in Arup is a very enriching and positive one which fulfils many of the requirements for best leadership and management practice. Arup can be judged to be a highly successful business from many different perspectives: revenue growth, employee commitment, innovation and contribution to the building world.

CMS CAMERON MCKENNA

CMS Cameron McKenna is a UK-based international law firm employing 1500 people in offices in the UK, and Central and Eastern Europe. The firm has 137 equity partners and provides a full range of legal services across all business sectors. Specialised areas include corporate, banking, energy, insurance, commercial and global industry.

While not among the 'magic circle' law firms, Cameron McKenna is the primary counsel to 20 of the FTSE 350 companies, and has acted for 103 of these companies in 2004–5. In addition to its own international offices, the firm has a further 45 associated offices worldwide, as part of the CMS network.

The firm's strategy is based on the achievement of competitive advantage through excellence in client services and providing value for money. Considerable time is spent focusing on the effective management of human capital. The firm prides itself on delivering client service through people. Its strategy has four core components: better people management, effective teamwork, personal development and better client relationships.

The client service strategy is based on building long-term relationships with clients, based on trust, honesty and openness. The goal is to live and breathe clients' business issues almost as well as clients do themselves. This approach is backed up by the fact that 90 per cent of client revenues are derived from repeat business, which is clear evidence that the strategy is working. Present customer satisfaction levels are an average of 4.2 on a 5-point scale, and the goal is to raise this to an average of 4.5.

To support its clients' focus, Cameron McKenna has commissioned independent customer research to gain accurate feedback about how clients perceive its service delivery.

Feedback is sought against five core headings:

- understanding of clients' needs
- quality of advice
- ability to manage work
- value for money
- overall satisfaction.

Independent interviewers are used to talk to clients face to face on a regular basis, and the results suggest that the firm is hands-on, proactive, flexible and human.

THE CMS CAMERON MCKENNA PSYCHOLOGICAL CONTRACT

The firm's approach to clients is very much underpinned by its approach to managing people. It has given credence to its emphasis on people through its People Report, which it published in 2005 and is available on its website.[2]

In recruiting, Cameron McKenna seeks people who have an interest in business and are therefore in a position to understand and relate to its clients' issues and concerns. This broader focus is also reflected in its development programmes, which contrast with those of many law firms by including personal and business skills.

While the HR team does not use the psychological contract explicitly there is an 'employee commitment' statement which lists 13 things that employees can expect from the firm. Interestingly, the other side of the coin, that is what the firm expects from its people, is not quite so explicitly formulated. This is however partly addressed by a recently produced career booklet by the firm, 'Charting Your Course', which spells out what the firm expects from people, and

---

2   CMS   Cameron   McKenna   website: www.law-now.com/cmck/pdfs/nonsecured/ peoplereport2005.pdf

what they can expect from the firm – in essence a picture of the psychological contract.

A conversation with Head of HR David Leech suggests that the psychological contract in Cameron McKenna has the components shown in Table 7.2.

Table 7.2   Cameron McKenna's psychological contract

CMS Cameron McKenna expects from employees	What employees expect from CMS Cameron McKenna
Client focus: drop almost anything for a client	Interesting and challenging work which people enjoy doing
Put themselves out for the firm: go the extra mile	Difficult or bad news to be handled gently, so that the individual can grasp and accept it
Collaboration and teamwork: working closely and supporting colleagues	Never to be alone: employees expect to be supported by colleagues, and receive consistent and open communications
To have a balanced life: in contrast to some law firms, people are not expected to give up the rest of their life for the firm	Respect for individuals as human beings – both their dignity and personal lives
Look after their own professional development – both legal and non-legal	Robust training to support their development

An example of teamwork in action occurred on the day of the London terrorist bombings in July 2005. The Head of HR together with a number of his colleagues in the London head office spontaneously talked and decided to set up emergency communications of events to all staff hourly, so that people were continually informed. The same group of senior staff jointly made the decision to allow staff to leave work early and return home.

The importance of this example is that the group of senior people who decided to manage the situation did it collaboratively, rather than through one senior person taking charge and instructing people what to do – they decided to take collective responsibility for handling the situation on behalf of the firm.

A similar situation occurred when a group of staff at an office overseas decided to defect to a competitor who made them offers they could not refuse. A small number of senior people spontaneously decided to work together to reflect and take stock of what had happened. They quickly decided on actions they could implement to address the situation, and they also decided how to handle the crisis in the best way for the firm and its clients. The team at the overseas location was quickly rebuilt.

At a more personal level, the Head of HR described a meeting to which he was called by one of the partners, to evaluate and discuss a particular proposal to change working practices. It did not take long for the meeting to establish that the basic idea was not sound, and had little merit. In other organisations, once a meeting arrived at such a conclusion, it would have stopped quite promptly. However, in Cameron McKenna once the conclusion was apparent to most of the people, the meeting continued to explore diverse aspects of the idea in a thorough and comprehensive way. The reason was not that people had failed to appreciate the conclusion, but that no one wanted to upset the individual who called the meeting, to avoid him losing face and instead let him down gently.

One of the important results of the Cameron McKenna psychological contract is that it has been placed in *The Sunday Times* 100 Best Companies to Work For survey. It won the award in 2002, 2003 and 2005.

CHALLENGES ARISING FROM THE CAMERON MCKENNA PSYCHOLOGICAL CONTRACT

The awards for being a great place to work provide a clear indication that the psychological contract has distinct value for the firm and its people. Discussions with the Head of HR suggested that these strengths may also create some downsides.

In Leech's view, the very strength of the psychological contract in terms of valuing people and teamwork might, in the medium to long term, also create a downside of allowing people to become complacent. The fact that the firm is such a pleasant place to work, and that it achieves over 90 per cent of fee income from existing clients, might allow people to rely on their present success and become relaxed about winning sales from new clients.

There is a danger that if the firm loses two or three of its major clients through no fault of its own, for example a big client being taken over by an organisation which uses a different law firm, then its employees may find it challenging to replace these big clients. The lack of apparent perceived high levels of hunger for new business among professional staff might simply allow them to become complacent about the need to continually build new client relationships. The firm is looking to sharpen and increase the hunger for new business among senior professionals.

Because of this danger, one of the priority people issues for the firm is development of 'more of a performance' culture. Leech's ideal is to keep people fleet of foot and focused so that they do not become complacent. This will involve more than honing the existing performance management processes and systems, by making sure that people really do give each other robust feedback, so that opportunities for increasing individual contribution are identified and acted on.

The challenge that the firm faces in becoming more performance focused is to make sure that it does not weaken the very positive features of teamwork, collaboration and support, which are important assets of the firm and its people.

The methods and approaches put forward in later chapters, focusing on leadership and culture, may add potential value to CMS Cameron McKenna in helping them raise the performance element of the culture, while retaining its other very positive features.

RICHER SOUNDS

Richer Sounds stands out in the world of audio-visual retailing. Established in 1978, it now trades from 43 stores in 35 towns and cities in the UK. Although Richer Sounds has relatively few outlets, they are the largest UK hi-fi, home cinema and flat-screen TV retailer. The firm takes great pride in its huge turnover per square foot of store, which is the highest of any retailer, and has landed them in the *Guinness Book of Records* for the last thirteen years.

Originally purely a retail store, Richer Sounds now trades over the web, and as a result of an employee's suggestion has recently extended its sales reach from private individuals to corporate customers. As well as offering among the lowest prices, Richer Sounds provides high levels of customer service, including genuine advice on equipment – something its web and high-street competitors are not renowned for – not to mention high levels of after-sales care.

A feature of Richer Sounds' head office in south-east London is making work fun, something which may have contributed to it becoming Britain's largest hi-fi retailer. Among the desks, computers and hard-working employees, there is a whole army of wacky artworks, including a life-size Elvis and Fido, the world's most welcoming (and overexcited) dog.

Julie Abraham, the Stock Control Director, says: 'I spent four years with IBM, where everybody did everything "properly". I came here, and people wear jeans and shorts in the summer. I wasn't sure if it was going to work for me, but you just get hooked. Everybody's completely mental.' An impressive 90 per cent of her colleagues find their teams fun to work with, and 91 per cent say that they can have a laugh with colleagues.[3]

THE RICHER SOUNDS PSYCHOLOGICAL CONTRACT

The psychological contract at Richer Sounds appears to have created real business and employee value.[4] Of the 1.3 million companies in the UK, Richer Sounds ranked as one of the top five British-owned businesses to work for, for three years running, in *The Sunday Times* 100 Best Companies To Work For survey. As stated in *The Sunday Times*, according to Teresa Chapman, Julian Richer's PA: 'The appeal is obvious. You can speak to people at all levels. If anyone wants to see Julian, he'll see them as soon as he can. That's policy.'

'We all know what we're working for and how our work fits in,' says Lol Lecanu, the Marketing Manager. 'Everybody is singing from the same hymn book, and it made me understand my role and how I have an impact on the company.' Communication is excellent, with all staff having ample opportunity to give feedback at seminars, suggestion meetings and branch dinners.

Salaries are high for the retail industry: a senior sales assistant can expect £18 000. The perks are also impressive: the loan of holiday homes in locations such as St Tropez and Venice, trips in the company jet, free massages, facials and pedicures at Christmas. There is even a take-your-pet-to-work scheme.

Promotion from within is the norm; the majority of head-office staff have worked on the shop floor. Ricky Faust had been working for the company for more than 20 years when he came up with the suggestion of corporate sales: 'They said, "Well, try it out." I was managing the Holborn branch and I wrote to 100 companies and got a 10 per cent response.' Now he is Corporate Sales Director. The suggestion scheme, with a cash bonus of at least £5 for each idea and quirky incentives for the best, has been remarkably successful, producing an average of 20 suggestions a year from each employee. Richer Sounds is also socially responsible, giving one of the highest proportions of any UK company of pre-tax profits (5 per cent) to charity. It is not surprising that 86 per cent of employees say they are proud to work there.

3   Richer Sounds website: www.richersounds.com/home.php?cda=vacancies
4   Based on presentation by Julian Richer to CIPD Annual Conference – Harrogate, 2004

The company-wide psychological contract looks something like Table 7.3.

Table 7.3   Richer Sounds' psychological contract

What Richer Sounds expects from its employees	What employees expect from Richer Sounds
High performance: people are expected to devote their full energy	Fun at work
To adapt working hours to customer activity levels	Recognition: 'Golden Aeroplane Award'
Low shrinkage: employees do not take stuff from the company	Reward: senior sales people earn £18K with weekly profit share and holiday homes and so on
High levels of customer service	Loyalty: promote from within, loyalty lunch at Ritz
Improvement of the business, through putting forward creative ideas in the suggestion scheme	Opportunity to make a personal difference

Importantly, this psychological contract combines expectations about hard work, service with engagement, fun and high reward.

The Richer Sounds' psychological contract refers to things that employees do that contribute directly to business effectiveness. These include flexible hours and a working week that match customer buying patterns across the year. People in Richer Sounds are encouraged to work longer hours in the run up to Christmas, but fewer hours during the months when customers visit its stores less frequently and spend less.

The tangible rewards for employees in Richer Sounds are significant, and differ from the psychological contract offered by most other retail organisations. Employees are among the highest paid in the high street, and receive rewards such as use of company holiday homes. More tangible than these is the profit share that occurs each week. At the end of Saturday trading, the profit of each store is calculated and the employee share of this is handed out in cash to each individual. The amount each person receives is influenced both by the total profit taken by the store and by satisfaction ratings made by customers after completing sales transactions with staff. Performance bonuses and emphasis on customer feedback help create an atmosphere which encourages store employees to think about customer service.

What makes the Richer Sounds' psychological contract special is that it operates in a very live and tangible way, semi-independently in each store. As employees increase store profitability, their personal reward increases. In this way, the psychological contract is much more than a static statement of the mutual expectations between the organisation and its people. Rather, it has become a core process for driving performance in the organisation. As employees raise their performance and business results, they in turn receive more from the company.

Achieving the highest sales revenue per square foot of any retail organisation is a real achievement. Despite the lack of space, which customers experience when visiting stores, this is more than overcome by the approach and service from employees. Employee performance is also significant, as indicated by the high retention rates; average length of service across the stores is over seven years, which is all about it being one of the top places to work in Britain.

The special feature of the Richer Sounds' psychological contract is that it works in the interests of the company, its customers and its employees. It provides an example of how a win-win psychological contract can add value to the business and its people.

CHALLENGES ARISING FROM THE RICHER SOUNDS PSYCHOLOGICAL CONTRACT

All the evidence points to the real value of Richer Sounds' psychological contract. The main downside is that because of its success, over a number of years people could become complacent. At present, there is no evidence of this – quite the reverse – people are engaged and committed, and the business results are very positive. The challenge will be to continue to foster the stretch factor in people's work, so that they continue to provide exceptional performance for customers and the business. The long-term challenge is that if the foot is taken off the accelerator, the business could perform less effectively and this in turn could impact the value people bring to the business.

This creates a challenge for top management to continue setting demanding stretch corporate goals which continue to be relevant to the fast-moving market place in which Richer Sounds operates, and which brings out the best in its people. The danger in the longer term is that if the company becomes less successful employees may spontaneously decide to contribute less. This may not be apparent quickly, but over time could impact performance, rewards and the standing of the business in the high street. It is a similar situation to an athlete who has competed successfully in national and international competitions, and then fails to win a particular prize. Because of this one failure, the individual might then become disheartened and decide to put less effort into their training, and in turn into the next competition they enter. Despite their string of successes, because they fail on one particular occasion the individual may become less confident and in turn put less energy into other competitions. This could become a downward spiral.

PARALLELS BETWEEN THE THREE COMPANIES' PSYCHOLOGICAL CONTRACTS

Although all three companies are very different, and operate in very different markets, there appear to be important parallels and similarities between their psychological contracts. Almost all the themes described below emerge from all three companies' psychological contracts, and in two cases the themes are explicitly referred to by two of the three companies.

The high-level similarities between what the organisations expect from their people include:

- achieve high levels of personal and business performance;

- go out of your way to deliver customer service;

- take personal responsibility for your work and life;

- enhance your personal contribution at work.

In the case of what employees can expect from these companies, there are also important similarities:

- opportunities to make a personal difference;

- stimulating environment – fun and a challenge;

- care and respect for the individual;

- longer-term opportunities to grow and develop.

One of the most important questions this comparison gives rise to is whether it is possible to identify a type of psychological contract which will in itself cause or give rise to high business performance and high employee engagement and commitment. While we do not have rigorous empirical evidence on this, the similarities between the psychological contracts of Arup, CMS Cameron McKenna and Richer Sounds seem unlikely to be just a coincidence. We might therefore view the similarities between their psychological contracts as a hypothesis about how a high performance psychological contract might look.

We can be confident that the high level of employee engagement and commitment in these three business organisations is in no doubt, because of their previous positions in *The Sunday Times* 100 Best Companies to Work For survey. Also from a business perspective, all three organisations have grown significantly in recent years, as well as having significantly increased their profitability and financial performance. Therefore the people and business metrics broadly suggest that these organisations are high performing.

Despite evidence which has so far to be viewed as less robust than would ideally be desired, the idea that there may be a type or types of psychological contract which give rise to high business and people performance could be of major value to business organisations. If there is, it would raise the importance of the psychological contract as something which is not just of interest to business psychologists and HR practitioners, but which is of critical importance for business managers and directors. Instead of being of academic concept, the psychological contract may have the potential to be one of the most powerful practical drivers of business success.

If there is a type or types of psychological contract which contribute more to business performance, this would assist all of us involved in maximising the performance of organisations, whether line manager or HR specialist, with an important tool in our armoury for creating business value. One of the leading experts on HR practices, Dave Ulrich, proposes that the principal purpose of HR is to create business value.[5] The psychological contract, or as we refer to it in other chapters, the personal deal at work, potentially provides such a vehicle for creating business value.

The potential of the psychological contract to add real business value will, I hope, encourage some of the energy that has recently been directed to research and measure the impact of breach of the psychological contract to instead focus on the type of psychological contract which is most associated with high performance in organisations.

Undertaking such research would involve measuring the psychological contracts in business organisations which are achieving high levels of business performance, including those that have achieved high levels of employee engagement and commitment. It would also involve measuring and comparing the psychological contracts in organisations which are underperforming, as

---

5   Ulrich, D. and Brockbank, W. (2005), *The HR Value Proposition* (Boston, Massachusetts: Harvard Business School)

well as those that have changed their position from high to low, or from low to high, performers.

Research in the UK by the Institute of Personnel and Development[6] relates people practices to high levels of business performance. This found that 19 per cent of the variation between medium-sized companies' profitability was accounted for by people management practices. This variation in performance is greater than the variation accounted for by factors such as strategy, technology or research and development.

While this is important evidence about people practices that contribute to high performance, the research so far does not take account of company expectations about people's performance on business performance. Researching the psychological contract components which are associated with high levels of business performance has the potential to provide important tools for business leaders to help them enhance the performance of their organisations.

Obviously, it is important not to draw more than a hypothesis from the review of psychological contracts of the three successful business organisations considered in this chapter. The potential of the hypothesis and tentative conclusions arrived at, however, is that they point towards an important step forward towards the grail of creating high-performing financial and people businesses.

If there is an ideal or optimum type of psychological contract then one of the obvious questions will be how this can be created in an organisation. One of the key issues which we will pursue in the two chapters which follow is how direct interventions can be made to change the psychological contract in an organisation to make it more effective.

CHAPTER SUMMARY

- The psychological contracts of three different business organisations were explored to identify any similarities between them. The three organisations were Arup, a firm of engineers in the construction sector, CMS Cameron McKenna, a law firm, and Richer Sounds, an audio-visual retailer. These organisations were chosen because

---

6   Patterson, M., West, M., Lowthorn, R. and Nickell, S. (1997), *Impact of People Management Practices on Business Performance* (London: Institute of Personnel and Development)

they are in different sectors and have all achieved sustained levels of business and people performance.

- The psychological contract descriptions are based on in depth conversations with senior managers in each of these organisations.

- The Arup psychological contract involves:

Arup expects from people	Employees expect from Arup
High performance from everyone	Freedom to express their individuality
Take responsibility	Have their voice heard
Failure to be allowed	Honesty and transparency
Ask for the development they want	A long-term career
Have their own lives and careers	A humane and caring employer

- The CMS Cameron McKenna psychological contract involves:

CMS Cameron McKenna expects from people	Employees expect from CMS Cameron McKenna
Client focus	To handle bad news gently
Put yourself out for the firm	Interesting and challenging work
Collaboration and team work	You are never alone
Have a balanced life	Respect individuals as human beings
Look after your development	Robust training

- The Richer Sounds psychological contract involves:

Richer Sounds expects from people	Employees expect from Richer Sounds
High performance	Fun at work
Adapt hours to customer activity	Recognition
Low shrinkage	Reward
High levels of customer service	Loyalty
Improve the business	Opportunity to make a personal difference

- There are important similarities between the psychological contracts of these three high performing organisations:

What business expects	What employees expect
High performance	Make a difference
Delivery of customer service	Stimulating environment
Take personal responsibility	Care and respect
Enhance your contribution	Opportunities to develop

- The similarities which emerged between the psychological contracts of these three business organisations raise the important possibility that there may be a type of psychological contract which contributes more to high levels of business performance. Researching what this psychological contract is may provide not only very significant value to HR professionals and psychologists, but potentially a powerful tool for business leaders to create higher-performance organisations.

CHAPTER 8

Using the Personal Deal to Improve Leadership Effectiveness

Leadership is one of the most widely written people issues in business. This is illustrated by a recent search of Amazon's online book store which identified 27 748 books on leadership. In this chapter, we explore how the personal deal can be used to provide a powerful but simple tool to enhance leadership and business performance. Despite the availability of a vast array of leadership techniques and methods, I believe you will find the approach based on the personal deal one of the most practical leadership development techniques available.

The chapter will first explore the nature of leadership and then consider how the personal deal has been used by business leaders, individuals and organisations to achieve enhanced results. The value of the personal deal approach will be explored in the context of ideas from the international leadership expert, Robert Quinn.[1] Finally, a radical way of thinking about leadership will be proposed, based on the personal deal.

NATURE OF LEADERSHIP

With so much being written about leadership, it's easy to forget the basics. Essentially, there are three features which characterise leadership: direction, relationships and a blend of right- and left-brain thinking. These components of leadership were described by Richard Boyatzis[2] respectively as hope, compassion and mindfulness.

DIRECTION (HOPE)

Direction lies at the heart of leadership. It's about going from where we are today to where we aspire to be in the future. This applies equally at an individual, team or organisation level. The direction might be about overall results for an organisation, such as launching a new product range, entering a new market, achieving business turnaround, improving customer satisfaction or simply

---

1   Quinn, R. (2004), *Building the Bridge* (San Francisco, John Wiley)
2   Boyatzis, R. (2006), *Resonant Leadership* (Boston, Harvard Business School Press)

increasing sales and profits. The direction might also be about enabling goals such as implementing major organisation change, fulfilling an organisation's resourcing needs or introducing a new IT system.

Our discussion about leadership direction takes account of some of the truly great international leaders who brought about change at a national and international level, such as Nelson Mandela, Mahatma Gandhi or Winston Churchill. These and a few other international giants achieved their standing as a result of the very clear direction they identified and fulfilled for and with their nations and people.

At its heart, leadership is about fulfilling direction – which is implicitly about change – achieving something which is not present today. A gallop through any of the major pieces of literature on leadership supports the idea that leadership is about change.

RELATIONSHIPS (COMPASSION)

The second core component of leadership involves influencing people to fulfil the direction that has been targeted. This therefore involves implicitly *relationships* with others through whom the direction is to be achieved. We have leadership relationships with people in our team, our business department or unit or, indeed, across the organisation. One of the special things that made Mandela, Gandhi and Churchill stand out was their skills in relationships and influencing. An essential quality of effective leaders is their capability to persuade people to achieve the direction they want. These influencing skills can take many different forms.

Until recently, most organisations, not just the military, relied on command and control relationships to persuade people to implement the ideas of those at more senior levels. The logic was something along the lines of 'I hold a more senior role than you, therefore I have the right to decide, and to tell you what and how to do things'. This no longer works in twenty-first century organisations, especially if we want people to be engaged and committed to the work they are undertaking and to the organisation. The thinking is increasingly that effective leadership involves gaining the emotional buy-in of people to do what is required; otherwise they will only follow out of fear, rather than a genuine commitment to achieve the results and direction needed by the organisation.

If we think about the immense results achieved by leaders in recent years, a large part is because of the effectiveness of their relationships with followers. This applies to people like Andy Groves (Senior Advisor, and previous Chairman and President, of Intel Corporation), Richard Branson, Tony Blair and many others.

RIGHT- AND LEFT-BRAIN THINKING (MINDFULNESS)

The third core component of leadership involves engagement of people's *right and left brains*. One of the significant discoveries of recent years is that the two sides of our brain operate differently and control different functions.[3] In essence, it was found that the left side of our brains involves the use of logic, analysis and reasoning, while the right side of our brains involves the use of emotions, feelings, intuition and so on.

The use of logic involves rational problem solving, analysis and interpretation of data, calculations and forward projection based on evidence. On their own, these capabilities are often insufficient to create long-term sustainable change. The missing ingredients are passion for the result that is being pursued, as well as the use of imagination, creativity and intuition to provide new perspectives and insights that logic alone cannot provide. All the truly transformational changes in organisations – for example IT businesses such as Intel, Google, Amazon, and Apple, as well as more traditional organisations such as Toyota and Tesco – are due to a combination of right- and left-brain behaviours.

One of the important findings from successful organisations is that their success is due to the engagement of people's right and left brains together. The work of Harvard Professor John Kotter, for example, emphasises the importance of using logic and reasoning as well as passion and intuition.[4] Use of the two together gives an infinitely superior result than the use of either one on its own.

DETERMINING DIRECTION THROUGH OBJECTIVE SETTING

The way most business organisations clarify direction for individuals and teams is through 'objective setting'. This is typically built into organisations' appraisal, performance management, and review systems. Performance management systems take different forms to suit the requirements and style of the organisation they are considering and are regarded as one of the key people processes.

Objective or goal setting involves leaders meeting with team members to agree goals and outcomes that the team member will achieve in the period

---

3   Springer, S. and Deutsch, G. (1997), *Left Brain, Right Brain: Perspectives from Cognitive Neuroscience* (New York: W.H.Freeman & Co Ltd.)

4   Kotter, J. (2003), *The Heart of Change* (Harvard Business Books)

ahead. These goals then become the outcomes that employees are expected to achieve, and are used as the future basis for measuring and evaluating how well the individual has performed their job. The outcomes or goals that are agreed most often take the form of specific business results such as achieving £X sales revenues, or fulfilling the manufacturing plan for products of Y, or completing implementation of new software applications. Output goals frequently are SMART (that is, Specific, Measurable, Achievable, Realistic and Time-Oriented). An increasing number of organisations now supplement output business goals (which I shall refer to as 'what' goals) with softer goals which involve display of specific organisation behaviours or competencies (which I shall refer to as 'how' goals). Examples of behaviour 'how' goals might include team-working, integrity, customer service, commitment to the organisation and so on.

Many leaders and managers also use the objectives or goals that have been agreed as a basis for less formal regular discussions on a monthly or quarterly basis to review, progress, coach and support individuals. In many organisations, future pay increases are either directly or indirectly influenced by the extent to which the individual has exceeded, achieved or fallen short of their targeted objectives.

Setting objectives is claimed to have a number of benefits. They:

- create a clear target or outcome for focusing individuals' energy;
- create common understanding between colleagues about direction;
- provide a structure within which employees can work;
- provide a context for setting day-to-day priorities;
- help people relate their activities to company objectives and goals.

While these benefits are all valid up to a point, this approach to objective setting as used by most companies is quite limited. Setting objectives is all about what the employee will deliver to the company – and typically makes little or no reference to what the company will deliver to the employee. What mostly happens is that the manager comes up with what seems appropriate objectives for the employee and checks that the individual understands them, and is not too upset by them. A more enlightened leader may ask the individual to come up with their objectives and then discuss or challenge these if they fall short of what is expected or required by the business.

While objective setting as described above involves a veneer of employee involvement, much objective setting implicitly supports the traditional command and control approach to leadership and management, that is, managers decide what will be achieved and how, and employees do as instructed. I know of many senior managers who accept the goals and objectives of those above them even if they believe the goals are less than optimum, because to significantly challenge the objectives of one's manager is not okay. Despite the claimed benefits, it is not surprising that objective setting becomes less motivational or inspirational than it ought to be.

Even when managers make comments like, 'If you achieve these objectives, you will get a high performance rating and in turn more money', these comments are often, by their nature, vague. The exception is for people in sales roles, or where clear financial performance targets can be set and measured, for example bond and currency traders, where financial rewards can be clearly linked to individual business achievement. For people in roles where individual performance is more difficult to measure, and this applies to many managerial and professional roles, objective setting is more difficult to relate to achieved employee outcomes.

The fundamental weakness of traditional performance management approaches, based on SMART objectives, is that they are mostly quite one-sided as they frequently do not involve the manager in finding out or even taking account of employees' issues and perspectives. As a result, objective setting often does not encourage development of the leader–employee relationship, and consequently does little to develop trust, openness or real engagement. In many businesses, the focus of the objective-setting discussion is one-sided: it's almost entirely about what I as an employee will do for the organisation in the period ahead, and in the overwhelming majority of cases makes little reference to what the organisation will do for the individual, apart from identifying the size of the challenge they will face.

A further flaw in many performance management systems is that they do not inherently encourage innovation or creativity. Because the process assumes that organisation rewards are provided against a static set of rules, there is often little incentive for managers or employees to step out of the box, think and deliver radical solutions, and receive equally radical rewards. The process of objective setting for many organisations therefore tends to encourage 'more of the same' thinking and, as a result, stifles creativity and innovation.

There is one large UK organisation where the author has worked as a consultant, which has a highly complex procedure for setting and recording objectives which are then carefully policed by the HR function. At the end of each year, leaders sit down with their team members and go through what each person has achieved, and then provide an overall performance rating. They also discuss and set objectives for the year ahead. Similar systems are used by many other large corporations. The process is very logical and rational; however, differences between what any individual can earn as a result of achieving an 'exceptional' as opposed to merely 'effective' result is quite often small – usually less than 10 per cent of earnings. So, there is limited financial benefit for an employee putting themselves out to achieve an exceptional rating. This is particularly the case where objectives are regularly changed throughout the course of the year.

HOW TO USE THE PERSONAL DEAL TO IMPROVE PERFORMANCE

The personal deal can be used with great effectiveness by leaders to engage more successfully with their people, clarify direction and significantly uplift performance. The personal deal can be used at any level to engage more positively and gain greater commitment from people. What makes this possible is that the personal deal provides a genuine two-way process for engaging and involving people more, clarifying and agreeing mutual goals and actions for the future, which will address the needs of both the leader and the follower.

In essence, the process involves the employee and leader jointly identifying and discussing what they each want from the other, then sharing and discussing their mutual needs and how they can best be fulfilled in the context of business realities. We call this process 'making a personal deal'.

The steps involved in making a personal deal are as follows:

1.   The team member prepares for the meeting by identifying the few really important (realistic) things they want from their leader and the organisation, and also the value they can bring to the leader and the organisation. They also anticipate the things they believe their leader wants from them.

2.   The leader prepares for the meeting in a similar way, by identifying the most important (realistic) things they and the organisation want from the employee and what they and the organisation can give

to the employee. They also anticipate the things they believe the employee wants from them and the organisation.

3.   The leader and employee meet to share and discuss the things they want from and can give each other. First one individual describes what they want from and can give the other. The exchange might include discussion of the extent each party is already giving the other party what it wants, and also what they anticipate the other wants from them. The other individual then shares what they want and the extent to which they perceive these things are currently fulfilled.

4.   Once the team member and the leader have shared their respective wants, perceptions of current fulfilment and what they can offer the other, they seek a win–win personal deal about what they will realistically give each other in future. The leader might have to say that they are unable to provide some things the employee may want – for example promotion within 12 months, a 30 per cent salary increase and so on.. Similarly, the employee may feel unable to provide some of the outputs the leader may want. When this occurs, it is important to have an honest and open dialogue and interchange about what each can and cannot realistically give the other, until they can agree a personal deal that works for both of them and for the organisation.

5.   Subsequent business meetings between the leader and team member then centre on the personal deal, where the leader and team member give each other feedback and discuss how they can both maximise fulfilment of their joint personal deal.

The possible types of things that a leader and the organisation might want from an employee and the possible things an employee might want from their leader and the organisation were listed earlier in Chapter 3. The diagram of the personal deal shown in Chapter 3 has been modified in Figure 8.1 to show the four core questions leaders and team members are recommended to cover to help agree an effective personal deal.

An important feature of the making a personal deal discussion which the diagram seeks to illustrate is that it makes the relationship between people more explicit and more equal. Most company performance management systems focus on the two lower boxes in the diagram – 'What does my leader and the organisation want from me' and 'What can I give my leader and the organisation'. The two boxes at the top of the diagram concerning the things

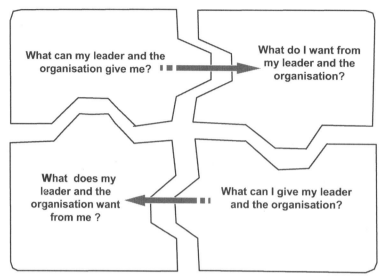

Figure 8.1   The four key questions when discussing personal deals

my leader and the company can give me and what I want from them are left unsaid or vague, and typically omitted from the discussion. Managers may refer to or imply certain things, such as if you achieve this you will be a great contributor, or you could be considered for promotion, but these comments in most cases only make up a very small part of the conversation.

The making a personal deal discussion is an entirely different type of conversation. It is similar to many performance management discussions in focusing on what the employee will deliver to the organisation. But in complete contrast to the performance management discussion, the personal deal discussion gives equal prominence to what the leader and the organisation will provide the employee. As a result, the making a personal deal discussion is genuinely two-way and is about what each party wants from and can give the other.

By making the relationship between leader and team member more two way and explicit, we believe we are making possible a step function increase in trust, engagement and, in turn, business performance. The practical business benefits of applying this approach at an individual and corporate level are considered below.

In most performance management discussions, followers get to hear what really matters to their leader and the organisation, and what they want from them. As a result, one of the outputs from performance management systems is that people have a reasonably shared understanding of the objectives their leader expects them to achieve. Therefore, the personal deal discussion may add little to this. However, in other areas the personal deal can add a great deal:

- *Clarify what matters to the team member*   The leader gets to hear what their team members really value and want. For example, the leader might hear that what matters most to one individual is hearing about how the individual's work has contributed to customers, and that they are not satisfied with feedback which goes beyond the usual 'good work'. Another team member may mention that they really want to be given stretch projects which require creativity and innovation. In contrast, a different person may say that what really matters to them is being able to leave work at 15.00 each Friday. Such things are typically omitted from performance management discussions.

- *Feedback for leaders*   The leader receives feedback about the extent to which they are fulfilling what really matters to the employee. It might be real news to the leader that the comment 'good work' does not count as real recognition by their team member or that only being given a very rare piece of work which requires innovation is not appreciated. It might also come as a surprise that another employee would be quite happy to put in additional time and effort earlier in the week but would really value being able to leave by 15.00 on Fridays.

- *Improved mutual outcomes*   By sharing mutual expectations, it is possible for both leader and team member to negotiate outcomes which might otherwise never have been discussed or thought possible. By sharing mutual needs, both leader and team member have an opportunity to create new opportunities for each other. A good example might be a leader who has a new project which has to be delivered, and who hears in their personal deal discussion that a team member is looking for more innovative and different work. Because of their new directly shared understanding, the leader has found someone to whom they might be able to allocate the new project.

- *Improved relationships and trust*   Another major benefit of the personal deal is increased trust and understanding. By sharing more about their mutual needs and expectations the leader and team member are likely to develop more respect and trust for each other. In turn, this will lead to an improved relationship. This aspect of the personal deal has been found to make a real difference to leaders and organisations who have implemented the personal deal.

- *Increased engagement*   People who have used the personal deal on a regular basis say that the single most valuable return is greater employee engagement between team members, with the leader and the organisation. By increased openness, and potentially creating better opportunities to fulfil employee needs, individuals will become more engaged with both the leader and the organisation. All the evidence suggests that engagement is one of the most important drivers of business performance.

People who use the personal deal as part of their day-to-day leadership suggest that these benefits make the additional effort more than worthwhile.

A LEADER'S ONE-TO-ONE USE OF THE PERSONAL DEAL TO ENHANCE PERFORMANCE

Tony, a managing director I recently coached, had concerns about how he could enhance the performance of one of his people, Jim, who ran a geographic profit-responsible business unit. Jim had had a successful track record until three years before. Jim's performance was considered to be less than successful in the last three years, and Tony had serious concerns about how to improve the performance of Jim and his business unit.

After finding out about the personal deal, Tony decided to use the approach with Jim, and the two men had a very honest and open discussion about their personal deal. Tony helped Jim to realise that things were not going well for either of them as they were now and that it was in both their interests that the situation should change. Importantly, Tony also heard and acknowledged that he had not been giving Jim as much support as he needed to raise his performance. The primary result of their discussion was that Tony and Jim agreed a number of things they would now undertake for each other. Jim acknowledged that he needed to raise the performance of his business unit and that this included working more effectively with his own team and spending more time on new business sales, something which Tony felt had been neglected. For his part, Tony agreed that Jim could obtain access and support from people in one of the other more successful geographic business units. They agreed that Jim could spend time with that unit to learn how they worked and what enabled them to achieve increased performance.

Tony's view is that the personal deal discussion was a real breakthrough in understanding and commitment between themselves. Tony felt it was the first time Jim really acknowledged that his performance was falling short of what was required. He also felt it was the first time that he had really offered to take constructive actions, in which Jim believed would help him.

At the time of writing, Tony commented that he was seeing signs of Jim's performance improving significantly as a result of their personal deal discussion, and that he was on the way to achieving the results required by the business. Tony has also learnt much about what he needs to do to enhance the performance of his individual team members.

ORGANISATION-WIDE USE OF THE PERSONAL DEAL TO IMPROVE PERFORMANCE

Personal deals are helpful for individuals to achieve change. Our experience is that the approach can be even more powerful when implemented across an organisation. The first major organisation-wide application of the approach occurred in Parkside Housing Group, a group of social businesses which provide high-quality, affordable housing and care across the South East of England. Parkside manages some 5000 homes south of London, and also runs care homes for the elderly and for adults with learning difficulties, autism and challenging behaviour.

The brief given by Group Chief Executive Colin Sheriff to the consultants was to develop leadership and culture in Parkside in ways which would sustain the 30 per cent year-on-year growth of the business. We first undertook an organisation diagnosis involving focus groups and one-to-one interviews to identify the enablers and barriers to change. This helped us clarify some of the priorities that we would need to address during the implementation phase. Three important conclusions emerged: that leadership in parts of the organisation was less consistent; that people are open and willing to take personal responsibility for their work; that some teams and functions were often insular, and tended to work in silos.

Following this diagnosis, we undertook some initial work with the Executive Directors, who then appointed an internal steering group to work with the consultants and lead the change process. The consultants were invited to become accountable to this steering group. The experience proved quite surprising for the steering group and the consultants. When we started, members of the steering group knew little about organisation change, or even why they had been selected to be involved in the change process. After a number of months, the group shaped the direction of the intervention and became real advocates of the change process across the business. This group of enthusiasts supported by the consultants set the tone and the pace for the total leadership and culture change process.

The first priority of the steering group was to raise the effectiveness of all leaders across the business, so we designed and ran a series of two-day workshops which developed leaders' skills in one-to-one coaching, and undertaking personal deal discussions. The workshops provided input sessions, individual 360 degree leadership feedback, and practical demonstrations of the skills being developed. Most importantly, the workshops provided opportunities for participants to practise and hone their new skills. Once all leaders had gone through the workshops, they were invited by the Chief Executive and HR Manager to implement personal deals with each of their direct reports.

Following the success of these workshops, and to reinforce the change among leaders, a series of one-day workshops were run for all staff, which the consultants designed and members of the change steering group personally delivered, to raise their and colleagues' awareness about the changes in leadership practices and behaviour and particularly use of the personal deal.

Because the diagnosis identified some isolationism and friction between departments and functions, we recommended that personal deals should be created not just between individuals, but also between functions and teams in the business. On some of the leadership workshops, we arranged for discussions about personal deals to take place between representatives of different functions – for example between finance and operational business units. These initial discussions were followed up by further meetings after the workshops, and resulted in the creation of succinct personal deals between people across departments. Interestingly, these personal deals quickly replaced the long and complex service-level agreements that had been previously drawn up between departments, and which were ignored as too difficult.

The original leadership workshop designed by the consultants is now run entirely by the company for all new professionals and leaders who join the organisation from outside, and the staff workshops are run on a number of occasions each year for all new joiners. This way, the original messages communicated to all staff continue to be passed on to newcomers to the business.

An independent evaluation of the change programme over time has been made by Investors in People (IiP), a UK Government sponsored body which sets standards in people management practices and evaluates organisations' performance against these. The workshops received high acclaim immediately after they were delivered in 2003, and the comments of the inspector who carried out the inspection in 2003 have already been quoted in an earlier chapter.

In October 2005, Parkside was again evaluated by Investors in People two years after the initial leadership workshops were delivered. The results achieved were summed up by Sue Turner, HR Manager for Parkside Housing Group, when she said: 'This is the fourth time that Parkside has been assessed and each time we have demonstrated real progress in improving our performance.' Sue Granshaw, the Investors in People assessor, said: 'Having first achieved the Investors in People accreditation in 2000, you have taken quite a leap to now exceed our criteria in a number of areas... Well done on such a strong performance – a lot of organisations are not reaching Level One of the revised standard, so Parkside Housing Group are setting high standards which other organisations should be striving to achieve too.'

A quote from the the Parkside Housing Group website reads:[5]

> *The Investors in People assessors also highlighted that the Group's overall main strengths were found to be 'the planning of learning and development to meet their business objectives and involvement of staff in decision-making to encourage ownership and responsibility.*

> *In particular the Group was seen to promote good practice through the introduction of the 'Deal' agreement between managers and staff. The 'Deal' sets out the behaviour expected of each other in terms of management, leadership and work performance and forms the basis of a contract between different parts of the Group's business divisions.*

Managers in Parkside have found the personal deal to be a highly effective vehicle for enhancing and improving relationships between leaders and their teams and, in turn, improving the performance of the business.

---

5   Parkside Housing Group website section on news, 18 October 2005, www.parkside.org.uk/ C2B/PressOffice/display.asp?ID=14&Type=2, last accessed 10 October 2006

While it has not been possible to empirically prove the link between the use of the personal deal and the performance of Parkside, the evidence and feedback from managers clearly suggests that there is one. This is well illustrated by the comment made by Colin Sheriff, the Group Chief Executive of Parkside:

> *When we commissioned Business Transformation to work with us on an organisational development program we were focussed on achieving excellence for our customers. The contract or Deal concept grew from that. Customers have clear views of what they expect and will have equally clear views about what they will deliver. The perfect customer experience comes when those views are in harmony with the supplier. It is important for the Parkside Group that there is consistency right through the businesses about how people can expect to be treated and to treat each other. If we need that kind of deal with customers then we need that kind of deal between the business and its employees and between managers and their staff.*
>
> *We wouldn't argue that it has been universally implemented yet – we are all human after all; where it has been successfully implemented we see improvements in service and in customer satisfaction. Staff polls after implementation show improved perceptions of communication, participation and engagement with the organisation. In short – it works.*

The impact of a further organisation application and implementation of the personal deal is given in Chapter 9, which focuses on Organisation Culture.

HOW THE DEAL COMPLEMENTS FUNDAMENTAL LEADERSHIP

One of the most powerful recent approaches to leadership has been developed by Robert Quinn[6], from Michigan University in the US. The approach known as 'fundamental leadership' emphasises a shift towards four distinct behaviour patterns:

- *Becoming more externally open, and less internally closed* This involves a shift away from our own internal lens and comfort zones which denies external signals, towards one which increasingly takes account of the perspectives, feedback and views of others.

- *Becoming more results-centred and less comfort-centred* This involves a move away from reactive and problem-solving activities towards

---

6   Quinn, R. (see page 131)

one which focuses principally on clarifying the results and outcomes to which we are committed and engaged.

- *Becoming more other-focused and less self-focused*   Instead of putting our own ego and selfish personal and material interests first, we shift towards a state where we give priority to the welfare of others, developing trust and the common good, and become more transparent and authentic in our relationships.

- *Becoming more internally directed and less externally directed*   This involves a move away from defining our identity through external resources, objects and trappings in our life, towards being more directed by our personal values and developing personal confidence and security based on who we are.

An important feature of the personal deal discussion is that it involves a shift towards all four of these states: externally open, results-centred, other-focused, and internally directed.

Personal deal discussions which focus on the needs and wants of both the leader and team members will inevitably be broader and more wide-ranging than discussions which focus purely on the needs of leader and the business. After a leader has held personal deal discussions with all their team members, they will have acquired a broader perspective of the team and individual members in it than they had previously. Personal deal discussions will therefore encourage people to become more *externally open*.

A team leader who has more wide-ranging discussions with their people will at least obtain a bigger picture of what others want and think. At best, it could result in both leader and team members gaining a fuller, less parochial and more externally based view of their roles and the business.

By having a personal deal discussion which focuses on a few really important things, rather than on very detailed outcomes, the employee and the leader will have an exchange which will encourage both to think differently and more holistically about what they are here for. By setting fewer but more salient goals, the discussion will shift qualitatively to what really makes a difference to the business, the leader and team members. Leaders and team members will therefore become more *results-centred*.

A team leader who talks about fewer outcomes, but at a higher level, will encourage their team members to view and think about their roles differently. At best, it will focus attention and energy on the things that make the most difference, rather than allowing the discussion to focus on the detail, which is often comfortable but avoids the important issues.

Using the personal deal approach to goal setting and leadership, instead of the traditional approach to performance management, involves a huge shift which takes more account of the needs of our team. Instead of just focusing on what we personally want our colleagues to do and achieve, the personal deal discussion means we have to ask and listen to what they want from us. Having a personal deal discussion with our team members therefore implicitly makes us more *other-focused*.

A team leader who listens to what each team member wants from the leader will become more aware of what team members themselves want from their work. It may also provide new ideas to the leader which enable them to organise the work of team members in ways which make it more fulfilling and engaging, and therefore more productive.

A personal deal discussion between leader and team member will inevitably rely more on personal values than one which purely focuses on team members' goals and outputs. Inevitably, it will touch and raise questions involving personal values, such as what is a fair exchange for what I give you, or you give me. At a deeper level, it will encourage both parties to think more about the quality of their exchange, and therefore contribute to making the discussion more *externally directed* rather than go through a fairly mechanical process of goal setting purely for the team member.

A team leader who has to undertake some negotiation with each member of their team will raise awareness about the values which underpin the way the company and its people interact. At a deeper level, it may also raise deeper discussions about the meaning of fairness and lead to an exchange of personal beliefs which impacts each party's expectations of the other.

A RADICAL ALTERNATIVE APPROACH TO LEADERSHIP BASED ON THE PERSONAL DEAL

The conventional view of leadership is that it involves a set of behaviours which focus on the three areas mentioned at the beginning of this chapter: direction, relationships and the use of the right and left brain. In the last few years, the behaviours approach to leadership has evolved to focus on particular aspects of these three core components of leadership. In addition to Robert Quinn's fundamental approach, other interesting treatments have emerged including

Goffee and Jones' four qualities of 'reveal your weaknesses', 'sensing', 'tough empathy' and 'being different'.[7] There is also the approach of 'situational leadership', which became very popular in the 80s.[8] A further approach is that of Daniel Golman, who focuses on the emotional state of the leader.[9]

Viewed through the lens of the personal deal, leadership becomes a very different issue or concept. Instead of focusing just on the leader's behaviour, the approach involves focusing on the inter-relationships and behaviours between leader and followers. This potentially changes the purpose and function of a leader to:

Leaders create personal deals with colleagues which enable the purpose and vision of individuals, teams and/or organisation to be fulfilled.

Instead of focusing on the behaviour or mindset of the leader, this definition of leadership focuses on the output of what the leader does with people, which contributes to the future of the unit or organisation in which they work. Instead of advocating a single set of behaviours or mind state as the route to effective leadership, this approach focuses on the mutual expectations of leaders and team members. In practice, this means that effective leadership involves aligning the leader's expectations to those of team members and, in turn, aligning both sets of expectations to the actions required to sustain the team or unit's survival.

To appreciate the value of the personal deal approach to leadership, we might look at the implicit expectations and personal deals two very different leaders have with their people. We can then use the understanding of the personal deal to understand their actual behaviour. Two very contrasting personal deals were adopted by Ghandi and Hitler. Hitler's personal deal with his people was something along the lines of:

- The German Aryan people are the superior race.

- I know best what is right for you and everyone else.

- Do as I tell you – and do not even think about arguing.

- We will use violence and force, and exterminate our opponents.

- Human life of non-Aryans is expendable.

---

7   Goffee, R. and Jones, G. (2000), *The Character of a Corporation: How Your Company's Culture Can Make or Break Your Business* (Harper Collins Business)
8   Zigarmi, P., Zigarmi, D. and Blanchard, K. (1985), *Leadership and the One Minute Manager: Increasing Effectiveness Through Situational Leadership* (Pfeiffer Wiley)
9   Golman, D., Boyatzis, R. and McKee, A. (2002), 'Primal Leadership' (Harvard: Harvard Business School Press)

This is almost opposite to the things that Ghandi expected:

- All people and nations have an equal right to exist and determine their future.

- I have ideas and beliefs which involve respecting those of others, including those who think differently.

- If you follow my way, it will help to liberate you and other people.

- Respect all other people and use non-violence to achieve your goals.

- Human life is very precious.

If we look at different business leaders, we can see that they too have very different implicit personal deals with their people.

VALUE OF THE PERSONAL DEAL FOR LEADERSHIP

This very brief review of what leaders do suggests, I believe, that the personal deal is a powerful way of viewing and understanding the approach and style of leaders in business. In the same way that it provided a clear picture of internationally renowned leaders, can it not also be used to describe the approach of leaders you know in your organisation? To bring the idea of the leadership personal deal to life, you may want to reflect on the implicit deal you perceive for some leaders you know, and how it manifests itself in their actions and behaviour in your organisation.

The value of exploring leadership through the personal deal is that it provides a very focused approach, which takes account of the needs of individuals as well as the organisation. The recipe for leadership effectiveness is not that leadership is reduced to some behaviour categories, but rather that leadership involves discussing and agreeing personal deals with people.

While followers in the past expected or at least tolerated leaders who were assertive, structured and did not show much consideration for their needs, this is no longer the case. Employees today are increasingly less willing to just be told; they want to be involved in decisions and to have their needs listened to and fulfilled. The leader of today, while helping to clarify direction, will only gain the real commitment of their followers if they create relationships with them which take account of their needs. The personal deal provides a practical vehicle which can do this.

This initial exploration of leadership through the lens of the personal deal has, I hope, illustrated its important advantages:

- The personal deal approach directly acknowledges that leadership is a function of the interaction of the leader and followers; viewed in isolation, leadership is meaningless.

- By exploring the expectations of both leaders and followers in a business situation, the personal deal opens the eyes of leaders and followers to the broader organisation and people context in which leadership is being exercised. Leaders such as Tim Smit of the Eden Project, or Julian Richer of Richer Sounds, clearly know this.

- The personal deal discussion focuses the leader on the all-important decision of when and how to fulfill followers' expectations, or when to challenge or shape these expectations. One of the reasons many organisations decline is because followers' expectations fail to take account of the new realities brought about by competitor activity. MG Rover in the UK went broke largely because of this, and there are many signs that General Motors may be in danger of the same thing happening.

- The personal deal approach gets to the heart of the issue of engagement. When leaders fulfil their followers' expectations, they will engage their hearts. Our work with Parkside Housing Group, and more recently Royal Mail Sales, has borne this out.

The individual leaders and organisations to which we have introduced the concept of the personal deal have all found it adds a powerful practical tool for enhancing engagement, commitment and, most importantly from a business point of view, performance.

CHAPTER SUMMARY

- Effective leadership involves three core components:

  - clarifying and communicating *direction* for the unit, team and individual;

  - effective *relationships* between the leader and followers, which involve influencing others to commit to and achieve the direction;

- engaging people's left and right brain simultaneously, which help analyse and reason logically, and enable the use of intuition, emotions and creativity, respectively.

- The way most organisations clarify direction at an individual and team level is through objective setting. This occurs through performance management systems and involves the leader and follower agreeing SMART objectives (Specific, Measurable, Achievable, Realistic and Time Oriented) for the future. These have the advantage of creating shared understanding between leader and follower, providing a focus for channelling energy, and providing a context for the leader's and follower's work.

- Objective setting suffers from the disadvantage that it is in most cases quite a one-sided process, which focuses almost entirely on what the individual will do for their leader and the organisation. It mostly pays little attention to the needs of employees, even though for jobs where the employees' financial contribution can be easily measured – such as sales – contingent financial rewards for employees can be specified. In many cases, objective setting reinforces traditional command and control leadership, albeit under a guise of involvement.

- Four key questions lie at the heart of the personal deal discussion, which need to be honestly and realistically answered:

  - What do I want from my leader and the organisation?

  - What can I give my leader and the organisation?

  - What do my leader and the organisation want from me?

  - What can my leader and the organisation give me?

- The value of the personal deal discussion is that the conversation is much more balanced than most performance management discussions, because it makes explicit reference to what each party wants and can give each other. This sharing of mutual needs and contribution results in a more balanced discussion, which encourages significantly more engagement than typically occurs in most performance management discussions. Ultimately, it can help create improved mutual outcomes which increase trust, engagement and performance.

- The personal deal was implemented as part of a leadership and culture change programme in Parkside Housing Group. All leaders were trained and given experience in coaching and undertaking personal deal discussions, as part of a two-day leadership development workshop. Following the workshop, the majority of managers held one-to-one personal deal discussions with each of their people.

- Two years after the leadership workshops were implemented, the results were independently audited by Investors in People. As well as commenting on the high standard of people practices in the business, the audit commented that: 'In particular the Group was seen to promote good practice through the introduction of the "Deal" agreement between managers and staff. The "Deal" sets out the behaviour expected of each other in terms of management, leadership and work performance and forms the basis of a contract between different parts of the Group's business divisions.'

CHAPTER 9

Using the Personal Deal to Change Organisation Culture

The idea of culture has been used in anthropology for a long time to describe the values, mindset and informal rules which govern the behaviour of people in different communities and nations. While anthropologists usually talk about pre-industrialised communities, the term was adopted by business thinkers more recently to describe the characteristic behaviour of workgroups and complete business organisations. Organisation culture is described by Schein as 'the learned shared tacit assumptions on which people base their daily behaviour – and is popularly thought of as "the way we do things around here"'.[1]

In this chapter, we first explore what organisation culture is and the basic approaches proposed by some experts for changing culture. We will then use these ideas as a context for describing the way we used the psychological contract and personal deal to change culture in part of the UK Royal Mail. Based on our experience we will explore how the personal deal adds a broader and insightful perspective of organisation culture. I believe the personal deal provides important insights and a pragmatic perspective that we can use to better understand and more successfully manage and change organisation culture.

The idea of organisation culture has gone through two distinct phases. During the first phase from the late 1960s to the mid 1980s the idea of culture was viewed as a soft and fluffy notion that was only of interest to academics and specialists in organisation behaviour. Since the mid-1980s the subject of organisation culture has been taken much more seriously as evidence has accumulated that culture is one of the most important drivers of organisation performance.

WHAT IS ORGANISATION CULTURE?

I learned about organisation culture in the late 1970s when, as a young personnel executive, I was sent on a troubleshooting assignment to a new factory

---

1   Schein, E. (1999), *Corporate Culture Survival Guide* (San Francisco: Jossey-Bass)

in the North West of England. The factory had been set up on a green-field site using what was then revolutionary new technology based on computer-controlled machine tools. Top management made the bold decision to locate the new factory in a completely new location rather than seek to modernise the outdated and tired manufacturing facility in North London. The business goal for implementing the new manufacturing technology was that it would reduce factory lead times from raw materials to finished product from an average of 13 weeks in the old factory to three or four days in the new factory and thereby achieve a significant increase in return on capital employed. By adopting the new technology the business aimed to slash inventory costs of part-manufactured precision products by over 12 weeks, and therefore more than pay for the investment in new technology.

I was asked to go to the factory some six months after it opened to investigate why inventory levels of raw materials were consistently out of line with production requirements. After two site visits I found that the purchasing clerks regularly changed their orders for raw materials from those specified by the computer printouts they received. Most of the eight purchasing clerks in the new factory had been relocated from the old factory because of their established relationships with suppliers. As a group they prized use of their experience (from the old factory) to tell them how much raw material to order based on inventory levels at any point in time. When the purchasing clerks received a computer printout which specified purchase order volumes which were different from what they considered correct, they just crossed out the numbers and wrote down what they believed from previous experience was the right amount to be ordered. Because of this practice they over-ordered some raw materials and under-ordered others. Inventory levels of raw materials in the early days of the new factory were therefore consistently out of line with requirements and from what was specified by the new compuer-based inventory control system.

My challenge with the production manager was to convince the purchasing clerks over a period of weeks that they should simply trust the computer printouts and place orders at the volumes specified, rather than double-guess what the correct volumes should be. It took about two months for the purchasing clerks to completely give up double-guessing what the correct order volumes should be and just order the volumes given on the printouts.

What the production manager and I were faced with was changing a long-established organisation culture among the purchase-order clerks. They had for many years been expected and rewarded for using their judgement to decide optimum raw material order volumes, so the factory would run with just sufficient raw materials to keep production going. While the purchase-order clerks had been trained in the use of the new computer printouts, they were reluctant to give up the skills which their team culture valued for working out how much raw material to order. They believed they knew best what the correct order volumes were. Changing this belief took quite a number of weeks. The purchasing clerks were not bloody minded or trying to sabotage the new factory, they just had a long-established belief that they knew the correct raw material quantities to order, based on knowledge of the old factory. While their beliefs were valid and helpful for the old factory they were totally inappropriate for the new factory.

This experience was a real learning point for me and demonstrated the power of team culture and values in driving behaviour. Viewed in terms of the personal deal, the box 'What the leader expects from me' had changed to no longer requiring individuals to adjust or correct the purchase volumes. The purchase clerks' willingness to just go along with the volumes specified by the computer print had however not yet changed in the box 'What I give my leader'. My challenge was to encourage the purchase clerks to shift their behaviour in line with management expectations. As we realised, rational discussion to get people to change their behaviour was on its own not sufficient. What was required was a series of team discussions and dialogues, backed up by information about the accuracy of the new computers to persuade the team of purchase clerks that they should change their long-established practices and expectations about determining order quantities.

In its second year of operation almost all the early teething problems of the new factory were eliminated. The business result achieved by the factory was a 40 per cent return on capital employed in its second year of operation – an outstanding business result by any yardstick.

My experience of the power of culture in the new factory was something of an eye opener. Only in the last two decades has the notion of organisation culture become appreciated as something which is important for business performance. The idea of organisation culture became popularised by the book *In Search of Excellence.*[2] This was based on research which sought to identify the principles, many of which were about organisation culture, which were fundamental drivers of business performance. Since then an increasing number

---

2   Peters, T. and Waterman, R. (1982), *In Search of Excellence* (New York: Harper Row)

of bottom-line-focused entrepreneurs have begun to recognise the impact of culture on business performance.

Before exploring the idea of culture change it would be useful to explore what makes up culture? According to Schein organisation culture has three components: artefacts, expressed values and underlying assumptions.

Artefacts refer to the physical objects, buildings and physical surroundings. This may refer to the building an organisation inhabits, the state of the offices, its unique way of packaging or presenting its products. One of my favourite examples of an organisation's artefacts is the bright orange colour used by easyJet. As well as the airplane tailfins, the colour adorns cabins in its latest venture easyCruise. Every organisation which has its own locations will display physical artefacts which can be seen by employees and/or clients to reflect its culture, even if these are not as bright or in your face as those of easyGroup.

Expressed values refers to the values expressed overtly by an organisation – either to its employees or to its customers. One of my favourites in the high street is the Prêt à Manger 'passionate about food' tagline which they use to underpin the quality and wholesomeness of their sandwiches. A rather longer one is contained in what is known as 'The Key Speech' by the founder of Arup consulting engineers, Sir Ove Arup. This is one of the most profound and comprehensive statements of company ethos and values[3] that I have come across. The Key Speech is required reading for anyone joining the company and its values continue to underpin the way people in the company think, behave and operate today.

Underlying assumptions are the few core ideas and beliefs that underpin what an organisation is and how it operates. In many cases these assumptions go back to the founders of the organisation. Two world-class organisations owe their recent improved fortunes to challenging and changing their founders' original values. Reuters has for many years been a very successful information and news provider. Until 1999 the company main board directors were mostly journalists (which was the original core skill that made the company successful), and their behaviour exhibited typical journalist values of intellectual rigour, highly analytical and so on. Another company, Apple, was until the mid 1990s dominated by its founders' belief in engineering and technology values. Reuters'

---

3   See Arup website: www.Arup.com, from the home page visit 'About Us', then 'History & Culture' for access to 'The Key Speech' by Sir Ove Arup; www.arup.com/DOWNLOADBANK/ download5.pdf, last accessed 11 October 2006

and Apple's decline in the late 1990s was due to the continued adherence to their founders values in markets that had moved on. By 2005 Apple has once again become highly successful as it grasped values related to product design and functionality – as epitomised by the iPod. Because of the shift in underlying assumptions Apple is again thriving. Reuters is now in the middle of a shift to IT and dotcom values and its fortunes are also beginning to be restored as a result.

These three components of culture hopefully illustrate that culture is only in part about relationships between people. The colour orange adopted by easyJet is one of its ways of highlighting its adoption of non-traditional approach to doing business. The value of 'being passionate about food' underpins Prêt à Manger's approach to providing customers only with wholesome food, without artificial colours, preservatives and other unnatural ingredients. The shifts in underlying assumptions of Apple and Reuters are impacting on how and what work gets done inside the organisation to provide products and services for customers. Many organisations' culture, including easyJet, Prêt à Manger, Arup, Apple and Reuters also include beliefs about people. The important point is that personal relationships between people are only one component of organisation cultures. Equally important are beliefs about how to do business, ways of working, what is delivered to customers, quality, design and other ways of working.

EFFECTIVE APPROACHES TO CULTURE CHANGE

Many people have put forward ideas for changing culture to make an organisation more productive and generate increased profits. While we do not need to cover many of these approaches, a summary of some of the more powerful and practical ideas will provide a helpful context which influenced our approach to implementing culture change in Royal Mail Sales.

One of my favourite quotes about organisation change comes from John Kotter:[4]

> *The central issue in change is never strategy, structure, culture or systems. These are important. But the core is always about changing the behaviour of people, and behaviour change happens in highly successful situations mostly by speaking to people's feelings.... People change what they do less because they are given analysis that shifts*

---

4   Kotter, J. (2002), *The Heart of Change* (Harvard: Harvard Business Press)

their thinking than because they are shown a truth that influences their feelings.

These four sentences focus on two profound principles about culture change. Changing behaviour is fundamental if a business wants to get people to do things differently – as I learned in my work at the computer-controlled factory in the North West of England. The other is that people change less by rational analysis but more by awareness of truths that influence their feelings and, in turn, their behaviour.

While straightforward, these two principles are often ignored in organisation change initiatives. Many businesses seek to implement changes – for example implementation of Customer Relations Management (CRM) systems, adoption of new distribution channels, launch and market new products or create a new organisation structure – by explaining the business reasons for change and assuming that people will therefore adopt the change once the logic has been communicated to them.

Examples I have encountered where logic alone did not bring about change include:

- Explaining the impact of overseas competition on the need to change business practices resulted in lots of talk but almost no change in what people did in a factory.

- Following continued critical customer feedback a major IT supplier continued to undertake the final development of its products on customer sites. Despite its technological innovation, this and other poor customer practices resulted in the demise of the organisation.

- Despite talking and explaining to a manager about the impact of his behaviour on colleagues the individual continued to behave in the same way. When asked why he had not taken action to address the feedback the individual said he could do nothing about it.

- Training front-line retail professionals in the need to become more customer focused following major changes in the marketplace proved insufficient on its own to bring about changes in retail staff behaviour with customers.

- Despite repeated talking to product developers across the globe about the need to set realistic completion goals, they continued to set unrealistic times for new product development. As a result major new product launches were consistently delivered late to the market.

- Implementation of new HR processes including performance management took much longer than expected even though staff were carefully briefed about the new procedures and their part in this. HR were quite surprised by the difficulty in implementing the changes.

- Implementing one of the largest CRM systems in Europe took three years instead of the one year originally planned. The delay resulted in considerable shortfalls in business performance that the organisation desperately needed to avoid.

You will certainly have your own examples and war stories of where planned rational changes in work practices and procedures failed to fulfil the original implementation goals or did so in extended timeframes. These all support Kotter's notion that it is behaviour rather than anything else that requires most effort to be changed and that change occurs most effectively when we buy into it emotionally.

To address these issues and barriers and implement enduring and sustainable change Kotter proposes eight broad steps for any change programme to go through to achieve success. It is important to mention Kotter's eight stages[5] briefly as they significantly influenced how my colleagues and I tackled our change assignment with Royal Mail Sales. The eight stages are:

1. *Create a sense of urgency* – bring to opinion leaders' attention the reason why things have to be done differently in future.

2. *Put together a guiding team* – create ownership for change among a small group of advocates who will take on personal responsibility for driving change through, even when barriers are encountered and resistance takes place.

3. *Create vision and strategies* – create a simple but bold and emotionally compelling picture of what change looks like.

4. *Effectively communicate vision and strategies* – communicate the new vision to everyone in the organisation in a way that grabs their attention and interest.

---

5   Note that the titles of the eight stages shown in italics above are taken from Kotter's book but the short descriptions are my own words

5.   *Remove barriers to actions* – take steps to bring the change to life in parts of the organisation.

6.   *Accomplish short-term wins* – create opportunities for small wins which helps people see and hear how the changes have made a difference to the business.

7.   *Keep pushing for wave after wave of change* – after the initial change interventions, put in place additional mechanisms, processes and actions which reinforce change.

8.   *Create new culture to make new behaviour stick* – make the new behaviours part of the way we do things round here.

These eight steps for implementing change do not guarantee success. What they do provide is a powerful blueprint for how to think about and plan effective organisation change. We have used these stages not in a mechanistic way, but rather as a tour guide for a foreign town, to help us make decisions about the sequence of places to visit. The way we undertake the journey and the precise steps we follow is up to us.

BUSINESS CONTEXT OF CULTURE CHANGE IN ROYAL MAIL SALES

Royal Mail is one of the largest employers in the UK, with over 180 000 people in 2005, as well as one of the most trusted consumer brands in the UK. It is a state-owned commercial enterprise charged by the government to provide a universal postal service to everyone in the UK and make modest profits. What is less well known is that of its annual £7 billion revenues the vast majority comes from commercial contracts with business organisations – such as banks, mail-order houses, publishers and so on. Providing services to private consumers using stamped mail makes up a relatively small amount of its revenues, and is loss making.

For over 350 years since its creation, Royal Mail operated as a monopoly supplier, and as a result was able to dictate terms to private and business customers. Deregulation of postal markets has allowed competitors to dramatically challenge the dynamics of the business. The first phase of the UK postal market opening was in 2002.

In 2002 McKinsey consultants were called in to provide a blueprint of how the postal market should be segmented to achieve more profitable relationships with business customers. Our first involvement with the business involved supporting implementation of this new structure. This included definition of the new job roles, the behaviours required for success in these, and the assessment and selection of existing sales personnel into the new structure. People were placed in the new sales organisation towards the end of 2003.

While the new structure was in place this on is own was not considered sufficient to achieve the performance levels required by the business. In 2004 the author and his colleagues were invited to assist in the creation of a more commercial and customer-focused culture in the business. The reason for the culture change was simple – to support the organisation to compete successfully in the new deregulated postal market.

We heard of many examples of practices which people at different levels wanted changed. Some examples included:

- inability to respond positively and flexibly to new customer requirements and needs – for example large time delays in dealing with customer issues;

- unwillingness of many sales people to engage with customers on their commercial issues and needs – for example reluctance to discuss customers real business issues, rather than their immediate next sales order for postal services;

- disempowering and bureaucratic systems and ways of working – for example managers with allocated budget were not allowed to authorise expenditure to previously agreed limits without many other peoples' signatures;

- inability of the organisation to create and bring to market new products which fulfilled customer needs – for example new products would often take years to bring to market.

The case for changing the organisation culture among the sales force was very clear. Traditional ways of thinking and behaving towards customers needed to change if the business was to succeed in the new competitive world.

CULTURE CHANGE INTERVENTION

The culture change programme started with the consultants running a one-day culture change workshop for the Sales Executive Management Team. This increased the directors' understanding of the issues involved in changing organisation culture. At the end of the workshop the directors confirmed that they were committed to change the culture, to become more commercial and add more value to the business. They also agreed that the consultants under the guidance of the Head of HR should undertake research to identify the key features of the new aspirational culture and come back to the Sales Executive Management Team with ideas for them to make decisions about the shape of this new aspirational culture.

The consultants conducted interviews with 30 different people across the business unit to gain their views about the state of the business, enablers and barriers to effectiveness, and views about the present culture. An important feature of these interviews is that we intentionally did not limit discussions to views about culture, but covered views about the business and broader enablers and barriers to future success. This was a tangible implementation of our view that culture is not just about relationships, but about much broader issues and beliefs which impact total business performance.

Because of the importance of relating culture to business goals we separately analysed and interpreted the five-year business plan to identify implications for the culture. One of the key issues addressed by the plan was a forecast of the impact of competition on the business as a result of deregulation of the UK and European postal market. This provided powerful indicators that the business would need to become much more commercial to thrive in the new deregulated postal market.

When we analysed the data we collected on both the present and future culture the consultants were aware that our proposals for describing the new aspirational culture needed to be very clear and easy to communicate. Our proposals needed to appeal as much to a junior sales employee working in a call centre as they did to a senior relationship manager of a major account.

To fulfil the requirements of impact, simplicity and relevance to the business the consultants identified what we called 'touchstones' for the new culture. When designing the touchstones the consultants took account of the culture and values of other major UK organisations including Tesco, General Electric (GE) and a competitor FedEx.

Our intention in using the word 'touchstone' to describe the new culture was that it implied something which is tangible for every job in the business, provides a unifying message for people across the whole sales force and which, if implemented, would make a real contribution to business performance. What we did not want was something which was bureaucratic, cumbersome and viewed as irrelevant by people.

The three touchstones were:

- drive the profit and loss (P & L)

- personal touch

- stretch comfort zones.

The Sales Executive Management Team agreed these three culture touchstones and to make sure we got them right it was decided that we would test their relevance and provide some seven or eight behaviour indicators which would illustrate each touchstone and demonstrate whether it was being implemented. Feedback from the testing strongly validated the relevance of the touchstones, and we started using them on a limited basis to create personal team deals with those teams involved in the testing.

Rather than run separate special meetings to test the new culture touchstones we decided to attend ten different regular business meetings held by teams across the business. We inserted a one-hour slot in these business team meetings to present the three culture touchstones and gained input and reactions from sales employees. The reactions were very positive and we also obtained powerful feedback which we used to refine and modify all the behaviour indicators so that they more fully reflected the issues and perceptions of people.

An example of behaviour indicators for one of the culture touchstones is shown in Figure 9.1.

Our goal in creating the behaviour indicators was that we would provide at least one example of each touchstone which could apply to every job in

- Do it now — create a sense of urgency
- Set step-change goals for you and the team
- Challenge people who do not allow you to make decisions
- Continually raise the bar
- Do not be afraid to take risks
- Challenge the business to 'think customer'
- Determination and effort

Figure 9.1   Touchstone behaviours

the organisation. The 'Stretch comfort zones' behaviour indicator of 'Set step-change goals for you and the team' may not be realistic for some jobs; in such cases the indicator of 'Do it now – create a sense of urgency' may be more relevant as well as more realistic.

Feedback from our meetings with the ten business teams suggested that the three headline touchstones were highly appropriate at an organisation level to describe the aspirational or targeted new culture for the Sales division. As well as gaining an attitudinal reaction to the three proposed touchstones we also asked people what implementing these behaviours in their team would do to performance, and the consistent response was that together they would add significant value to performance. The team meetings also helped us shape the behaviour indicators we produced for each of the touchstones, so we were confident that they were not just relevant across the business, but that they were relevant to people in different teams and job roles.

IMPLEMENTING THE CULTURE TOUCHSTONES THROUGH THE PERSONAL DEAL

Having created the culture touchstones the challenge was now to get these implemented in the organisation. What we did not want was a polite reaction from people which would result in the culture-change programme becoming yet another well-intentioned initiative which would be forgotten 12 months later.

We decided that the route to embedding the touchstones would be through their inclusion in team deals across the business. With input from HR and the Sales Executive Management Team we decided that implementing the touchstones could occur more effectively through team deals rather than personal deals. Our thinking was that people in the Sales organisation mostly work as integrated members of business teams. Different teams focus on sales to different market segments (for example financial services, or local government), and to different types of clients (for example to large customers, or many smaller customers), for which different approaches were adopted by each sales team.

The Managing Director (MD) and Sales Executive Management Team asked every sales team to formulate their own team deal. We suggested that the team deals should make at least one reference to each of the touchstones and that they could if desired include things which had nothing to do with the culture touchstones. Our intention was that every team deal would describe the behaviours to which each team would commit as their contribution to enhance the performance of the business.

Once each team deal had been formulated it would become the way of working to which the team committed. The team deals would be used to support change in the business. One frequent application that teams used their team deal for was as a way of reviewing performance of the team at the end of meetings.

In the sample team deal shown in Figure 9.2 the team committed to 'Give each other feedback about our contributions'. At the end of team meetings those present would go round the group and ask each other for feedback about their contribution and also check whether they really had spoken their minds to one another. In some teams the team deal was put on a flip chart at the beginning of the meetings and used as a way to identify opportunities during the meeting where people might 'open their networks with one another'. This would signal to everyone where they would be expected to share contacts, and so on.

All the teams signed up to team deals, including the Sales Executive Management Team, and these were created within some nine months of the culture-change programme being started.

Early on we realised that while some sales teams would be enthusiastic and find it easy to clarify their team deals, others may not. We therefore decided to put a vehicle in place to provide local advice and support. The Sales organisation had already created a network of some 80 'champions' to

	We get	We give
Add the personal touch	Personal support to help me do my job better, and to learn and grow more than ever	I support my colleagues to address their really difficult stuff, and to learn and grow
Own the P & L	Opportunity to make a real difference to the business, across different areas	I only bring major breakthrough issues impacting the whole business to the team (£1m+)
	Involvement in more things in the business than before	I will engage in discussions where I am not an expert to increase my involvement and responsibility to the business
Stretch comfort zones	Space to really engage and use all my talents	I listen and provide input of my ideas, challenge, options, passion and energy to team discussions

Figure 9.2   Sample team deal

support implementation of the European Foundation for Quality Management (EFQM) model. As the champions had already been selected for their openness to change and ability to support colleagues, it seemed sensible to leverage this group's talents to help create team deals across the organisation. To make this possible we ran a one-day training workshop for all the 80 existing champions to equip and encourage them to apply their skills to the implementation of team deals.

Once the champions went through the training day the MD decided to go ahead and formally launch the culture-change initiative across the business unit. Keeping the touchstones relatively low key up to that point in time had given the change process a selective and special flavour. While some people had been involved in the initial testing of the culture touchstones, quite a few more were involved in the first wave of creating team deals. When we chose teams to initially test the behaviour indicators we did so purposely with teams who were seen to be influential and role models in the organisation. This initial implementation therefore began to create rumours among people and this made others curious about what was going on. Word was beginning to get out about the new touchstones – and people were beginning to ask questions.

Once the champions were trained the MD announced the approach to the whole organisation at a sales conference. On the advice of the Head of HR this was undertaken in a low-key way so that this intervention did not go down like so many previous initiatives in the business. He did so with the specific request that every team should formulate its own team deal. The MD's presentation was followed by one from the Head of HR who presented how teams could actually formulate their own team deals. People were also advised that the champions were ready and trained to support their efforts.

We believe that one of the reasons for the success of the programme is that as soon as the new culture touchstones were announced people were asked to do something with them by creating their own team deals. Momentum to implement the culture touchstones had already developed as a result of the early informal testing of the touchstones. Support had been created around the organisation and we were confident from the previous testing that the touchstones would strike a chord with people. The low-key launch of the new aspirational culture included a specific task for everyone – to formulate their own team deal. Support was also available from inside the organisation from the champions. To raise the impact every employee was sent a CD with basic ideas about the need for culture change, the culture touchstones, a description of the personal deal and instructions on how to formulate team deals.

During autumn 2004 almost every team in Royal Mail Sales completed their own team deal. Consistent feedback from people was that the approach made sense and that the team deal was a powerful vehicle for implementing new ways of working.

REASONS FOR SUCCESS OF THE CULTURE-CHANGE PROGRAMME

There are many signs that this culture-change intervention has added considerable value to the organisation. The most obvious sign is that people inside Sales are talking about the culture touchstones and about team deals. This is not just apparent to people inside the division but to people from other parts of Royal Mail who work and interact with Sales.

Feedback from Head of HR David Prince is that 'We have progressed much faster than I had expected when we started and now find that we have arrived at a place that I thought might take us 18 months to two years but has taken us only 12 months.' David went on to say:

> The key to rapid progression in my view was that the approach we took showed people that we were serious about changing behaviours and about providing some direction, but we were also serious about not dictating those behaviours.

> We engaged people very early on in the formulation of the behaviours and the Executive Committee had some very difficult feedback to swallow and respond to. To their credit, they were so bought in to the concept too, that they responded positively and learned from it.

> In a time of uncertainty and upheaval our people needed something to grab a hold of that said things are different now. The culture touchstones gave them a framework to buy into, something they could take and use on a daily and personal basis.

Royal Mail has a measurement system for evaluating how employee opinions and commitment change over time, a system known as 'Have Your Say', or HYS. David commented about the results:

> Our HYS scores have typically improved across the key measures by up to 30 per cent. Bearing in mind that we were coming out of a major change programme and feeling the affects of deregulation, this is really quite an achievement. I feel that the culture touchstones gave people

*something tangible to work with, it helped them to make sense of their
new world and how they wanted to operate in it.*

In the view of the Sales MD, implementation of the culture touchstones
is one of the contributing factors why the Sales business unit successfully
achieved their targets in the year ending 2005.

We believe there are two important reasons for the success of this culture-
change programme.

Firstly, a simple business-focused definition of the new aspirational culture
based on the touchstones was used. The three culture touchstones are simple and
straightforward to understand and were carefully tested so that people in the
business could be confident that they were relevant to the tasks and challenges
faced by the business. To make sure the touchstones were relevant across the
business we created a small list of behaviour indicators for each one. At least
one or two of these behaviour indicators could be applied to any role and level
in the organisation. We were particularly pleased that the Executive Committee
wanted to only have three touchstones. This ensured that the new culture was
easy to talk about and that everyone could understand it. This contrasts with
definitions of culture introduced by some organisations which have lists of up
to a dozen different culture factors. In our view defining the new aspirational
culture with three touchstones meant that they could be remembered by people
and therefore were more likely to be spoken about and acted upon.

Secondly, we used the personal deal in the form of the team deal to
implement culture change. One of the big reasons many culture-change
programmes fail is that they remain at a theoretical level – remote from what
people do day to day in their work. By asking all teams to formulate their
own team deals people were encouraged to bring the touchstones to life and
make them part of the way they worked. The value of the team deal is that it
brought the new aspirational culture described by the touchstones into focus
and therefore into the lives of every business team. Importantly, the personal
deal approach encouraged people to shape and mould the culture touchstones
to something that had meaning for them.

One of the ironies of many culture-change programmes is that they are
implemented in an essentially command and control way. Typically, what
occurs is that internal or external change agents design the new culture and
then advocate 'this is what you must now believe in and implement'. By using
the approach of the team deal we were encouraging teams to integrate the new

aspirational culture in a way that made sense for their jobs and their working lives.

As far as we know, Royal Mail's implementation of a new target culture is the first time it has occurred in the form of the team deal. I suspect that this approach has exciting implications for other organisations' approaches to culture change, and also for our inherent understanding of culture.

VIEWING CULTURE AS THE PREVAILING PERSONAL DEAL

The definition of organisation culture given at the beginning of this chapter described it as 'the learned shared tacit assumptions on which people base their daily behaviour'. I suggest that the words 'tacit assumptions' could be replaced with the words 'expectations and personal deals'. This would then give us a definition that reads:

> *Culture is the learned shared expectations and personal deals between people across the organisation, about what they will receive and what they are expected to contribute, on which people base their daily behaviour.*

I suggest that this definition of culture has a number of important benefits. First, it is more explicit about what culture is: it is all about expectations that people have in their heads – about how a person should behave.

More important than its explicitness, this definition of organisation culture provides a more dynamic perspective of culture. Traditional definitions of culture focus on the way people typically behave in the organisation. As we indicated in Chapter 3 the personal deal is a two-way process: it is about what the organisation gives the individual and what the individual gives the organisation. Adding a personal deal perspective to the way we think about culture provides this two-way perspective. In addition to the current perspective based on how people behave (which is included in the usual definition of culture) the personal deal perspective adds a component relating to what the culture is expected to do for the individual, as well as what the individual is expected to contribute to the culture. Our perspective of culture therefore becomes broader as well as more embracing.

Conventional perspectives of organisation culture emphasise the typical behaviour of people in the organisation. Viewed through the personal deal, culture now has the added component of what the culture does for people. This two-way view of culture therefore takes much more into account than the traditional view. Figure 9.3 shows the components of organisation culture.

As well as viewing organisation culture in a wider perspective, this model provides some real practical pointers for understanding how culture can be sustained or changed.

If the goal is to sustain a given type of culture, then actions can focus on one of three boxes: 'What the organisation gives people'; influencing 'What people expect from the organisation'; and 'What the organisation expects from people'. The organisation cannot directly influence what people give the organisation, as that is their decision.

A simple example might be where a culture emphasises the importance of teamwork. The route to sustaining a teamwork culture therefore could focus on any of the three boxes. The organisation might focus on what it gives people, so that they are encouraged to behave in a more teaming way. This might include training, organising people into self-contained work teams, providing opportunities for people to work in additional teams to their core teams – for example on projects. The second area of intervention is to communicate to people what they can personally expect to gain from the organisation. An obvious one could be to emphasise the benefits and value to individuals of working in teams – for example more personal support, more learning and more sociable work experiences. The final area the organisation might focus on is what the organisation expects from people. In this case the organisation

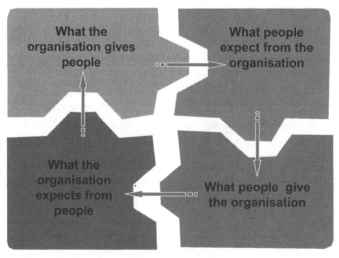

Figure 9.3   Personal deal perspective of organisation culture

would emphasise that it expects people to display team behaviours of certain types – for example to make team decisions or that people support their colleagues in certain ways.

The importance of the personal deal perspective of organisation culture is that it expands our perspective of the options we have to sustain a particular organisation culture. Equally, however, this perspective can be used to encourage different perspectives of how best to change organisation culture.

The conventional view of organisation culture implies that focus should be given to the box in the diagram 'What the organisation expects from people' and this is where many culture change programmes focus exclusively. The personal deal perspective however broadens our perspective to include the other two boxes 'What the organisation gives people' and influencing 'What people expect from the organisation'. I believe this broader view of culture creates a useful step in our approach to understanding, thinking about and most importantly changing culture.

CHAPTER SUMMARY

- The concept of organisation culture refers to the informal rules which govern behaviour in a team or organisation, colloquially expressed as 'the way things get done round here'. Organisation culture, even if we are not aware of it, is something we experience at three distinct levels:

  - artefacts – physical objects, offices, colours in the organisation;

  - expressed values – these refer to the values reflected in the way people behave with one another or with customers;

  - underlying assumptions – the few core ideas and beliefs that underpin how an organisation operates.

- Changing organisation culture involves getting people to change their behaviour and engage emotionally in what is involved, not just understand the logic behind change. There are eight basic change steps which can be used to significantly increase the likelihood of successful organisation change.

- The requirement for culture change in Royal Mail Sales followed a structural reorganisation. While this was perceived to have set the foundations, it was on its own not seen to be sufficient to create the behaviour required for commercial success in the new competitive market place faced by Royal Mail.

- After gaining the top team's commitment to the goal of culture change the consultants conducted research among employees, as well as analysis of the business plan to identify the critical priorities for the new aspirational business culture. From the research results we identified three simple powerful 'culture touchstones' which captured the changes required in the culture: drive the P & L, personal touch and stretch comfort zones.

- The Sales Executive Management Team approved the touchstones so we tested them by attending a number of sales business team meetings. Using their feedback we refined the touchstones and produced a small number of behaviour indicators for each which applied across different level jobs in the business.

- Sales teams across the business unit then created their own team deals using the team deal toolkit. We asked teams to keep their team deal simple, and to include at least one item from each of the touchstones. We allowed them the option to include some team deal items which had nothing to do with the touchstones if they so wished. Eighty champions in the business were trained to support and facilitate the creation of team deals.

- Reactions to the total culture change programme were seen to be highly positive, and both the MD and the HR Director valued the results we achieved for the business. A large part of the success of the project was due to the simplicity of the touchstones, the way we leveraged the touchstones into business teams through the team deal and the way we built up momentum for the change.

- The final part of the chapter proposes a new definition of organisation culture: culture is the learned and shared expectations and personal deals between people across the organisation, about what they will receive and what they are expected to contribute, on which people base their daily behaviour. This definition has important benefits for organisation change practitioners.

CHAPTER 10

How Human Resource Practitioners Manage Personal Deals

Increasingly, the human resource profession is now represented at board level of companies through the appointment of HR and resources directors; this was the exception only a few years ago. This change demonstrates in a very tangible way that business organisations have a need for representation in board discussions of what is seen to be the single most important asset of most businesses – people. Despite HR's increasing representation at the board table, one of the hot debates among HR professionals centres on their role and business contribution.[1]

This chapter views the role of the HR profession through the lens of the personal deal. After some practical examples we will explore how the HR function has evolved to address ever broader aspects of personal deals at work. We shall look at how the personal deal should be one of HR professionals' fundamental focus. The proposition I want to make in this chapter is that one of the fundamental purposes of the HR function is to help business leaders shape and manage their personal deals with people.

HOW HR SHAPE PERSONAL DEALS

My first proper job was as a Personnel Officer with a company called Fisons. In my first week with the company I met one of my new more senior colleagues who sat me down to talk about my membership of the company pension fund. After various preliminaries, including being given a book describing the rules of the pension fund, he went on to talk about money. He mentioned how much pension contribution would be deducted from my pay each month and how much the company would add as their contribution to my pension. All of that seemed reasonable; however the number which took me by surprise was his calculation that based on my starting salary I could expect a pension when I retired in 2014 of some £1122 per annum!

---

1   Ulrich, D. (1997), *Human Resource Champions* (Boston, Massachusetts: Harvard Business School Press)

My surprise was not that my pension could be worked out so precisely or even about the sum of £1122 which was after all some 60 per cent of my salary at the time. What surprised me was the implicit assumption that having just joined the company aged 23 that I would be staying with this organisation for the next 42 years until I retired.

At the time the recently created notion of the psychological contract meant nothing to me. But with hindsight I realise that this conversation was a wonderful illustration of the way people in personnel (as HR was then called) promote and reinforce the psychological contract or personal deal. In this particular case my colleague assumed that having joined what was then a blue-chip company I would, of course, want to spend my entire working life with the organisation. It was taken for granted that such an established company would continue to thrive and that, providing I played my part, that I would naturally want to continue in employment until I retired.

As a son of refugee parents who had fled across Europe to Britain to escape the Holocaust, I had been brought up to understand the impermanence of things. Despite this, here I was being told in all seriousness by my new colleague that my anticipated pension from the company in 2014 would be £1122 per annum!

I talked to some of my friends about my future pension and we all laughed. In fact what I was really laughing at (even though I did not realise it) was the personal deal that the organisation was proposing: a lifelong career which at the end offered me what, at the time, seemed a tolerable retirement income. Events subsequently showed my laughter appropriate: I have since then held full-time roles with seven other business organisations, and Fisons as a company has now disappeared. I am not sure what happened to the original pension fund either!

At the time the conversation my colleague had with me and other people who joined was meant in all seriousness. It reflected the genuine belief among management at the time that when an individual joined an established company like Fisons, that they would be there until retirement. While the conversation at one level was about how the pension fund operated, at a deeper level it was about the mutual expectations and personal deal I could expect to have with the organisation.

RESHAPING PERSONAL DEALS IN AN ORGANISATION

For most of us, work involves some great times and other times where we feel less positive about what we are doing. One of the less good times for me – as a 30-something-year-old personnel manager – involved breaking the personal deal that the organisation had with some people.

In the early 1980s I worked for ICL, a large UK computer company, which in 1979 employed some 30 000 people. By 1984 the workforce had been cut to some 22 000 people and part of my role in Personnel was to make people redundant. People were told in large meetings by a senior manager that they were being declared redundant and my job was to have detailed individual conversations with colleagues about the timing, leaving payment, pension options, holiday entitlement and the job search support that would be provided to them.

Conversations about terminating the employment of people of my age or younger were no fun, but tolerable. It was an altogether different matter with people who had been employed by the company since the 1960s and were under the impression that, having joined ICL as a young man or woman, they had a career for life. Having a redundancy conversation with individuals in their 40s and 50s, with significant family commitments, was an altogether different matter. While everyone I talked with kept control, I knew many of these people were going through real anguish about their future.

While the company offered reasonable financial terms, and my colleagues and I did our best to support people who lost their jobs, we knew we were breaking the expectations of many people who had devoted their working lives to the company. They thought they had a job for life: I had to talk to them in detail about how that expectation was being broken and the terms of their leaving. The underlying reality was that my job in talking about leaving terms with people declared redundant was helping the company break the personal deal it had with a number of people.

My experience in Personnel during my time in ICL, fortunately involved other activities which fulfilled and reinforced the positive personal deal between people and the company. A notable activity was running assessment and development centres to identify people for promotion. This was an activity which helped the organisation fulfil its personal deal with people rather than break the personal deal.

Having shared two personal examples where HR was closely involved in shaping or breaking personal deals with people, we can now turn to the wider perspectives of the HR function and its role in business.

EVOLUTION OF THE HUMAN RESOURCE FUNCTION FROM THE WELFARE FUNCTION

It is generally agreed that the role of personnel or human resource management has evolved significantly since it emerged in the late-nineteenth century.[2] Three broad stages can be identified: the original welfare role which involved concern for employees; a role involving increased professionalism which I will call professional personnel management; and the more recent evolvement of HR which involves contributing to direction of the business. This is often called strategic human resource management (SHRM), which we shall consider later in the chapter.

The second half of the nineteenth century saw the emergence of the welfare function among the more enlightened industrial concerns, particularly those run by the Quakers – such as the chocolate manufacturer Cadburys and the breakfast cereal manufacturer Quaker Oats. Welfare workers were originally female members of the owning families, but then became appointed to roles in the more progressive companies at a time when hours were long and factory conditions were harsh, unpleasant and uncertain. The role of welfare workers was to take care of the physical and mental welfare of employees – for example provide assistance if someone was sick, became disabled or faced disastrous personal circumstances.

The role of the welfare worker was to inject some humanity into the otherwise tough personal deal operated by most business organisations. In terms of the four personal deal types mentioned in Chapter 6 (relationship, traditional, mercenary and developmental), the welfare worker was primarily enabling the relationship personal deal. This involved feelings and trust, and the welfare workers provided nurturing, emotional and material support to those in real need.

---

2   Torrington, D., Hall, L. and Taylor, S. (2002), *Human Resource Management* (London: Prentice Hall)

PROFESSIONAL PERSONNEL MANAGEMENT

From the end of the first quarter of the twentieth century right through to the end, the old welfare departments evolved into personnel departments which became increasingly professional. This evolution occurred in three distinct areas: supporting scientific management; the implementation of standardised techniques and approaches in the management of people; and involvement in industrial relations.

One of the important developments of scientific management was the introduction of psychometric testing for selection, as pioneered by the Institute of Industrial Psychology in the 1930s in Britain, and the implementation of standardised techniques and methods included things such as contracts of employment, job evaluation, grievance and disciplinary procedures and so on. The intention was to provide routines and procedures for dealing with a wide range of people issues. The final area of personnel professionalism centred on industrial relations, including the collective bargaining and negotiated union–management procedural agreements. The driver for standardisation and industrial relations was to enable management to retain control of the workplace in response to increasing demands and pressures from employees and trade union representatives.

The increased professionalism of personnel management involved all four personal deal types; however, particular focus was given to traditional and mercenary personal deals. The focus on standardised procedures and industrial relations placed considerable emphasis on the creation of traditional personal deals with their emphasis on rules and processes for handling people as well as the emphasis on fairness and equality. Because many of the procedures impacted on the provision of financial rewards, this area therefore focused on the mercenary personal deal with its focus on pay and financial rewards for employment.

THE HUMAN RESOURCE PROCESS

Having viewed the link between the personal deal and human resource management at a high level, we will consider the link at a practical operational level in human resource work. Human resource work, like much other work, can be thought of as contributing to a process or flow. In the case of HR the flow is of people through the business. It starts with people joining the organisation and involves their flow through the organisation until their departure – either voluntary or involuntary. HR activities contribute to this flow through the organisation in six different ways according to Ulrich and Brockbank.[3]

- Buy *
- Build *
- Borrow
- Bind
- Boost *
- Bounce. *

The operation of the personal deal in four of these activities, (marked with an * above) will be considered in the sections that follow. Practical examples will be given which show how these activities shape the personal deal between the individual employee and the organisation.

BUYING – RECRUITING PEOPLE INTO THE ORGANISATION

It has been suggested that bringing new people into the organisation is the single most important thing HR people do, as it involves making decisions on how the business will allocate its expenditure on people – typically over 70 per cent of all business costs. Hiring staff involves relationships with the labour market, attracting and selecting the most appropriate staff for today and tomorrow, and their induction into the organisation.

Organisations invest increasing resources into the selection of staff and this involves use of advanced assessment methods such as psychometric profiling and assessment centres, as well as what I believe is the most cost-effective method – behaviour or competency interviews. These methods, if professionally implemented, have been demonstrated to make a real difference to the quality of candidates brought into the organisation. From my experience the use of advanced assessment methods, combined with speedy decision making, can also make a profound difference to the attractiveness of the organisation to candidates – they imply a better personal deal.

My colleagues and I were invited to help improve the selection process of a well-respected law firm in the UK. The organisation wanted to improve its selection effectiveness without making the selection process excessively complex or cumbersome. We recommended three vehicles for improved

---

3   Ulrich, D. and Brockbank, W. (2005), *The HR Value Proposition* (Boston, Massachusetts: Harvard Business School Press)

selection: a high-level verbal reasoning questionnaire, a group discussion and a test of ability to grasp complex arguments and present these in a succinct form, in addition to the interview which they continued to use. The verbal reasoning questionnaire evaluated individuals' ability to solve complex problems and the group discussion evaluated their ability to work and relate with people. The exercise we were most pleased with was the test of ability to grasp complex arguments. From our analysis of the job of a young lawyer we believed that a critical personal skill for lawyers is the ability to grasp and get to the heart of complex issues. Even at a senior level we believe this is one of the critical skills of a successful lawyer and something which underpins use of legal knowledge and expertise.

One of the most important outcomes from introducing this selection process was that in the partners' eyes the quality of graduate intake into the firm was significantly improved. A less-expected but equally important outcome was that the rate of take-up of offers made also went up considerably to well over 80 per cent. The combined benefit of this was that better quality candidates were being identified and offered jobs and fewer jobs now needed to be offered because of the higher acceptance rate.

The reason for the increased offer take-up is one which other organisations have experienced following the introduction of more rigorous and relevant assessment methods. From a candidate's perspective the use of apparently more rigorous selection methods over other companies (we say 'apparently' because candidates do not know the selection methods work) suggests that the organisation really values its new entrants and their role in the organisation.

This suggests that the organisation places more emphasis on the two personal deal boxes 'What the organisation expects from me' and 'What the organisation gives me' than competitors. This at a deeper level implies that if the company want more from me then they will also invest more in my training and development so that they can get the most out of me. From a young graduate's point of view this is good news and an overall better personal deal than is offered by other firms.

This example of the law firm shows how recruitment methods and processes impact the personal deal. From the organisation's point of view, recruitment provides powerful signals about how it works and what it wants and expects from people. In this way recruitment begins to shape prospective employees' behaviour when they join. From a prospective employee's point of view, the recruitment process provides information the individual can use to decide if the personal deal on offer from the organisation is one they want at work, and whether they should accept any job offer that is made.

BUILD – TRAINING AND DEVELOPMENT

The purpose behind training and development is to increase organisation capability. Typically training takes one of two forms – either people attend formal off-the-job training programmes or it involves the provision of opportunities to learn directly from workplace experience, for example short-term assignments and projects.

Coaching is an interesting half-way house between the two types of training and development. When coaching occurs with someone who is not in our immediate team it involves off-the-job meetings and discussions. Coaching with an immediate colleague – for example our boss or a colleague on the same level – is more of a workplace experience.

Many apparently straightforward training programmes imply a new and different personal deal. When a company sends an individual on a 'finance for non-financial managers' workshop, it provides employees with an opportunity to develop new finance skills. At the same time, whether explicitly stated or not, there is an implied change in the personal deal between the employee and the organisation.

By giving an individual financial skills there is an implicit message that the individual has a part to play in managing the financial well-being of the company. In other words by training an individual in these new skills there is also an expectation that they will use them in their work. The personal deal is that the company is giving you these new skills – which you are now expected to use as part of your day-to-day work. After attending the training you will be responsible for using your finance skills to help the company improve its financial performance.

One of the key purposes of training and development, even if not explicitly stated, is that by giving an individual new skills they did not previously have, they are implicitly expected to use these and include them as part of their work. Quite simply as a result of training there is a suggestion that the personal deal about the contents of people's jobs has started to change to include use of the newly acquired skills.

One of the most successful training workshops I have been involved in was for a large corporation to help people manage their careers. Historically, part of the implied personal deal in the organisation was that individuals' careers would be managed and taken care of by the organisation. An important awareness of the HR director in 1995 was that it was no longer realistic for the organisation to attempt to fulfil this part of the personal deal unilaterally. The core goal of the workshop was therefore agreed to encourage and equip middle and senior management participants to take more personal responsibility for managing their careers. Viewed another way, the goal of the programme was to change the personal deal so that individual employees now had significantly more responsibility for their careers.

While we called the programme a 'development workshop', it differed significantly from the conventional development centres which typically involve over 70 per cent of workshop time on assessment of participants' skills using business exercises. This programme involved two, two-day events, separated by a six-week gap. Most significantly we spent less than a day on assessing individuals' skills, but a lot more on facilitating individuals to reflect on their own personal and life goals including work and exploring their personal work issues and barriers.

Feedback from participants puzzled the training director. On the one hand the programme obtained the highest average ratings of all the training programmes run by the organisation. At the same time the programme also regularly obtained a small number of quite low ratings from one or two people on each event. This puzzled all of us – those sponsoring the programme as well as the consultants running the programme.

These unusual results can be interpreted through the lens of the personal deal. For the vast majority of participants the programme provided a powerful learning experience and one which enabled them to rethink how they could better manage their future careers. The majority of participants viewed the programme experience as a new and additional item which falls into the personal deal box 'What the organisation gives me'.

For a very small number of participants however we believe the development workshops challenged their mindsets about the previous personal deal which promised that the organisation would take care of individuals' careers. For those few people who did not welcome the organisation changing the previous personal deal the workshop probably felt like the organisation was now reducing the box 'What the organisation gives me' and increasing the box 'What I give the organisation'. Viewed in this way their lower ratings for the programme are quite understandable. Using this knowledge we revised the pre-workshop materials and the first workshop session.

The way organisations train and develop people provides many varied messages about their personal deal with the organisation. Very importantly, as we found with the development workshops, training and development can also provide a very effective vehicle for changing personal deals in the organisation.

BOOSTING – PROMOTION AND SUCCESSION

There are many windows organisations provide which offer direct access to their culture. One of these is the physical layout of offices including the reception area, another is the boardroom – even when none of the directors are present. Another important window is how people are groomed for future senior positions. In my experience the people who are groomed for top management typically closely epitomise the culture and behaviours that are most valued in the business.

Typically individuals who are selected to join high-flier programmes mirror the characteristics most valued by people at the top of the organisation. This is because people at the top usually seek to sustain the qualities and culture of the business. The selection process for people to join high-flier programmes, whether systematic or not, involves a matching of their characteristics against the desired and valued characteristics of the organisation.

When an organisation decides to implement new mechanisms and processes for selecting the next generation of top people it usually occurs after long and heated debates among top management. It's not just that selecting future senior talent matters: at a deeper level discussion about the qualities and values of future senior people is fundamental for the organisation going forward. The introduction of a new high-flier system usually is more than a decision to select and develop people in a new way. It is a signal that top management want to introduce a new culture and mindset in the business – at least at the top end.

One sector where promotion and succession processes are clear indicators of culture is in professional service firms, such as accountancy, law, engineering and so on. In traditional law firms the process for becoming partner is often shrouded in mystery. It was said to me by the head of HR in a successful law firm that the route to partnership starts when one of the partners 'taps you on the shoulder and says that in 12–24 months you may be considered for partner'. In many law firms there is no process for applying for partnership and no selection criteria are published. What simply happens is that a particular partner decides you are up to it and advocates your candidature with other partners. If they agree to back your sponsor, you are then tapped on the shoulder and told to prepare for being considered. In law firms the process often involves a formal business case being prepared and an interview with a panel of partners.

In a big-four accounting firm I know, the partner selection process has become increasingly more complex over a number of years. In the early 1990s a 'partner assessment centre' was introduced, where the decision to promote an individual to partner was made. A 'senior management development centre' (essentially another assessment centre) was subsequently introduced for people some two years before they were likely to attend the partner assessment centre. One of the main goals for this event was to weed out people who were unlikely to pass the partner assessment centre. I was then asked by one of the UK regions to design and implement something we called a 'personal development centre' for people 12–24 months before they attended the senior management development centre. Over seven years or so the partner assessment centre had spawned two further hurdles for people to be selected for partner at increasingly earlier stages of their careers.

During a period of very rapid growth in an IT company people were changing jobs typically 2 or 3 times a year. Many of these job changes involved promotions and salary increases. HR's pragmatic responses for dealing with this whirlwind pace of change was the introduction of a rule that an individual could not get promoted unless they had groomed a colleague to take over in their present role. This created a whole new incentive for people development in the organisation. Quite dramatically the onus for development was no longer HR or the system – responsibility for the development of colleagues rested with the people themselves if they wanted to share in the new job opportunities in the business.

In organisations where new job opportunities arise less frequently the prevailing view of development is that it involves the acquisition of new skills and experiences through lateral moves, rather than to a role at a higher grade. The role of HR in such cases is to create mechanisms and processes for individuals to move across the organisation to take on jobs in areas where they have no previous experience.

These examples of organisation prmotion and succession practices illustrate the importance of the role of HR. In each of the different examples HR played a part in putting in place mechanisms which addressed the needs of the organisation. Concurrent with changes in the promotion processes, HR was making critical changes to the personal deals in the organisation.

BOUNCE – PEOPLE LEAVING THE ORGANISATION

People leave an organisation for either voluntary or involuntary reasons. If the reasons are voluntary it is because the individual chooses of their own free will to go to more exciting or better prospects in another company or because they can get more money in another company. Alternatively, people leave because of involuntary reasons – for example they have attained the normal retirement date (but this is likely to become illegal shortly in Europe), they may be declared redundant as a result of a downsizing or cost-reduction exercise, or they may be dismissed for poor performance.

One of the main reasons people leave an organisation voluntarily is because they feel their personal deal has been breached or broken. While people may in their exit interview say that they were offered a job with greater prospects or better pay, this begs the question of why they bothered to apply for the new job. Often the reason someone looks in the job pages of websites or newspapers is because they feel their expectations about the way they should be treated by the company have not been fulfilled. Frequently, there is a specific incident when they suddenly decide that their personal deal has been broken or breached and it is time to move on.

A few years back my manager in a big company where I worked said that if I delivered a particular piece of work successfully that he would put me forward for promotion to the next level, and I knew that this grade carried a company car. Shortly after I delivered the work to positive acclaim, including appreciation from the MD, I asked my boss about the promotion we had discussed. He said that things were difficult at that time and that there was pressure not to increase the number of people in more senior grades. I felt really let down: quite simply my boss had broken our personal deal as I was not receiving what I expected from my leader or the company in return for delivering a successful project. Shortly after, I decided to search for a job which carried a company car elsewhere. Within six months I was offered a more senior role in another organisation with the company car I had wanted. What I underwent is illustrated in Figure 10.1. I experienced less in the box 'What my leader gives me' compared to 'What I expect from my leader'. By indicating

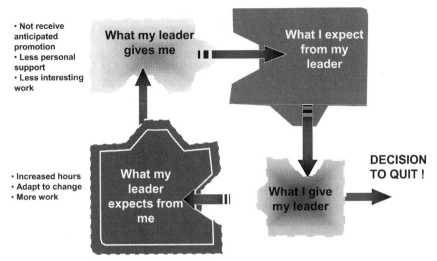

- Not receive anticipated promotion
- Less personal support
- Less interesting work

What my leader gives me

What I expect from my leader

- Increased hours
- Adapt to change
- More work

What my leader expects from me

What I give my leader

DECISION TO QUIT !

Figure 10.1   Broken personal deal experience

that I was likely to get a promotion with a company car my boss had raised my expectations. By not fulfilling that expectation I perceived that my leader was giving me less than I expected.

Increasingly organisations today expect more from their people than in the past. This may involve an expectation that people take on more work, work longer hours or adapt to an ever-increasing change agenda. This would manifest itself in the diagram as a larger box; 'What my leader expects from me' compared to in the past. A classic example in the UK in 2006 is that all the high-street banks – Barclays, HSBC, Lloyds TSB and NatWest/RBS – now expect their retail branch staff to sell products and services to customers, not just to execute counter transactions. A similar thing is happening in Post Offices, where staff who respond to the needs of the general public are now also expected to identify opportunities to sell other products and services, including insurance, personal loans and so on. Business pressures now make it essential that Post Office employees sell as well as execute transactions. From an employee point of view, however, the organisations and their leaders are now expecting more than in the past. The personal deal has changed: implicitly the old personal deal is now broken.

The personal deal provides a concise framework for understanding how employees may experience their personal deal to be broken. They may feel that what their leader and the organisation give them falls so far short of what they expect, or they may feel that their leader and the organisation are now expecting more from them than they want to give. If alternative employment is available, these two types of changes in the personal deal may lead individuals to decide to terminate their employment.

The personal deal can also be used to understand situations where employees leave an organisation involuntarily – because of company action. An organisation may invoke performance or disciplinary procedures when an employee's performance and contribution are seen to fall short of what is required. In terms of the personal deal diagram the employee box 'What I give my leader' is less than the box 'What my leader expects from me'. A leader may feel that the employee has broken their personal deal for many different reasons: lower output, poor attendance, disruptive behaviour, unwillingness to change, incorrect decision making and so on.

On the personal deal diagram the poor match between what the employee provides and what their leader and the organisation expect results in the leader and the organisation changing what they give the employee. In the extreme case the ultimate sanction that can be invoked is that the organisation ceases to give anything further to the employee – they are fired.

STRATEGIC HUMAN RESOURCE MANAGEMENT

The most recent evolution of the human resources function has been towards what is now increasingly called 'strategic human resource management' (SHRM) or simply 'human resource management' (HRM). At its heart SHRM involves a broader view and alignment of people to the business itself. The value of SHRM is that it adds value to the direction and execution of business strategy, whereas professional personnel management is primarily about improvements in efficiency, that is, reducing costs. SHRM creates step-function greater business value by impacting organisation outputs as well as managing processes and costs.

SHRM involves making decisions and implementing people actions which align and integrate with everything else that is going on in the business and its environment – the formulation and implementation of business plans, alignment to brand and marketing strategy and tactics, operational and technology strategies and activities. As Ulrich and Brockbank put it so succinctly:

> The HR value proposition means that HR practices, departments and professionals produce outcomes for key stakeholders – employees, line managers, customers and investors.

SHRM provides a new raison d'être for human resource professionals. Instead of being just a service function that responds to the demands of line managers (which has and continues to be an important part of its purpose), HR now has an additional role and purpose which is to contribute to the direction of the business. The overall way in which SHRM contributes business value is described by Storey[4] in Table 10.1.

Table 10.1   Strategic human resource management

Beliefs and assumptions	
1	HR give organisations competitive edge
2	The aim of SHRM is not just compliance with rules but employee commitment
3	Employees need to be carefully selected and developed
Strategic qualities	
4	HR decisions are of strategic importance
5	Top management involvement in SHRM is important
6	HR policies stem from, contribute to and should be integrated into business strategy
Critical role for managers	
7	Because HR practices are critical they cannot just be left to HR specialists
8	Line managers need to be involved both as deliverers and drivers of HR policies
9	Greater attention needs to be paid to the management of managers
Key leavers	
10	Managing culture is more important than managing procedures and systems
11	Integrated action is required on selection, communication, training, reward and development
12	Restructuring and job design allow devolved responsibility and empowerment

The SHRM focus on culture and the achievement of business outcomes implies greater focus on developmental personal deals rather than those of a mercenary, traditional and relationship type.

The importance of development personal deals for SHRM is reinforced if we refer back to the list of 12 characteristics of SHRM identified by Storey above; four of the items specifically refer to development:

---

4   Storey, J. (2001), 'Human Resource Management Today: An Assessment', in Storey, J. *Human Resource Management: A Critical Text* (London: Thomson Learning)

- no. 3 refers to the importance of development;

- no. 9 refers to the importance of management of managers, that is, leadership development;

- no. 11 refers to the integration of development with other HR activities;

- no. 12 refers to devolved responsibility, which implicitly involves development.

The SHRM approach to specific HR activities is also very different from the professional personnel management approach. The professional personnel management approach to recruitment might focus on the use of more effective assessment techniques to help appoint more of the right people. This would emphasise reduced recruitment costs which might otherwise have been incurred – for example through the use of assessment centres in the place of traditional interviews to assess candidates. While the cost of designing and administering an assessment centre is much higher than the use of biographical interviews, their reliability for identifying candidates who have the necessary skills for success is also much higher. The economic value of assessment centres for assessing candidates is accepted more and more by the HR profession and hence they are increasingly used for graduate middle- and senior-level selection.

The SHRM approach to assessment centres extends beyond the actual selection of candidates and encompass a wider perspective on the impact on organisation culture. The SHRM view considers how assessment centres contribute to the creation of a culture which includes a consistent understanding of how behaviour impacts performance. An SHRM perspective might also include how assessment centres contribute to the creation of a culture which focuses on managing people in a more systematic way and the impact on other people management processes such as performance management. The performance culture would in turn be expected to impact the quality of business results achieved by the organisation.

In this example the SHRM view of assessment centres is both broader and more business focused than the purely professional personnel management perspective. The outputs of SHRM extend beyond the efficiency of people processes themselves to outputs and results achieved by the business. An empirical model created by David Guest illustrates the value of SHRM,[5] and is shown in Figure 10.2.

---

5   Guest, D. (1992), 'Employee Commitment and Control', in Hartley, J. and Stephenson, G. *Employment Relations* (Oxford: Blackwell).

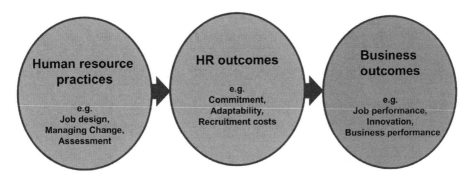

Figure 10.2   How SHRM creates business value

The broader focus and contribution of SHRM has significant implications for the type of personal deal that it facilitates in the business. A major focus of SHRM, in the view of Ulrich, Storey and Guest, is organisation culture. Shaping and changing organisation culture involves a more developmental personal deal as it involves changes in outlook and behaviour. In Chapter 6 we described the developmental personal deal as future focused, centred on how individuals take in, apply and share knowledge in their work to serve the organisation. As businesses become increasingly dependent on the use and application of knowledge, the developmental personal deal becomes increasingly important.

While SHRM implies that more emphasis should be given to developmental personal deals this view on its own is, I believe, too simplistic. One of the big challenges facing HR practitioners is to decide where to focus their energies and attention. I believe we can match the four personal deal types to different high-level priorities for HR. The HR implications of the four different personal deal types are described below.

Traditional personal deals are appropriate where an organisation has significant numbers of people fulfilling stable roles in a relatively stable environment. The key requirement for success of the organisation is continuity and stability. Such personal deals prevailed in organisations such as Government departments, Barclays and others.

In such organisations the role of HR was primarily to enable and foster long-term employment relationships with employees, which are controlled by impersonal processes and rules, as well as principles of justice and equity. The work of HR people is likely to be characterised by complex procedures and rules. One of the challenges for HR is not to allow processes to become ends in themselves – but to retain line of sight between processes and the purpose and goals of the organisation.

Mercenary personal deals are most appropriate in organisations which are ambitious to deliver standard vanilla products in a competitive market. Two types of employee are critical to the success of these businesses: armies of temporary workers where costs are controlled tightly, as well as ambitious leaders who have the energy to lead the organisation in its tough market environment. Organisations of this type include Coca-Cola, Citibank and Ford.

The priorities for HR in mercenary organisations are split between the need to manage efficient relationships with people on short-term contracts and the key role in the recruitment and development of people with high energy, determination and dynamic leadership skills. HR will also have a key role to play in the management of change. The work of HR people is likely to be characterised by pace and focus considerably on performance management. A key challenge of HR will to be to justify its existence in an organisation which is continually demanding increased efficiency and cost savings.

Developmental personal deals involve medium-term relationships which focus on the development and application of knowledge. The key to success in such organisations and indeed for their success in the marketplace is the way individuals acquire and use knowledge. Examples of such organisations are professional service firms such as Ernst & Young, Arup and research-based organisations such as biotech companies. The leadership challenge in such organisations is both to encourage colleagues to learn and to leverage their knowledge.

The most important focus for people in developmental organisations is to locate, recruit and develop creative talent. Individuals have value to such organisations so long as they continue to acquire and use knowledge in pursuit of the organisations' goals. The purpose of HR therefore is to facilitate development and retention of people with talent. One of the big challenges facing HR in such organisations is to select business leaders from among the population of technical experts. The challenge here is to identify people with the potential to change career focus away from their professional focus – whether it is accounting or engineering – and become business leaders.

Relationship personal deals focus on the quality of relationships and one of the major priorities of organisations that use such deals is the quality of the relationship itself. The key features of personal deals are trust between people and the creation of mutual long-term respect and well-being. Not surprisingly, there are not many organisations that use deals purely of this kind in the commercial world. However such organisations certainly do occur among some social businesses where the relationship between people reflects the relationship they adopt towards customers. There are some family-run businesses of this type where high emphasis is placed on employee well-being. A few examples also exist in the commercial world which are significantly, if not totally, relationship focused. Examples include firms which are largely controlled by employees – such as John Lewis, Arup and Gore. While these are not pure relationship organisations, they place a stronger focus on relationship personal deals than competitors in their respective marketplaces.

The role of HR in organisations with a high focus on relationship personal deals is one of supporting and nurturing people. The focus will include helping people achieve their potential – not so much for the business but simply for their well-being. The contribution of HR will also involve creating harmony between people. One of the key challenges facing HR in relationship organisations is to make sure that HR genuinely adds business value and becomes more than an updated physical and emotional welfare provider.

The role of HR in organisations with the four different types of personal deal are summarised in Figure 10.3.

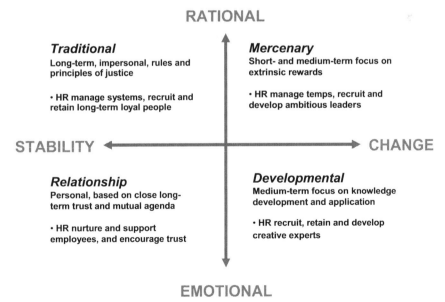

RATIONAL

Traditional
Long-term, impersonal, rules and principles of justice

• HR manage systems, recruit and retain long-term loyal people

Mercenary
Short- and medium-term focus on extrinsic rewards

• HR manage temps, recruit and develop ambitious leaders

STABILITY ←――――――――→ CHANGE

Relationship
Personal, based on close long-term trust and mutual agenda

• HR nurture and support employees, and encourage trust

Developmental
Medium-term focus on knowledge development and application

• HR recruit, retain and develop creative experts

EMOTIONAL

Figure 10.3   Matching HR priorities to different personal deals

In this chapter we have seen how diverse HR activities are seen to impact and influence the state of personal deals in organisations. This is not a coincidence or an accident. These different examples of HR work all point to the conclusion that one of the core purposes of HR in a business is to shape and manage personal deals between an organisation and its people. While it does so directly in some instances, in others the role of HR is to provide the tools and techniques for business leaders to manage their personal deals more effectively with their people. At a strategic level a critical contribution of HR is to decide what types of personal deals an organisation needs to have with its people to be successful. By influencing the personal deal, HR is impacting what people receive from working in the organisation as well as what and how they contribute. This has to be one of the most critical contributions anyone can make to the future of the business and the people who work in it.

CHAPTER SUMMARY

- Many HR activities involve shaping and fulfilling the personal deal between employees and the organisation. When people join an organisation HR plays a key role in creating the new personal deal they have with the organisation. However, when HR is involved in making people redundant this involves supporting the organisation breaking the personal deal with people.

  The HR function has evolved through three distinct stages:

  - original welfare function from the late 1800s;

  - professional HR which started to emerge from the 1930s;

  - strategic human resource management from the late 1980s onwards.

- As HR has evolved it has got increasingly involved in wider aspects of the four personal deal types mentioned in Chapter 6: relationship, traditional, mercenary and developmental.

- The purpose of the welfare function was to inject some humanity into the tough business organisations of the late-nineteenth century. Its purpose in personal deal terms was to support the relationship personal deal between the organisation and the employee. The welfare function might typically display some care towards individual employees, for example, who suffered injury while at work, or who faced a close family bereavement.

- Evolution of the welfare functions into professional personnel departments involved things such as the introduction of systematic selection, standardised terms and conditions of employment and industrial-relations collective-bargaining negotiations. The professional personnel department got involved across all four personal deal types, in particular those of a traditional and mercenary type.

- At an operational level the human resource process, which is the primary focus of attention of professional personnel departments, involves the flow of people through an organisation from recruitment through to eventual departure from the organisation. It involves six different activities according to Dave Ulrich: buy, build, borrow, bind, boost, and bounce.

- Personnel practices and procedures can either reinforce the prevailing personal deal, or help reshape it. Sending an individual on a training course to learn new skills creates an implied revised personal deal that they will subsequently use these new skills in their work. Managers promising promotions which they then do not deliver are a classic example of how a manager can break their personal deal with an employee.

- Professional personnel/human resource functions and professionals are increasingly expected to contribute to the formulation and execution of business strategy – strategic human resource management (SHRM) – and involves particularly high focus on development rather than the other three types of personal deals.

- One of the strategic challenges facing HR today is to focus its activities to support and complement the prevailing personal deals that exist in the organisation. Alternatively if there is a business requirement to change the prevailing type of personal deal in the organisation then HR can play a key part in this by re-shaping the way it delivers its services to the business.

CHAPTER 11

How to Shape Your Personal Deals

So far we have viewed the personal deal and the psychological contract as an idea and approach at an organisation level. This chapter adopts a different focus and explores what practical steps we can personally take to manage and shape the personal deals in our work life. The chapter is intended as do-it-yourself actions which you can personally use with your colleagues at work.

The chapter will start by looking at the preconditions for a useful one-to-one personal deal discussion with a colleague. We shall then consider the practical steps involved and preparation required for having the personal deal discussion and how a personal deal toolkit dedicated to your specific organisation can enhance the quality and reduce the time involved in the discussion. After looking at the process of the personal deal discussion itself we will consider the type of training that is recommended to develop the relevant personal skills and mindset to maximise implementation of personal deal discussions.

Most people rarely have personal deal discussions. Probably the most frequent occasion is when a couple exchange marriage vows. The traditional English marriage vow involves the couple both agreeing that they will:

> *... take you to be my husband/wife, to have and to hold from this day forward; for better, for worse, for richer, for poorer, in sickness and in health, to love and to cherish, till death us do part and this is my solemn vow... I give you this ring as a sign of our marriage. With my body I honour you, all that I am I give to you, and all that I have I share with you.*

One of the important features of this marriage vow is that it creates identical expectations each partner can have of the other. In practice each partner in every couple will bring slightly different things to their relationship. One partner may bring in more money than the other, one partner may spend more of their time taking care of children, one partner may be more sociable and organise more social events, one partner may be the practical one who fixes and repairs things, one partner may help both of them handle difficult feelings and so on. What occurs in every marriage relationship is that each partner will bring slightly different things to the relationship, many of which are important and valuable to the other.

The traditional marriage vows take no account of these differences and indeed the different expectations and contributions of each partner may only emerge later. Useful as the marriage vow is, it does not do justice to the real differences in expectations that occur within a close relationship. As a couple get to know each other better these different strengths emerge, and one partner will tend to rely on the other for the particular and unique contribution they bring to the partnership. Often these different strengths may be taken for granted by one or both of them, perhaps not even overtly discussed, and over time become the way the couple behave together because it suits both of them.

When things go wrong in a marriage it is frequently because the particular strength or quality one partner brings to the relationship is either no longer valued by the other, or because one or the other partner decides either consciously or unconsciously to change or withdraw a particular feature of their contribution to the relationship. So if one partner who has taken the lead role in the relationship in taking care of the couple's social life, or the one who brought in most of their income decides not to, or is no longer able to continue doing so, then this changes the dynamics. A very frequent cause of breakdown is when a couple have both assumed that they will have an exclusive sexual relationship together, and one of them decides to have an extra-marital relationship. When one person in the relationship unilaterally decides to do something different than has been agreed – implicitly or explicitly – then things start to go wrong. There are many parallels in the relationship we have with our manager to the relationship we have with our life partner – even if the content and context of the relationships are very different.

In work relationships it is unrealistic that people should expect identical things from their colleagues that they expect from the manager. As occurs in a marriage, each employee typically brings different things to their work relationships. For the personal deal to be meaningful therefore it cannot be uniform for both parties, but rather needs to reflect what each party uniquely brings the other.

This chapter provides ideas for what is involved in preparing and undertaking personal deal discussions at work which acknowledge each person's unique and different needs and contribution to their work relationship, and how these different contributions can be sustained or changed when business requirements and circumstances change.

PRECONDITIONS FOR DISCUSSING OUR PERSONAL DEALS

Discussing our personal deal with someone involves a discussion about our relationship with each other, and this is something many of us do not find easy or straightforward. You may have encountered occasions during your life when you found it difficult to discuss your relationship with another person. Even if we and the other person are willing to have the conversation, it may not be easy for any of a number of reasons: perhaps due to our own narrow beliefs or to those of the other person. Both our national and organisation culture impact our ability to discuss our relationships with others. While Israelis and New Yorkers may find it quite easy to discuss their personal relationships, Germans and English people may find it more difficult. While it might be OK to discuss your relationship with a colleague in an advertising agency, it may be rather more difficult in a traditional law firm. There is considerable evidence that women find it easier to discuss their relationships with others than men do.[1]

There are five preconditions which need to be fulfilled for people to have a constructive discussion about their personal deal with one another:

- self-awareness

- personal communications

- candour and honesty

- open-mindedness and understanding

- view the relationship as a mutual and shared responsibility.

There are two further requirements for the person who initiates the discussion:

- understanding how the personal deal operates

- coaching and facilitation skills.

It is important that we look at these as if all five preconditions are not present to at least some extent, then the personal deal discussion may be difficult, or even impossible.

The most fundamental requirement for a discussion about our personal deal is self-awareness. This means that we have a mental picture of who we are, where we are in our life and what matters to us. This includes an idea of what we want from the person with whom we intend to discuss our personal

---

1   Grey, J. (1992), *Men are from Mars, Women are from Venus* (New York: Harper Collins)

deal. If we have no idea what we want from the other person it becomes almost impossible to discuss our personal deal.

Experts in emotional intelligence consider self-awareness to be the core competence for developing effective relationships.[2] It has three separate components. The first is emotional awareness, which is being in touch with our own feelings and values. The second is accurate self-assessment, which is being aware of our own strengths and weaknesses, and being able to maintain a balanced and open perspective on ourselves and the world. The third component is self-confidence, which is about having a belief in our own self-worth, capabilities and judgement.

The second precondition for a personal deal conversation is that both parties are able to communicate with each other. While the ability to string together words and communicate is fortunately possessed by most people, there are many situations when people for all sorts of reasons simply do not communicate with one another.

Over the years I have encountered quite a few leaders and managers who in their colleagues' eyes simply do not communicate with their people. This may be for reasons ranging from large spans of control, intense work pressures or geographical separation, any of which may create constraints on people being able to communicate.

Another reason people may not communicate is because of their very different personalities: for example one person may be highly logical and rational while the other may be highly intuitive and operates at a feelings level. In such cases the barrier is not about their individual personalities but more about the interaction of their different personalities and the different ways they see the world.

An increasing number of people complain about electronic communications. Many people resort to communications by email to colleagues who sit near to them, and this can be seen to be impersonal and make it difficult to transmit things other than facts and data. A case which received wide publicity in the UK in 2005 occurred when a company communicated the dismissal of a sizable part of its workforce by mobile phone texts. This is hardly a medium which will encourage goodwill or even understanding for such an important communication.

---

2   Goleman, D. (1998), *Working with Emotional Intelligence* (New York: Bantam Books)

The third requirement for having a discussion about our personal deal is that we are willing to express our views openly and tell the truth. It is easy to take openness and candour for granted; however, if we are unwilling or unable to express our ideas and wants openly then a discussion about our relationship with another person is almost impossible.

One of the adverse effects of a command-and-control leadership style is that it discourages people from engaging or communicating openly with people in authority. I recall a meeting I attended with a team who reported to a highly autocratic boss. When the boss put forward what was a totally ridiculous idea his subordinates simply agreed with him. They had learnt from past experience that their ideas and suggestions would not be listened to, so they saw no point in speaking up. There are many business situations when people may be able to communicate but are unwilling to do so.

The fourth requirement for a personal discussion is open-mindedness and understanding. Discussing our personal deal requires a willingness to hear things about ourselves which we may prefer not to hear! A manager might pride themselves on their consideration for others, but the colleague with whom they have the personal deal discussion might say that they really want the manager to take more account of their personal needs. While the manager might have a clear belief about their behaviour, this may not be shared by colleagues. The personal deal conversation may therefore throw up issues in the relationship which are uncomfortable to deal with by either party.

The important thing for us when discussing our personal deal is to be willing to understand the personal needs and concerns of the other person – even if these are completely different from our own. It is not that one person is right and the other is wrong: it is simply that we are different and our needs and motives may be different, and the way we perceive the state of the relationship may therefore also be different.

The final precondition for a personal deal discussion is that both people genuinely believe that they share some responsiblity for the quality of their relationship. If I as a manager believe that my relationship with my team members is entirely dependent on their enthusiasm for work, I am unlikely to engage in a proper discussion about what we both want from one another. Equally if I have a relationship with a forceful and highly assertive colleague and am convinced that because of his behaviour he must bear total responsibility for the state of the relationship, I might absolve myself of any responsibility for improving how we get on together.

It is easy at one level to think that responsibility for a voluntary relationship is shared by both parties and this notion is supported by relationship experts such as Schutz[3] and Rogers.[4] This issue is illustrated by occasions when we are in conflict with someone and may believe that the state of our relationships is entirely their fault. We might blame them for what has happened and therefore be reluctant to listen to their perceptions about our relationship.

The two requirements for the person initiating the personal deal discussion; understanding how the personal deal operates, and coaching skills, will be considered later in this chapter.

The five requirements for holding a personal deal discussion might seem obvious; however, they are important preconditions for us to hold a meaningful discussion about our personal deal with another person. At the beginning of a discussion about our relationship with a colleague it may therefore be helpful to briefly check that we both share the five assumptions about relationships. There are organisations where it is simply not the done thing for a person to talk about the quality of their relationship with a senior colleague. If having such a discussion goes against the cultural norm or will break an organisation taboo, then it is really important to set the scene first about the requirements for a personal deal discussion.

Before reading further you might find it useful to reflect on when you last discussed the quality of your relationship with your boss or with people in your team. Have you talked about your relationship recently, a year or two back, or never? If the answer is never then it is important to acknowledge that having a personal deal discussion will be quite a new and different thing for you and the other person.

STEPS INVOLVED IN HAVING A PERSONAL DEAL DISCUSSION

Having a personal deal discussion is not difficult; it does not depend on our education or our seniority. Some personalities may find it easier than others: two extroverts may find it easier than two introverts; even so, introverts are quite capable of having a very positive discussion about their personal deals. Providing the five preconditions described above apply, anyone can have a personal deal discussion. Any adult can have the discussion with any other

---

3   Schutz, W. (1984), *The Truth Option* (Berkeley, California.: 10 Speed Press)
4   Rogers, C. (1995), *A Way of Being* (New York: Houghton Mifflin Books)

adult, and adults can have the discussion with children – but that could be the subject of another book.

There are three simple stages involved in the personal deal discussion:

- setting the scene about what the personal deal is, the purpose and value of the discussion, and the preconditions;

- brief preparation by each person on their own, which involves answering two simple questions, preferably combined with some time for individual reflection. This preparation can be made even easier with the use of a personal deal toolkit;

- having the personal deal discussion about what each person wants and will give the other, including agreeing any trade-offs each will make for the other.

SETTING THE SCENE FOR A PERSONAL DEAL DISCUSSION

Setting the scene for the personal deal discussion is important but should not take more than about 15 or 20 minutes. The starting point is to introduce the concept of expectations and the personal deal to your colleague as something which occurs in all our relationships, in and outside work. You can do so using Figure 11.1, which was introduced in Chapter 3. Before talking about personal deals in business you may want to refer to a non-work example – for example the restaurant example described in Chapter 3, or some other example which will resonate with your colleague personally.

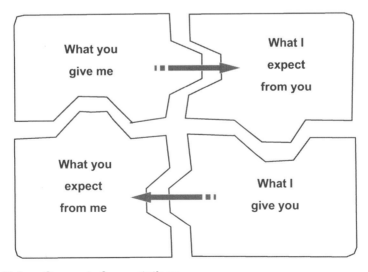

Figure 11.1   Concept of expectations

Once your colleague understands the concept you can mention that it applies equally to your relationship with them, and that they will have expectations about you and that you have expectations about them. It is important to give a specific reason why you want the discussion with them at this point in time. It may be because you have noticed strains in your relationship, or because you are or are likely in future to face some big challenges or you have not been achieving the results you should be achieving and so on.

From experience of working and supporting people to clarify their personal deals I believe it is important to carefully explain the specific benefits that you, your colleague and the business will obtain from having a personal deal discussion. The major benefits from my experience include:

- Employees understand better what they can do to enhance their contribution and be seen more favourably by their leader and the organisation.

- Leaders understand more about the personal expectations, needs and motives of an individual and their work, so that the leader can more effectively engage and support them to contribute.

- Increased mutual understanding, trust and quality of personal relationships between leaders and employees ensues.

- Leader and employee know better how to focus their joint energies and actions for each other and the business, based on the 80/20 rule. They also know which actions they can curtail because they are less valued by the other or the business.

- Clarifying personal deals across the organisation can help people to better align their efforts with what customers want, and with the strategic and cultural direction of the business.

These benefits are I believe extremely valuable. From the organisations where we have encouraged managers and employees to have personal deal discussions the benefits are both tangible and enduring. How these benefits were assessed independently was described earlier in Chapter 8 on leadership.

You may be thinking that these benefits are similar to ones which should accrue from performance management discussions and processes and, at a theoretical level, you would be right. However, in practice, many organisations find that performance management discussions often fail to deliver these benefits.

The final part of setting the scene is to ask your colleague to prepare for the personal deal discussion, as outlined below.

BRIEF PREPARATION FOR THE PERSONAL DEAL DISCUSSION

Preparing for the personal deal discussion is straightforward and easy. It requires both people to answer three simple questions:

- Identify the few important things you want from your colleague?

- Put yourself in the shoes of your colleague and identify what you believe are the few important things they want from you?

- Identify what you currently give your colleague and what you might give differently (more of, less of, or different) to better fulfil what they want from you?

This preparation is important because we have often found that people have never had a discussion where they were asked to say what they most want from their manager/leader. While leaders do talk to their people about their career aspirations and goals it rarely provides the full picture of what matters most to people at work.

Having a personal deal conversation can often raise unexpected issues for both leaders and employees. The leader may not know that their colleague would like to be able to leave work two hours early on Wednesday evenings to go to an evening class. Or it may be surprising to a leader to hear that while they believe they keep colleagues informed on what is going on, team members would like the team leader to spend more time communicating and hold a 45-minute meeting every Monday morning to keep them up to date. Even if it might be a surprise for the leader to hear that their communications are less effective than colleagues would like, they will be in a much better position to discuss options and ideas for taking more care of individuals' and the team's needs.

Equally, the employee may be surprised to find out certain expectations that the leader has of them – things which were never raised in the performance management or other discussion. It may be something about the way an employee responds and talks to customers, or the way they communicate with colleagues, which the leader has been concerned about but has never raised directly. In the personal deal discussion the leader can air his priorities for change so that team members become clearer about what is expected of them and about how they can add more value to the business.

When answering the three questions it is important to be aware that the things raised might cover a very broad spectrum: some items may refer to specific job outputs, others may refer to activities and others may refer to behaviours or attitudes. There are no constraints on what the leader or the employee can identify as the most important things they want from the other. The only thing that matters is that they are important in that person's eyes.

When asking someone to answer the three questions it should be mentioned that while things of an aspirational type are fine, they need to be within the realms of reality. While an employee may say that the most important thing they want from their manager is to be able to do the same work for double their pay, this is unlikely to be within the ability or interests of a manager of the organisation to provide while the individual performs the same job. It may however be something the manager can discuss with the individual for the long term.

Apart from answering the three questions from a realistic perspective, the only other advice we would give is that it is best if people allow some space and time for personal reflection before they meet to discuss their personal deal. While our first and immediate answer to these questions might be the right one, time for personal reflection may help reshape and provide a clearer and more personally powerful picture of what we want from someone else. We therefore recommend allowing at least a three- or four-day gap between the time someone is asked to prepare for their personal deal discussion and actually having the discussion itself. This can help both people get the most from their subsequent discussion.

Personal deal toolkit

There are many organisations, and people for whom the idea of having a discussion about what they would like from each other is a novel idea and indeed something they may never have experienced. Having our first up-front discussion with another person about what we want from them, with our boss, may feel quite daunting.

For someone who is highly introverted the idea of having an up-front conversation with anyone about what they want from them may seem like quite a challenge. Typically, a highly introverted person may not want to tell another person what they want from them unless they feel very strongly about the need for this – for example the boss has yet again let them down. If the relationship with the boss, however, is basically a good one an introvert may have little difficulty in having an up-front conversation about their relationship with them.

There are also some organisations or parts of organisations where it is not the done thing to be up-front with your manager. The informal rule might be that it is OK to express your ideas and views on business issues, but it is not OK to be up-front with your boss about what you want from them. This could simply be an extension of the old-fashioned command-and-control style or it might be that it is simply not part of the culture to ask for what you want from your boss. This might apply either to a whole organisation, a department or a section.

In one organisation I know people pride themselves on being open and up-front. In fact one of the things that really impressed me in a meeting some years ago was when one person argued against what a colleague said. Another person in the room then said, 'That's a good challenge.' This was not meant in a hostile or put down way to the first speaker, but as a compliment that the person who put the argument forward had raised the quality of the debate and taken account of broader business issues which had not been considered up to then.

But even in this organisation I have heard comments that there are discussions between senior people and their team members where people are less open and up-front about what they want from one another. In one large company it was decided that it would be useful to provide a vehicle to facilitate greater openness and candor between people. We discussed options for this and decided to create a dedicated 'personal deal toolkit' for this purpose.

The approach to the personal deal toolkit is similar to the approach we adopted with the case study presented in the leadership chapter. Essentially we created a set of cards which describe many of the things that managers might want from their people and a separate list of things that people might want from their manager and the organisation. The cards were based on the different categories shown in Table 11.1, which were earlier described in Chapter 3.

For each factor in the list below we produced three different items, providing a total of 33 different things that managers might want from their people, and a separate list of 33 things that an employee might want from their manager.

Table 11.1   What employees and managers want

Things employees want from their manager	Things managers and the organisation want from their people
Environment	Flexibililty
Direction	Commitment
Well-being	Care
Challenge	Performance
Development	Learning
Creativity	Improvement
Influence	Ambassador
Equity	Knowledge
Relationships	Collaboration
Recognition	Conformance
Security	Protection

Each item was presented as a self-contained statement, and printed on a separate card.

The important feature of these cards is not just that they described the things people want from their managers and managers want from their people: the words and phrases we used to describe each item used the prevailing words and phrases expressed by people in that business. We believed that for the cards to be used it was essential that they contained words and phrases which people were familiar with and which they had come across in their day-to-day discussions with others.

An example of the words we used on one of the cards to describe something a manager or the organisation might want from a colleague is:

Recognises own personal style and flexes this to display behaviours which, while not typical of them, respond to client and situation needs and influence people in order to contribute more to the achievement of business performance.

We formulated the words on the cards based on a series of focus groups we ran with representative of employees and managers from different parts of the organisation and at different levels. We used a range of questions which helped us identify the different things people wanted from their colleagues. We also used indirect methods including 'repertory grid',[5] which helped identify their thinking at a deeper level.

Our plan in creating the cards was that they could be used in a variety of different discussions between people in the organisation to facilitate and assist being more open and up-front about what they want and expect from each other. Some of the planned applications include:

- *Performance management* When leader and colleague meet to discuss the ways they can work together more constructively, the leader can use the cards to discuss their priorities for the team member and the team member can use them to describe what they want from the leader and the organisation.

- *Promotion/induction* When an individual makes a career transition the cards can be used to assist the new leader talk about their new expectations about the individual and their contribution. The individual can also use them to describe the support they want from their manager.

- *Understand what matters/motivates someone* When a manager feels they do not properly understand what matters to a team member they can show the cards to the individual and ask them to identify what matters most for them in work, and where they would like support.

- *Development* When an individual is seeking advice on what they need to do to prepare for a move to a different or more senior role they can discuss the requirements for the new role with a colleague so they can better understand where and how they should focus their energies.

- *Graduate trainee induction* One of the challenges faced by a new member of the workforce is to understand what is expected of them, and also what they might expect from their boss and the organisation. The cards can be used to help clarify these expectations.

The cards have been tested for use on different locations in the organisation with encouraging results. Feedback suggests that the cards have helped remove some inhibitions that people have when discussing what they want and expect from one another. In a smaller number of cases we have had feedback that

---

5   An interviewing technique that determines an ideographic measure of personality devised by George Kelly in 1955 – Kelly, G. (1992),*The Psychology of Personal Constructs* (UK: Routledge)

some mangers have found the cards helped them describe what they want to their people.

The personal deal toolkit is a powerful vehicle for describing the range of options that people might want from their leaders and managers, and the things that managers and leaders might want from their people. By having the different options clearly identified, expressed in language used by people in the organisation gives individuals permission to be more up-front than they might otherwise be.

HAVING THE PERSONAL DEAL DISCUSSION

There are many different ways to have a personal deal discussion. My experience is that people have the most fruitful and constructive discussions if the initiator does so using a coaching style. People who already have an effective level of coaching competence will find it fairly easy to undertake. Those who have not will benefit from training, as well as briefing in the personal deal. This is covered in the next section.

The personal deal initiator should start by reminding their colleague that the goal is to clarify their mutual expectations of each other and improve their working relationship and achieve the five benefits referred to earlier.

The initiator should then go through the following steps:

Share your expectations

1. You tell them what you believe are the five most important things they want from you.

2. Invite your colleague to tell you the five most important things they actually want from you. Do not interrupt them during this – except to ask for clarification if required.

3. Invite your colleague to tell you what they believe are the five most important things you want from them.

4. You tell your colleague the five most important things you want from them. Invite them to ask if anything is not clear.

5. Both of you should comment on the similarity and or differences in what you both want from each other compared to what you thought each other wanted.

Comment, clarify and trade expectations

6.   You comment on the feasibility of giving your colleague what they want, taking account of your preparation beforehand.

7.   Your colleague comments to you on the feasibility of giving you what you want from them, taking account of their preparation beforehand.

8.   You both explore creative ideas, options and trade-offs that you might agree to provide each other with more of what you both want.

9.   Summarise the options and agree what is realistic and practical for you to both give each other to maximise your joint fulfilment.

Confirm agreement for the future

10.   Agree a time when you will jointly review how you are fulfilling each other's expectations against what you said you will give each other.

11.   Give each other feedback about the discussion and share what you believe you have both learnt. Celebrate what you have achieved for each other and the organisation.

12.   Record your personal deal, when you will review it and your joint learnings from the experience.

I have purposely broken down the three stages into the detailed 12 steps involved in the personal deal discussion to make them clear and easy to follow. Obviously, the steps do not have to be followed in the precise order, and you may prefer to do it differently to suit your own personal style and the culture of the organisation. What matters is that you have an open discussion about your personal deal and that you are able to clarify and improve what you jointly give each other.

Our experience of working with people is that they conduct their personal deal discussions in varied and different ways. In some cases people have a more fluid and less structured discussion. The style does not matter so long as it works for you. Because of the different ways you can undertake the personal deal discussion we recommend that you practise it beforehand. Ideally this practice should occur in a training or briefing session, which is the subject of the next section. It is important to check that the personal deal we negotiated last year is still valid. Peoples needs and company needs change, therefore last years deal may no longer be valid.

PERSONAL DEAL TRAINING

Having a personal deal discussion should be quite straightforward. What gets in the way is that most of us rarely get involved in personal deal discussions. The idea of having an up-front discussion about what we want from another person and hearing what they want from us in an equally direct way may be unfamiliar. Because this is new territory for many people we may not know what to expect or how to go about the discussion. My work with the personal deal indicates that training can properly equip and prepare people to have personal deal discussions which have lasting business value. This is particularly important for the leader or manager who wants to initiate personal deal discussions with their colleagues.

I recommend the training should cover three basic areas:

- development of coaching and facilitation skills;

- understanding how the personal deal operates, including consequences when it is broken;

- practice in having a personal deal discussion.

This approach will do more than provide participants with information about the personal deal and skills to have the personal deal conversation. Very importantly, it will help change their mindset that it is useful and valuable to have this unusual type of conversation. You might want to ask yourself when you last discussed your mutual expectations of another person. How did you feel about the conversation and what did it add to your relationship?

We have found that the GROW coaching model provides an effective method for training people in coaching.[6] For people who have reasonable social skills a half-day training module provides sufficient opportunity to provide a live coaching demonstration, provide input about the GROW coaching model, and practise two brief coaching meetings. Having at least two practice opportunities to coach someone is fundamental in helping people learn, as well as beginning to develop their skills and confidence in coaching.

Many organisations provide training in handling performance management discussions. While this training can provide useful preparation for a personal deal discussion, in many cases it only covers part of the ground. In practice, most performance management discussions are quite one-sided, as they are about the leader telling his direct report what he expects. Most

---

6   Landsberg, M. (1996), *The Tao of Coaching* (London: Harper Collins)

time in a performance management discussion is about the way the employee performed over the previous time period and the objectives and behaviours the employee will pursue in the year ahead. While some time may be spent discussing what the leader will do for the employee, this mostly forms only a small part of the total discussion.

The personal deal discussion is a genuinely two-way discussion – it covers what the leader will provide the employee, and what the employee will provide the leader and the organisation. The mindset required for this conversation is very different than in traditional performance management discussions. Instead of the leader being in a more powerful position than the employee, the discussion is much more between two equals. For quite a few managers this is unfamiliar territory; therefore training and practice in conducting a personal deal discussion is really important.

Input on the personal deal, including discussion about the context, can occur in about an hour. It also really helps if people conduct practice personal deal discussions with colleagues in the training workshop. We usually ask people to work in small groups to undertake practice personal deal discussions. People fulfil three different roles:

- Person A – Would be themselves and lead a personal deal discussion with a person role-playing a real colleague in their team.

- Person B – This person would role-play the colleague of Person A, and would be told something about this specific person by Person A, before the role-play.

- Person C – Would observe the personal deal discussion and then lead and give feedback, principally to Person A on how well they conducted and led the personal deal discussion, and how they used different coaching behaviours for this.

In something over an hour each person in a trio can fulfil the three different roles, thus providing them with experience of leading a personal deal discussion, being on the receiving end of such a discussion and in observing the discussion.

Our experience of introducing the personal deal is that its success depends on leaders and managers understanding what is involved, and in having some practice in a safe environment of what for most of us is an unfamiliar discussion. This can be achieved quite easily in a one-day interactive workshop.

To maximise the learning we would recommend that a workshop should have about 12 to 18 participants, and either two or three facilitators to support the coaching and personal deal discussions.

The personal deal discussion is for many people a completely new and different type of conversation. Understanding what is involved, proper preparation, using the suggested steps in this chapter and using a coaching leadership style can make the personal deal discussion effective and valuable. In many cases it provides a new platform of understanding and collaboration between people which assists the creation of additional business value, as well as greater employee fulfillment.

CHAPTER SUMMARY

- One of the few common situations where people talk and make an explicit personal deal is when they get married. The traditional marriage vow in the UK states what each partner will give to the other, and can expect from the other. In most of our relationships we typically do not talk directly about what we will give and what we will receive from each other – our personal deal.

- There are five preconditions to having a personal deal discussion:
  - self-awareness
  - personal communications
  - candor and honesty
  - open-mindedness and understanding
  - view the relationship as a mutual and shared responsibility.

- There are two further requirements for the person who initiates the discussion:
  - understanding how the personal deal operates
  - coaching and facilitation skills.

- There are three simple stages involved in having a personal deal discussion:
  - setting the scene about what the personal deal is, the purpose and value of the discussion, and the preconditions;

- preparation and reflection by each person on their own for the discussion;

- having the personal deal discussion about what each person wants and will give the other, including agreeing any trade-offs.

- There are three questions we should seek to answer before having a personal deal discussion:

  - Identify the few important things you want from your colleague?

  - Put yourself in the shoes of your colleague and identify what you believe are the few important things they want from you?

  - Identify what you believe you currently give your colleague and what you might give differently to better fulfil what they want from you?

- Creating a personal deal toolkit specific for the organisation can considerably facilitate personal deal discussions. The personal deal toolkit describes the different things that employees may want from their manager and the different things that managers may want from their people, using the typical words used by people in the organisation. The value of this is that it provides a reminder to managers and employees of things that may be important to them, in the language of the organisation.

- Having a personal deal conversation involves three basic stages:

  - sharing perceptions and expectations of each other;

  - clarifying and trading future expectations;

  - confirm agreement for the future.

- Training people in personal deal conversations is important because it is such a new thing for most people. Experience in a number of different organisations suggests that it should include development of coaching and facilitation skills, understanding how the personal deal operates and practice in having a personal deal discussion. Training of this type, including experiential exercises, can be completed in one day and will add considerably to the quality of personal deal discussions.

CHAPTER 12

Behavioural View of the Personal Deal

This final chapter will view the personal deal from a very different perspective. We will explore the personal deal from a behavioural point of view between people, based on the framework of transactional analysis[1] or TA as it is often known.

After describing TA in the first part of the chapter I will describe five different types of personal deal behaviour patterns and relationships. In practice, almost no one has personal deals which are only of one type; however, many people have personal deals which are predominantly one or two of these. In the final part of the chapter I will look at options we have available to change our type of personal deal.

There are many behavioural frameworks that could have been used to describe personal deals – for example neuro-linguistic programming, Emotional Intelligence and Belbin's Team Roles. However, none of these, in my view, provide such a powerful yet practical vehicle for understanding and changing personal deals between people as TA. It has been used by many different practitioners including the author to develop and change behaviour and performance at work.[2]

INTRODUCING TRANSACTIONAL ANALYSIS AS A FRAMEWORK FOR UNDERSTANDING PERSONAL DEAL BEHAVIOUR

TA is a framework for understanding behaviour between people, including the emotions they express towards one another. It was created by Eric Berne, an American psychiatrist who wanted a simple language he could use to help his clients understand themselves. In contrast to the traditional language of psychology, incomprehensible to most people, Eric Berne developed transactional analysis, which we can use to describe our own and other people's behaviour. It is concerned with what people do and say to one

---

1   Berne, E. (1967), *Games People Play* (Middlesex: Penguin Books)
2   Wellin, M. (1978), 'TA in the Workplace', *Personnel Management*, July

another. Communication and behaviour were viewed by Berne as a series of exchanges or transactions between people. If I meet you and say hello and you nod your head and smile back at me, we have exchanged greetings; there has been a transaction between us. TA is the analysis of transactions between people.

TA is based on the 'ego states', three separate observable behaviour patterns which reflect states of feeling and thinking. Each of us uses all three ego states to varying degrees and we can observe the way people shift from one to the other ego stage through distinct changes in facial expression, vocabulary, gesture and posture. The manager who frowns when interrupted in a meeting by a ringing mobile phone is exhibiting certain ego state behaviours, as is the team leader who responds to the plan of the operations director by asking, 'What are the time scales for getting this done?' The salesman who jokes with his colleagues is in the third ego state. The behaviour of these three people is respectively described as 'parent', 'adult' and 'child' ego states. At any one moment we are in one of the ego states but have the capacity to switch quickly from one to the other and indeed we do so frequently.

PARENT EGO STATE

The parent ego state refers to rules, admonitions and beliefs. These can be expressed as critical and demanding (as in the above example of the manager who frowned) or may be concerned and sympathetic. The 'critical parent' sets limits and makes judgements. Phrases such as 'Never access the CRM system on your laptop when you are face to face with a client' or 'You must get this analysis finished by tonight', or 'Don't question my instructions – just do it' are typical critical parent statements, as are words such as 'never', 'must' and 'always'. Non-verbal communication which suggests that someone is in a critical parent ego state are a furrowed brow, pointed finger, head tilted up and peering down, and a scowl.

The sympathetic or 'nurturing parent' is also expressing judgements and beliefs with phrases such as 'Let me know if you get stuck and want help' and 'Don't worry, I'll sort it out for you'. Typical non-verbal behaviours which characterise the nurturing parent are the pat on the back and the benevolent smile. As with the other ego states the parent can be used in a variety of situations both positively and negatively. We might tell our team member 'You must provide the data for this client by tomorrow morning before he travels overseas'; this has a positive message in terms of achieving results according to timescales and is an example of constructive use of the parent ego state for business success. Equally, use of the nurturing parent in a conversation to a new colleague who has just joined our organisation may be appropriate: 'This is a confusing system to work with – if there is anything you are not sure about come and ask me'.

Much of our parent ego state behaviour originates from when we were very small and were told what to do and what not to do by our mother and father. As we got older and joined groups and organisations outside our family, such as schools, friends in the neighbourhood and business organisations, we took on some of their values, judgements and beliefs as part of our own parent ego state. Organisations in which we work have rules about how to dress, how you can speak to senior colleagues and about punctuality, even though many of these are not written down. To what extent have you adopted these rules in your behaviour? Do you wear the same clothes as everyone else or are you an individualist who dresses either more formally or more casually than your colleagues? You will have your own standards about timekeeping, the format of a good report, what makes a fair day's work and many other things. Your views on these are the internal parent rules you have for yourself and which you will express in your behaviour towards others.

ADULT EGO STATE

The adult ego state is made up of rational, logical and analytical behaviour. It is based on our objective experiences and exploration of the environment and develops throughout our life. Typical adult statements might be: 'What time is it?', 'Why did the system fail?', 'The statistics suggest that…' and 'The cost of launching the new product will be…'. Adult ego state behaviour selects data, works things out, evaluates alternatives and estimates probability. The adult ego state operates like a computer and, like a computer, is ruled by logic and does not show emotion or feelings. This is emphasised by the typical non-verbal behaviour of someone in their adult ego state: when we are in it we often have a straight-back, level eye contact and are aware and attentive to what is going on around us. Phrases such as 'has his feet on the ground' or 'level-headed' precisely describe the adult non-verbal behaviour of someone who spends much of their time in the adult ego state.

The adult ego state is a requirement for every job, irrespective of whether we work in front-line operations or the boardroom. We are involved in analysing data and problem solving; the problems might be about resolving a customer enquiry, a new product launch or estimating long-term oil supply implications – all require use of the adult ego state.

It is often believed that at work we spend most of our time in the adult ego state. However, while we may spend time analysing data, calculating, planning and other rational activities, for many of us this accounts for only part of the time we spend at work. While many business meetings have an objective and adhere to an agenda, a significant proportion of our time in the meeting may not be spent solving problems or giving and receiving pure information. How often have you attended meetings and felt afterwards that it could have taken far less time? When this occurs it is because either other people's adult ego states were functioning less well than your own or that their and perhaps your other two ego states were used more in the meeting.

CHILD EGO STATE

The child ego state expresses our feelings and responses to things going on around us or within ourselves. Our child ego state is the source of our energy and happiness. If we are eager to get on with a new project or feel bored about the people we are working with, this is due to the feelings in our child ego state. The feelings can be spontaneous and expressive as in the 'free child' or they may be compliant as in the 'adapted child'.

The free child represents the way we were when we were born, is self-centered, and operates without regard for other people, groups or organisations. It is carefree and expresses what we want directly with words such as 'I want…', 'I feel fantastic', and 'Ow'. Typical non-verbal behaviour would be laughing, loud talking, relaxed asymmetrical posture, cuddling, tearful and fists clenched. The free child provides charm and warmth in our lives and is the source of fun.

Our memories of family, school and our first job will have taught us that life in an organisation requires adherence to certain rules and standards of conduct if we are to continue as a member of that organisation. We were praised for doing the right things and sticking to the rules, and punished when we broke the rules. At school we were taught to attend lessons (even when we may have preferred to be playing in the school grounds) and to do our homework on time (even when it may have been much more fun to go to the movies). At work we almost certainly had some of those early rules from school reinforced, such as the need to be punctual. At work we also had new rules imposed on us, such as how to prioritise our work, not to disagree with the boss, or tell a customer to get lost. The above are all examples of the adapted child.

The words 'parent', 'adult' and 'child' used from a TA point of view have different meanings from those used in normal conversation. Grown-ups with youngsters spend a lot of their time telling them what they should and should not do – the parent ego state. When grown-ups are working together to solve business problems they exhibit the adult ego state. Children express their feelings as a rule much more readily than grown-ups, and joy, excitement, compliance and creativity can be readily observed in children playing. When we talk about a grown-up being in the child ego state we do not mean that they are behaving in a childish or immature fashion but that their behaviour expresses feelings.

The ego states provide a comprehensive framework for categorising people's behaviour. At any moment we are in one of the ego states and this applies now to you as a reader of this book. If you are thinking what you have read is rubbish you are most probably in the critical parent ego state. If you are reading this attentively, evaluating what has been said so far and comparing it to what you already know about behaviour at work you are almost certainly in the adult ego state. However, should your reaction be one of great enthusiasm, anger or total agreement with everything that has been said, then you are likely to be in one or the other part of the child ego state. You may want to consider your posture and body position as an indicator of your ego state. Does it match the ego state you think you are in?

Figure 12.1 shows the three TA ego states.

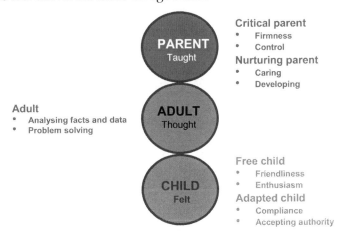

Figure 12.1   Parent, adult and child ego states at work

TRANSACTIONS

When two people communicate or engage in a transaction this involves behaviour from one of the ego states in one person to one of the ego stages in the other. Thus if a colleague asks you 'Have you seen the new product file?' and you reply, 'Yes, it's on Mary's desk' you have engaged in a conversation or transaction between your and your colleague's adult ego state. We can visualise transactions between people as lines going between two sets of three circles, each set of three circles representing the three ego states. A transaction occurs when person 1 in the diagram communicates with person 2 by giving a stimulus from one of their ego states to one of the ego states of person 2, and person 2 responds from one of their ego states to an ego state of person 1.

When communication occurs to and from the same ego state, as in the example above concerning the new product file, we say it is a 'parallel transaction'; quite simply the lines between the two individuals' ego states are parallel, as shown in Figure 12.2. Parallel or complementary transactions, as they are also called, can occur from one person's parent ego state to another's parent ego state, from one person's adult ego state to another's adult ego state, or from one person's child ego state to another's child ego state. Parallel transactions can also occur between the parent ego state of one person to the child ego state of another, and then the reply is from that person's child ego state to the other person's parent ego state.

However, an unexpected response may occur to a stimulus and the lines on the diagram may cross, leading to a blockage of communication. An example of this may occur if the colleague had responded differently to the question, 'Have you seen the new product file?' (adult to adult) with 'Do I have to find everything for you' (critical parent to adapted child).

When we get involved in crossed transactions we stop communicating smoothly and one of the people concerned will need to change their ego state if they want to continue to relate. A good indication of a crossed transaction is

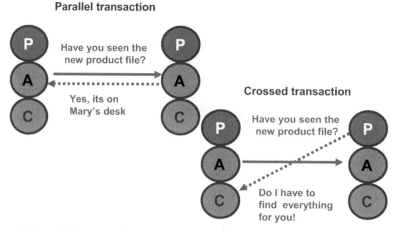

Figure 12.2   TA Transactions

when we say something to someone and they respond in an unexpected way and we get a sudden lump in our throat.

The third type of communication is the 'ulterior transaction'. Ulterior transactions involve one person sending messages simultaneously to two separate ego states in another. One example might be when a manager says to a subordinate, 'Will you have that report ready for tomorrow?' as in Figure 12.3. On the surface this could be seen as an adult to adult transaction; however, in the context this is only part of the message. Underneath it could imply a critical parent to child message at the psychological level – 'You will have that report ready for me won't you!' (shown by the dotted lines in the figure). We often use ulterior transactions when we want to convey messages in a disguised and socially acceptable way.

The giveaway that we are engaging in ulterior transactions comes from our non-verbal behaviour. If when the boss asks 'Will you have that report ready by tomorrow?' the question is accompanied by a furrowed brow, pursed lips, head pointed upwards or a slightly sharp tone, that is a give-away of non-verbal parent communication.

BEHAVIOUR UNDERPINS ALL OUR PERSONAL DEALS

Many personal deals involve repeated patterns of behaviour between people and these patterns endure often over long time periods, frequently over very different business issues. If the behaviour patterns between people occur repeatedly this suggests that that there is a consistent personal deal at an emotional level.

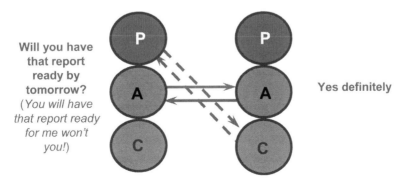

Figure 12.3   Ulterior transactions

TA can be used as a powerful vehicle to understand individual pieces of communications by people. As an observer of different people you will probably be aware that some people tend to have consistent relationships while others have very different types of interactions with different people. The value of TA is that once we are familiar with the basic ego states and transaction types we can quickly look out for the predominant ego states that are involved in different personal deals and can then identify the emotional tone of personal deals between colleagues including those we are involved in personally.

Before exploring the different behavioural personal deals that may occur, it is important that we acknowledge that in reality everyone is able to use all the different ego states. Even in a very well-established personal deal relationship, where the pattern of behaviour is consistently repeated, there will be occasions when either or both people use atypical behaviours. In a personal deal, for example, where one person mostly uses critical parent behaviours and the other mostly uses adapted child, there will be occasions when they change – for example they both communicate adult to adult, or child to child. They may even on occasions reverse the usual pattern and the individual who is mostly critical parent may communicate adapted child, and the person who is typically adapted child may briefly communicate as critical parent.

In the sections that follow, each of the six types of personal deal will be described. After you have read of these you may find it interesting to reflect on which type best describes your relationship with your manager or your relationship with individual members of your team. You might like to reflect how you would like it to be?

MASTER–SERVANT PERSONAL DEAL

This is probably the oldest and best known personal deal at work. It is epitomised by the relationship between landowner and servant in the Middle Ages or even earlier. The same style of relationship prevailed between mill owner or supervisor and workers, and is still to be found in many business organisations across the world.

The master–servant personal deal involves one person behaving in a predominantly critical parent way (master) towards the other person who responds in a predominantly adapted child (servant) manner. The master will give instructions and the servant will comply and agree with instructions as shown in Figure 12.4.

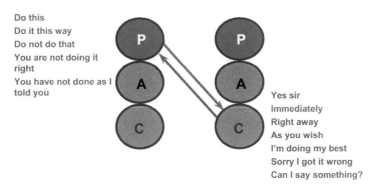

Figure 12.4   Master–servant personal deal

The expectations of the master are along the lines that they have the right to tell the servant what to do, organise their work and their time, correct their work and discipline them if they get it wrong. The master also expects that the servant will do as they are told, will follow instructions and accept any punishment meted out. The master probably believes that they know best – about everything, and perhaps that they are a better or superior person to the servant. People fulfil the master role either because they feel that is what others expect of them or because they have personalities that like to be in charge.

The expectations of the servant are broadly that their role is to do as they are told, follow instructions, jump when they are asked to jump and be disciplined when they get it wrong. This means that even if they know that a situation requires action they will not bother until the master has told them to do it. An individual may be happy to fall into the servant role either because it gets him things he wants – a job, pay, a quiet life and so on – or he may fall into this role because he has a personality with a large amount of adapted child.

One of the real downsides of the master–servant personal deal is that the servant is treated like a machine. As with mechanical machines, people who fulfil the servant role are not required to use their head or their initiative but to obey instructions. What happens is that they expect to be told what to do, so when they are not – even if they know it would be useful to the organisation to do something – they hold back until they are told. The result of the master–servant personal deal is that it really disempowers people.

The master–servant personal deal is still found in many different organisations and often goes under the label 'command and control'. When I have come across master–servant personal deals among knowledge workers they result in lower productivity and poor morale. I remember one meeting I attended when a senior manager wanted a master–servant personal deal with his team. In team meetings his people did not put their case, they never told the boss when he was wrong and they generally just complied for an easy life. The result was that the team's performance was well below what the organisation required, and indeed below what they were capable of delivering.

RATIONAL PROBLEM SOLVER PERSONAL DEAL

One of the prevalent personal deals among knowledge workers in functions such as accounts and IT is the rational problem solver personal deal. It is a personal deal which historically occurred between colleagues at the same level but is today increasingly a feature of relationships both across, up and down organisations.

The rational problem solver personal deal involves two people behaving towards each other in a very logical, rational and analytical way. Both people in TA terms are relating or transacting to each other through their adult ego states. Person 1 uses adult communication towards the other person, and they respond in turn using adult communication. The focus of their behaviour involves asking for and giving data, exploring consequences, working things out, clarifying procedures and so on. Like all adult behaviour it is like a computer – logical unemotional and void of feelings. It is great for solving problems involving the analysis of data – but it can be a bit dry and unexciting. The rational problem solver personal deal is shown in Figure 12.5.

The underlying expectation of both parties in a rational problem solver personal deal is that they work rationally together to solve problems. There is an expectation that each can ask the other for data, information and knowledge, and that the other will provide this data information and knowledge to help solve the problem in hand. There is an assumption that it is OK for one person to ask, and if the other has relevant information they will provide this. Even

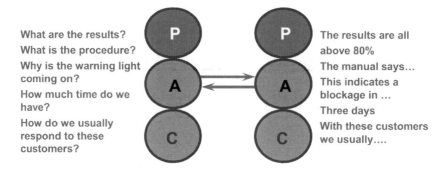

Figure 12.5   Rational problem solver personal deal

if one person knows more than the other, the assumption is that the more knowledgeable person will not act as superior or a step up from the other, but that they will willingly share their data and knowledge.

The real value of the rational problem solver personal deal is that it helps people to share information and ideas to work things out and solve problems. The downside of this personal deal is that it is void of feeling and emotions and therefore is not much fun. People who have predominantly rational problem solver personal deals are very analytical and dry; there is no humour, animation, fun, excitement. People with this type of personal deal talk together in monotones, do not raise their voices and spend a lot of time with both feet on the ground.

The rational problem solver personal deal is very often found in accounts departments, IT departments and financial institution back offices. When you visit people's offices with these sorts of deals the conversations are hushed, quiet and measured. A few years ago I did some change work with an IT department in the US. My client and I walked into the facility which was so quiet I thought no one was in the large open-plan office. As I walked through the office I saw many people working away at their workstations in isolation from anyone else. When I came across a few small groups working together they were huddled together around a monitor talking in hushed subdued tones. It felt quite dry. The physical environment probably also encouraged the rational problem solver personal deals: every person had their own desk and workstation and were surrounded by drab looking screens between them and the person at the next workstation.

BENEVOLENT INSTRUCTOR PERSONAL DEAL

This is another long-established personal deal at work. It has its roots in the days of traditional craftsmen who handed down their trade and skills to more junior apprentices. In the past these skills were typically manual – for example making swords, horsemanship and woodwork. The benevolent instructor tradition is carried on among senior professionals whether in architecture, accounting, law, medicine or IT whose role involves the development of more junior staff.

The benevolent instructor personal deal involves one person in behaving in a nurturing parent way towards the other person, who responds in a predominantly adapted child manner. The nurturing parent instructor will show by example, teach, coach, delegate tasks and give constructive feedback to the trainee who typically responds in an adapted child mode. The benevolent instructor personal deal is shown in Figure 12.6.

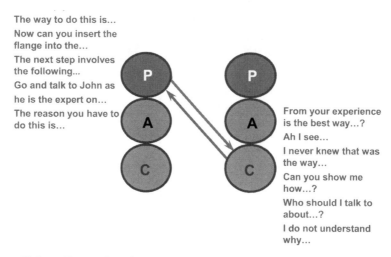

Figure 12.6   Benevolent instructor personal deal

The expectations of the instructor are that they have more expertise than their trainee who will respect them and be eager to learn from them. They also expect the trainee to put into practice what they tell them so that their performance and skill improves. While they will tolerate some mistakes they probably do not expect the same mistake to be committed twice. They expect the trainee to accept feedback positively rather than as a personal challenge and accept that they have the right to set the standards for performance.

The expectations of the trainee include that the instructor knows what they are talking about and has the expertise to answer their questions. They also expect that the instructor will be willing to share their knowledge and skills so that they can learn and develop. When they make a mistake the trainee expects to be told in a constructive way how to improve next time, rather than be bawled out or made to feel inadequate. They want to be told if they have got things right and praised for learning and doing a better job than they did before.

The benevolent instructor can be a really positive personal deal and one which adds value to both parties. The instructor ends up appreciating their expertise and feeling valued. The trainee learns new skills first hand and develops their overall repertoire and performance. One of the downsides of this personal deal is if it is perpetuated in the longer term, thus preventing the trainee from taking greater responsibility for their actions and performance.

The benevolent instructor personal deal is highly prevalent among many professional service firms. One of the key requirements for long-term success of professional service firms is the development of young blood to take over senior roles in future. This can only occur if those in charge today take on the task themselves of grooming the up-and-coming young professionals. Many firms institutionalise this personal deal by allocating interns to partners, setting up mentoring schemes, expecting them to get involved in graduate recruitment and so on.

CREATIVE GENIUSES PERSONAL DEAL

This is a very different type of personal deal. It is a personal deal which is all about new ideas, creativity, doing things differently, thinking the impossible and challenging mindsets. It is a personal deal that creative people in any field have. It is about bouncing around new ideas, each person building and being spurred on by the other to come up with ever more outrageous concepts and ideas.

The creative geniuses personal deal is essentially child to child communication. Person 1 may come up with a new idea they tell person 2. Person 2 then extends the idea further and shares it with person 1 who continues to add and extend that idea, and so on. As well as lots of new perspectives and ideas, creative geniuses personal deals involve lots of excitement, energy and enthusiasm. Creative geniuses have lots of fun with their ideas, exploring new paths, thinking the impossible and so on.

The underlying expectation of both parties between creative geniuses is that new ideas and thinking are exciting and worthwhile. There is an expectation that each can say and think the impossible and that the other will be interested to explore it. Creative geniuses thrive on complexity and the impossible. The expectation between them is that logic, rationality and practicality are less important than the excitement of the latest new idea and perspective. They will expect their enthusiasm and excitement to be mirrored by the other person who, like them, will not be bounded by the world as it is now. The creative geniuses personal deal is shown in Figure 12.7.

The value of creative geniuses is that they can be immensely creative. While individuals working on their own can be innovative, pairs or small groups who have creative geniuses personal deals can be absolute powerhouses for innovative and creative thinking. The upside of this personal deal is that it can lead to totally off-the-wall ways of thinking that go against the conventional

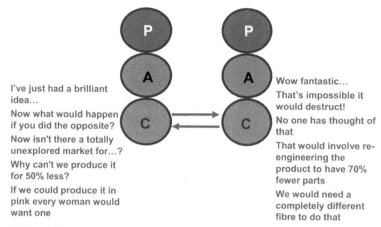

I've just had a brilliant idea...

Now what would happen if you did the opposite?

Now isn't there a totally unexplored market for...?

Why can't we produce it for 50% less?

If we could produce it in pink every woman would want one

Wow fantastic...
That's impossible it would destruct!

No one has thought of that

That would involve re-engineering the product to have 70% fewer parts

We would need a completely different fibre to do that

Figure 12.7   Creative geniuses personal deal

view. This can be very helpful for inventing new products and services and ways of behaving and living. Many of the things we take for granted today originated from creative off-the-wall thinking – for example electricity, human flight, nuclear energy and the computer. Which of these were the product of creative geniuses personal deals I will never know. What I do know is that groups, as opposed to single isolated individuals who come up with radical ideas, usually have creative geniuses personal deals. On occasions when I have overheard discussions between advertising people or between investment bankers it has sounded as if the creative geniuses personal deal is present.

The downside of the creative geniuses personal deal is that it can be totally unrealistic and lose touch with issues of practicality, cost and so on. Creative geniuses who forget about practicality may end up exploring dead ends or wasting millions. Notwithstanding this potential weakness, this personal deal will become ever more important for organisations to thrive in a world where future success depends on innovation and off-the-wall thinking.

SMOOTH CONTROLLER PERSONAL DEALS

The smooth controller personal deal appears to be very rational, logical and easy-going on the surface. At a deeper level however it involves subtle control by one person of the other, who accepts and goes along with the control. It is a very common personal deal in situations where the colleagues and subordinates accept and totally understand that they will fulfil the subordinate role in the relationship, so much so that they go along with the other person's authority – accepting it almost as a matter of right and without question. This personal deal is often portrayed in theatre and films in the way subjects behave towards a king or monarch, or the way junior gang members behave towards the gang leader – for example in films like *The Godfather*.

At its core the smooth controller personal deal appears to be not very directive – just making suggestions and putting forward ideas and proposals. This contrasts with the master–servant personal deal which is quite overt about who is in charge. The smooth controller however is listened to carefully by followers who are keen to do whatever is suggested. The smooth controller personal deal is shown in Figure 12.8.

The expectations of the smooth controller are that others will listen and obey with no need to clarify reasons or give explanation. The smooth controller expects others to understand that it is in their interests to comply and not be difficult, and even to marvel at their astuteness and wisdom.

There are organisations where smooth controllers still prevail, especially those which have a well-used command-and-control style. I recall one organisation I worked where the smooth controller was a senior person in charge of a £1 billion plus operation. People were too scared to ask the smooth operator about his thinking – they just waited until he issued his ideas and then got on with it. There was an unwillingness to challenge or question the smooth controller.

Subordinates of smooth controllers expect that by respecting and acknowledging the individual their position and role is secure. By waiting until the smooth controller speaks they believe that they will be valued and appreciated. Once the smooth controller has spoken then they express views and make supportive comments and suggestions which back up and reinforce what he has said.

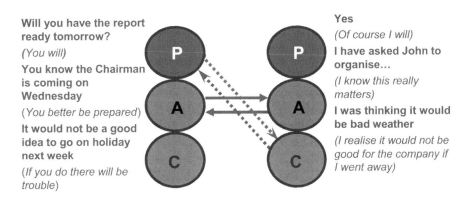

Figure 12.8   Smooth controller personal deal

The advantage of the smooth controller personal deal is that if the individual is highly revered and clever it can be a very efficient method of leadership. If the leader is wise and an effective decision maker, such as the widely respected Prime Minister Lee Kuan Yew of Singapore, then it can be a very efficient way of exercising power. Lee is credited with leading Singapore from a third-world British colony into the independent financial and economical powerhouse it is today. The downside of the smooth controllers personal deal is that if they are not so wise, or they require other input when making decisions, then it can be both unproductive and socially dysfunctional.

METHODS FOR CHANGING PERSONAL DEALS

While there are many different possible types of personal deal types, the five described above are, I believe, very common in the organisations and teams I have worked with. Obviously they do not portray all possible personal deals that can occur. From my experience however they are frequently found personal deal types and certainly ones I come across in organisations in different sectors and different sizes.

There is no such thing as a perfect personal deal – the right one is the one that the people involved feel is right. Sometimes external observers might view a particular personal deal and believe it is dysfunctional – but for all sorts of reasons it may prove worthwhile to the individuals involved. Equally we might observe other personal deals which we view as ideal and very positive, yet those directly involved and affected may consider them to be very far from optimum.

In this final section we will not attempt to evaluate types of personal deals. Our goal is rather to provide some insights and options which you may want to consider to use to help discuss and perhaps change your own personal deals you are involved in which you find less positive than you would like.

The first option before seeking to change behaviour of your personal deal is to be aware of what is happening in the relationship by listening and reflecting on your and the other person's behaviour. What ego states are you in and what are you doing with and to one another? Are there certain repeated patterns which show the cycle of how the relationship evolves over a time period? Are you in parent, adult or child ego state? What kind of transactions do you repeatedly use with one another? How successful is the relationship?

Once you are aware of what is happening in the relationship, the second step is to decide the changes you want to make in your personal deal behaviours. Do you want to become more assertive (parent), do you want the other person to be more understanding of you (nurturing parent) or do you want to laugh more (child)? Before seeking to change your personal deal it's important you are clear about the directions you would like it to move. Clarity about how you might want the relationship to change is no guarantee that it will happen – but it is a great start for where you would like the relationship to go.

Now you know the personal deal behaviours you have with another person and how you would like them to change you can take any of five actions to seek to bring about the changes you desire.

A subtle action which may encourage the other person to change their behaviour is to ask questions which, if they answer, will get them to engage different ego state behaviours. Some examples might be:

- 'I know you want me to produce the report by the end of tomorrow – but how will you use the report? Wouldn't a mind map be sufficient instead?'

- 'You have expressed your dissatisfaction with what I did – can you tell me how you would like this next piece of work done and who else does it the way you would like?'

- 'You have told me to do this work in a different way for clients, but how do you know they will notice, and even if they do, can you tell me what difference it will make to them?'

- 'This is the third time this week you have asked my opinion – instead of me telling you, how about you tell me what you think is the best way to deal with this, and why?'

Asking direct questions about the matters under discussion is an effective and direct way of getting someone to change their ego state behaviour, especially to shift them into adult ego state.

A more up-front way of encouraging someone to change their behaviour is to give feedback and tell them you would like them to behave differently. You can describe how you see their behaviour and tell them what you want them to do differently. Possible examples might be:

- 'You have given me five separate instructions about how to handle this work, I believe I know what I am doing and would much prefer it if you just left me to it. You can then give me feedback when I have finished. Is that OK?'

- 'You keep asking for my advice about what to do. I would really appreciate it if you tried to work it out for yourself before you ask my advice. Next time can I suggest that you work it out and then come and ask my view after you have your own view? I would much prefer that.'

- 'In the last 30 minutes you have told me at least three things that are wrong with my presentation. Rather than interrupt me half way, I would find it more helpful if you kept all your comments and feedback until I have finished, and tell me then.'

- 'You have given me lots of analysis about the data. What's missing for me is your clear recommendation about what should be done. Can you please tell me now what your recommendation is?'

Not everyone wants or is open to direct feedback and up-front requests to do things differently. You need to judge if this is the most effective way – especially if you are asking your manager how they would do things.

A different, but very powerful option to encourage people to change is to reflect back to them how you experience their emotional state towards you. You might say things like:

- 'You seem quite commanding/directing towards me?'

- 'A lot of the time I feel you are criticising me for what I have done.'

- 'I experience you as very rational, how do you feel about this?'

- 'The way I see you is quite emotionally needy – wanting my approval/reassurance.'

This is quite a dynamic way of giving feedback. Rather than just telling the person how you see them – you are providing feedback based on your personal experience – which makes it more likely they will be open to your comments and be willing to explore their behaviour openly with you. It then gives you an opportunity of how you would prefer to experience them.

A completely different way of encouraging someone to change their behaviour style is to start a discussion about your mutual expectations about one another. The steps for this were described in Chapter 11 earlier in some detail. Engaging in a discussion about what you give each other and what you would like from each other can be a great way of bringing the issues about behaviour into awareness between you.

For example, if you want the other person to do less 'telling to you' you can say that what you expect is more freedom to get on with the job rather than being told how to do it: 'What can we both do so that you can give me that greater freedom to get on with the job?'

As part of that discussion you might also learn about their thinking behind the way they behave towards you. For example, they may feel that if they did not always tell you what to do that you might forget. Talking and sharing the reasons you behave in particular ways towards each other and the assumptions you make about each other is a way to clear the ground for more positive and productive relationships.

A final way of helping to change the behaviour in your personal deal is to simply change your behaviour from the one you have used in the past: instead of behaving compliantly in servant mode to a master you could just stop behaving like a servant, but more like a master yourself. This may take them by surprise and cause them to change their behaviour towards you. On the other hand there is a danger that your changed behaviour could result in uproar and conflict. By saying 'No I will not do it that way, I am going to do it my way' could just cause some sparks. By giving the other person less of what they want might on the other hand unfoot them – and cause them to completely change. There are risks in this approach, so be aware of the possible outcomes if you decide to go for it.

There are no silver bullets for changing our patterns of behaviour with another person. The methods outlined in this chapter, based on the context of TA, have the potential of changing and improving our personal deals. There is no one best way – but try some of these described and see what happens. Before persevering with any approach after using it once – listen and watch how the other person responds. Then if a tactic proves unhelpful, you may want to use an alternative.

CHAPTER SUMMARY

- Transactional analysis of all the behaviour frameworks can be easily adapted to understand the behaviours and type of relationship involved in our personal deals. It is particularly appropriate because it views behaviour and interaction between people as a series of transactions.

- TA uses three ego states – parent (taught), adult (thought) and child (feelings) – to describe the different types of behaviour between people. Each ego state is characterised by distinct verbal and non-verbal behaviour which can be easily observed. Each of us can display all three behaviours, but we each have our own preferences for each ego state.

- Communication is viewed by TA as a series of lines between the ego states in one person and the ego states in the other. There are three types of communications: parallel transactions enable communication to continue; when crossed transactions occur communication becomes difficult; ulterior transactions are for sending emotional code rather than saying things directly.

- There are five personal deal types: master–servant, rational problem solver, benevolent instructor, creative geniuses and smooth controller.

  - The master–servant personal deal involves one person mainly being in critical parent ego state who assumes they are in charge, while the other is mainly in adapted child and obediently complies.

  - The rational problem solver personal deal involves both people in the adult ego state problem solving, sharing data, using logic and reason to get things done. While it is very reasoned, it can become boring.

  - Benevolent instructor personal deals often occur between senior and more junior professionals and craftsmen: the senior person displays nurturing parent towards the junior who is in adapted child.

  - Creative geniuses personal deals involves child to child behaviour and involving bouncing and building ideas between each other. It challenges convention and produces highly creative ideas.

  - Smooth controller personal deals operate at two levels. At one level they appear highly reasoned, but at a deeper level they involve subtle critical parent control by one person of another's adapted child ego state.

- There are a number of different ways of changing our personal deal behaviour with another person. The starting point is to be aware which type you are using and then decide the behaviour you would like to change to. Options which you can try include:

    - Use a different ego state;

    - direct feedback to the other person about their behaviour;

    - assertively ask the person to change their personal deal behaviour;

    - reflect the implicit feelings you are aware of in their behaviour;

    - have an open discussion and renegotiate your personal deal;

    - just change your behaviour in response to theirs.

Index

Publications are indicated by italic headings. Tables and figures are indicated by bold page numbers.

About the Author

Michael Wellin is Director of Business Transformation Ltd, a niche consulting firm specialising in organisation change, team effectiveness and coaching. He works primarily at board and partner level, delivering practical solutions which enable people and organisations to better achieve their goals. Michael has consulted to a wide range of organisations and sectors including companies such as Arup, Ernst & Young, Ford, Reuters and Royal Mail.

One of his principals which underpins Michael's workis that all of us have enormous talent, and our challenge as we travel through life is to bring out more of that talent for our and others' benefit. Michael has over 20 years successful consulting experience and a hallmark of his work is the creation and application of innovative practical methods which help people and organisations to leverage their talent.

In his earlier work he was one of the first users of Belbin's team roles and transactional analysis as vehicles for leadership and organisation change. In the 1990s he created a framework of effective board behaviours, and a generic framework of business behaviours – Talent Inventory®. Most recently he has pioneered techniques to help organisations use and improve their psychological contract, which culminated in the writing of his book.

Michael's interest in the psychological contract was stimulated both by his experiences of working in diverse business organisations across different sectors as well as his extensive personal world travel. Exposure to different cultures at national and organisation levels taught him that each culture has its own subtle conventions about acceptable behaviour.

Before taking up consulting Michael received a very good grounding in all aspects of human resources, working in the peronnel functions of large UK and international organisations, including Fisons, BOC, ICL and Continental Illinois National Bank. Michael brings to his work as a business psychologist an understanding of people and their behaviour with a strong drive to achieve business results.

He studied social psychology at Sussex University, and then pursued his interest in business psychology by gaining an MSc in personnel management at

City University Business School. In 1992 he was elected Chartered Occupational Psychologist and Associate Fellow of the British Psychological Society.

Michael speaks at conferences and has written several articles on people issues in business. His previous book, *Behaviour Technology*, advocated many of the people practices which are now common in organisations today.

He lives with his wife Ruth and son Zack in North London. As well as his family he is passionate about things Indian and Nepali. He loves trekking in high mountains, particularly the Himalayas, and also spends time with friends and cultivating a Japanese garden.

Michael can be contacted at: michael@michaelwellin.com